MEDITATION OVER MEDICATION

Ravi K. Puri, Ph.D.

authorHOUSE®

AuthorHouse™
1663 Liberty Drive
Bloomington, IN 47403
www.authorhouse.com
Phone: 833-262-8899

Published by AuthorHouse   06/29/2021

ISBN: 978-1-6655-2956-3 (sc)
ISBN: 978-1-6655-2955-6 (hc)
ISBN: 978-1-6655-2957-0 (e)

Library of Congress Control Number: 2021912579

Dedication

To my parents, for teaching true values of life comprising discipline, morals, and ethics. To Professor O.P. Sehgal for igniting my inner fire for the unknown.

> Do not pursue the past.
> Do not lose yourself in the future.
> The past no longer is.
> The future has not yet come.
> Looking deeply at life as it is
> in the very here and now,
> the practitioner dwells
> in stability and freedom
> We must be diligent today.
> To wait until tomorrow is too late.
> Death comes unexpectedly.
> How can we bargain with it?
> The sage calls a person who knows
> how to dwell in mindfulness
> night and day
> "one who knows the
> better way to live alone."
> —*Bhaddekaratta Sutra (Buddha's Teachings)*

Contents

About the Author

D r. Ravi K. Puri has served his profession for almost thirty years in teaching and research. He has a broad range of experience and excelled in the field of Pharmacy, Biochemistry, and Environmental sciences. He has taught and researched at the various renowned Universities in the USA and abroad. He has published nearly a hundred research papers and scientific reviews in the journals of international repute including chapters in reference books published by CRC Press and Lewis publishers. He has been on the review panels of many prestigious scientific journals in the USA and abroad.

He took an early retirement from the University of Missouri while working as a Group Leader at the Environmental Trace Research Center and joined the hospitality industry in 2000. He excelled in the hospitality business by dint of his arduous work and honesty. Today, the Puri Group of Hospitality is enjoying an excellent reputation in the state of Missouri, USA, and has international franchises like Hilton Garden Inn, Double Tree, Holiday Inn, Hampton Inn, and Comfort Suites along with restaurants like Garden Grill, Sapphire, and a couple of Cheerleader Grills.

He is the celebrated author of the book entitled *Natural Aphrodisiac: Myth or Reality*. The book is widely acclaimed by physicians, pharmacists, nurses, natural products chemists, and herbalists. It is one of the most comprehensive and informative compilations on Natural Aphrodisiacs.

Apart from being a scientist, he has also been practicing spiritualty. He has already published a book entitled "Consciousness: The Ultimate Reality." Many readers highly applauded the book. Present publication is the result of his continuing search and belief in spirituality.

Acknowledgements

First, I am extremely grateful to my consciousness who is the real author of this book. I sincerely offer my humble gratitude from the core of my heart to 'That' existence who gave me the strength and intellect to express my feelings. I could sense that invisible power directing, assisting, and protecting me during the various walks of my life. I am honestly indebted to 'That'.

I am incredibly grateful to Linda Castillon, Transcendental Meditation Teacher for writing the foreword and equally thankful to Elizabeth Davis, News Paper Columnist and Freelance Editor, for editing the manuscript.

My gratitude to my family for their support and encouragement. During the period of writing this book, my wife, Mrinal had an accident which resulted in a stroke and I had to abandon my writings for almost two years. This event has shaken my life dramatically. Everything got changed around me, suddenly. I could never ever imagine that she was a potential source of my life and all my activities revolved around her. She has been a great source of inspiration to my progress and achievements in my life. Her long illness was a great spiritual awakening for me that led to realization that we people unnecessarily shed tears for the past and worry too much for the future when there is no certainty of life in the next moment. I profess, we should live from moment to moment. Always hold fast to the present and remember, every moment is of infinite value.

"I learnt to live in the present moment, next moment is not mine."
—Ravi K. Puri

Foreword

From an early-stage Dr. Puri was a seeker of Truth, the Ultimate Reality. In his life journey and quest for spirituality, Dr. Puri learned the value of meditation. Through his earnest desire to help people, he has written this book to accentuate the importance of meditation. He has done an excellent job in illustrating the significance of meditation in modern life. He also demystifies any doubts, inhibitions or myth people may have about meditation.

Having been born in India, the land of the Vedas, Dr. Puri grew up in the culture most infused with the science of consciousness, and then supplemented that foundation with his doctorate in Pharmacy. This combination of profound familiarity with both Vedic Science and Modern Science provides Dr. Puri a foundation to appreciate and express the fundamental implication of meditation over medication to develop perfect health thereby enabling any individual to naturally fulfill the purpose of their existence and evolve their consciousness to its full potential, the state of enlightenment. This book is a compassionate gift to all who read it.

Linda Castillon, Transcendental Meditation Teacher,
St. Louis, & Cape Girardeau, MO.

"Shine like the whole Universe is yours."
—*Rumi*

Your Thoughts Create Your Reality

Thoughts are immensely powerful and can drastically change the life of a person. Whatever thoughts one carries in his or her mind will continue to influence the emotions, actions and finally personality of that person. In other words, the entire alchemy of the body is changed through *thought process*. We exist within this reality and create our own reality. *As within, so without.*

The belief system, feelings, emotions, and actions, if remain the same that would bring the same stereo type of results again and again in the life of a person. "Insanity is doing the same thing over and over again and expecting different results." Articulated by Albert Einstein. If anyone wants different results, one must change the pattern of thinking. That would eventually transform the feelings, emotions, actions, habits, and character of an individual. Controlling of thoughts is not an easy phenomenon. The more you persist them, the more they resist. However, deviation of thoughts is possible. Meditation is one of the ways to divert negative thoughts which dramatically control the life. *"The goal of meditation is not to control your thoughts; it is to stop letting them control you."*

— Ravi K. Puri

"He whose joy is within, whose relaxation is within, and whose light is within, that Yogi, being well-established in Brahman (the Supreme Power) attains to absolute freedom."
— Bhagavad Gita.

Preface

During the period of writing my previous book *Consciousness: The Ultimate Reality*, I came across several people who wanted to know the right technique of meditation. They asked many questions about the problems they were facing during their meditation program. Some of them believed it was a myth not a reality and were carrying many misconceptions about meditation. In fact, many of them are entirely confused about the concept of meditation since there are so many types of meditation available in the literature. They were not sure which one to follow to get positive results. They wanted a comprehensive, simple, and clear-cut review on the phenomenon of meditation comprising its definition, background, method of practicing and benefits with validations. At the same time, I had been confused as well about meditation for some time owing to contradictory reports available in the literature. In the process of writing this book and even far earlier, I have been seeking answers from mystics in India regarding some questions or doubts in my mind about meditation. I met several mystics and visited their communes in India but could not get satisfactory answers to my queries. Everyone has his or her own concept and technique of meditation. So, it was thought, desirable, to review and explain meditation in general and specific focus *on its scientific validated benefits*.

I am neither a mystic nor a preacher and do not belong to any section of faith or religion, but I do believe in spirituality. In my opinion, meditation is not a myth but a scientific technique to stabilize the restless mind to tranquility without the help of tranquillizers. However, I am not in favor of long retreats of meditation. Regular Meditation for 15-20 minutes daily can be assumed as exercise for strengthening the mind as physical exercise for strengthening the body. "A sound mind in a sound body" —is very essential for a meaningful life. I do hope the readers will enjoy and follow the phenomenon of any meditation and make use of this text.

—Ravi K. Puri, Ph.D.
Columbia, MO, USA.

"In the beginning, there was nothingness — a darkness that stretched out to infinity." — *Tony Del Degan*

God is an intelligent sphere,
whose center is everywhere and
whose circumference is nowhere.
                    —Hermes Trismegistus

Chapter One:
Inner Fire for the Unknown

"Ignite your Inner fire, explore it, and share it with the world.
—*Ravi K. Puri.*

During my childhood, I used to watch my mother, father, and grandmother practicing meditation. Occasionally, I also used to sit by their side and try to imitate them. Whatever mantras they used to speak, I followed them sincerely and repeated after them, though I could never understand the meaning of those mantras on account of their language which was in Sanskrit, the primitive version of the Vedas. Hindu deities of Shiva, Ganesha, Rama, Hanuman, Krishna. Goddesses such as Durga, Laxmi, Saraswati, and many more were kept on a platform, in a small room at home known as *mandir* (puja place). In the middle of the platform was a big, beautiful metal statue of lord Krishna standing on one leg playing a flute, behind him was a beautiful white cow. This big metal frame of Krishna was the attraction of the *mandir.* The image of the beautiful statue is still fresh in my eyes. I, along with my younger brother and sisters, sat in front of that stage with folded hands and followed our parents without asking any questions. My grandmother used to tell us the stories from the religious books about Rama, Krishna and related Gods and Goddesses. It touched my heart specially to go through the life of Lord Krishna, who was known as king of kings, handsome of handsomest, lover of lovers, intellectual of intellectuals', yogi of yogis and warrior of warriors. I was curious to know more about him owing to his talents.

My parents taught all the children during their childhood, "God is omnipresent, omniscient and omnipotent, you cannot hide anything from Him. He lives in the sky. He watches all your actions. If you are doing anything wrong such as lying, stealing, and cursing others,

He is going to punish you". This information, imbibed in me as well as in the other four siblings fear, and curiosity to know Him who knows everything and who is present everywhere: powerful, unborn, immortal, self-illuminated and invisible. Inner fire to know the unknown was ignited in me during my childhood. My mind was full of questions and self-inquiry was going on all the time.

Who is He? Where does He live? What type of house is He living in there in the sky? How can He live among the cloud? Is He alone? Is He married? Does he have kids? Do they have shopping centers there? What kind of food is available there? Do they have trees and other vegetation there? How does He control the entire Universe? How does He travel? What kind of transportation does He have? Why is He living in the sky? What kind of person is He? Is He handsome and charming? Or ugly and cruel? These questions used to gnaw at me all the time. I was reluctant to ask these questions to my parents or teachers. I was afraid; they may consider me a fool or a crazy boy. In fact, the more a person thinks about God, the more complex and imaginative the concept becomes.

As I grew up, my quest to know the Almighty God was also enhanced. I started reading books about religion. I was born in a Hindu family, so it was easier for me to know first Hinduism. By the time I was 16, I read two critical religious books Bhagwat Gita and Ramayana. I was very much fascinated by Lord Krishna's life and his preaching through Bhagwat Gita. However, Ramayana was a story of Rama's life, and there were specific descriptions in the form of Shlokas which were beyond my comprehension. However, I learnt from my mother how to read and recite shlokas of Ramayana. My interest was more towards Bhagwat Gita which preached more than a religion. In my opinion, Gita is above religion, mostly spiritual.

My parents were living in the neighborhood predominantly a Sikh community. Most of our neighbors were Sikhs families. They influenced my childhood and adolescent. The back side of our house was a Sikh temple known as *Gurudwara*. Early in the morning at

4 am Sikh priest started singing sermons of Sikh religion in the *Gurudwara*. While in half-sleep, I could hear them. Sikhism teaches philosophy of nonviolence and spiritualism. *Jap Ji Sahib* narration of Sikh Guru, Nanak Dev Ji impressed me a lot. Some of the sermons, I even remembered by heart.

I also got the opportunity to get in touch with Professor Sehgal who lived in our neighborhood. Our families were remarkably close. We used to visit each other on regular basis. He was a physicist but had an excellent knowledge of Hindu Vedic Philosophy. I learnt a lot from him and really admired him.

In 1965, during my final year of Pharmacy degree, I wanted to write an article on "Religion and Spirituality" for my college magazine. Professor Sehgal helped me to write that article which was greatly appreciated by Professor K.S. Chopra, one of my professors at the school of pharmacy. He encouraged me to explore this subject further. That was the turning point of my life and gateway to the path of spirituality. I started to explore and comprehend the meaning of spirituality.

Most of the population in my hometown was of Jains community who believe in a religion known as Jainism. Some of my close friends were Jains. I got the opportunity to explore Jainism. The Jainism religion teaches non-violence, non-attachment, and asceticism. Jains take five main vows: *non-violence, truth, not stealing, celibacy or chastity or sexual continence, and non-attachment.* These principles have influenced Jain culture to a great extent such as leading to a predominantly vegetarian lifestyle that avoids harm to animals and their life cycles. Jainism has between four and five million followers, with most Jains residing in India only. Some of the largest Jain communities are present in Canada, Europe, Kenya, the United Kingdom, Hong Kong, Fiji, and the United States.

I liked one of the aspects of Jain religion that there was no beginning and no end of the Universe. Every realized soul is God. However, there is one aspect about their Jain Gurus, walking absolutely naked bare footed in the procession among young and old people and wearing a mask around the mouth, did not captivate me. Though, wearing a mask has becomes a way of life today.

After completing my post-graduate studies in pharmaceutical sciences, I joined my *alma mater* as an assistant professor in 1970. I taught there for ten years and remained busy in teaching and research, got little time to practice or follow any religion. I was awarded post-doctorate fellowship for two years in 1980 to pursue research on anticancer drugs from plants at the University of Mississippi, Oxford, USA. After completing my fellowship, I decided to settle in the USA for the better prospects of my sons and accepted a faculty position there.

During my stay in the United States, I was influenced by some Christian friends and studied the life and preaching of Jesus Christ, too. I liked and admired most of Christian teachings, particularly the Ten Commandments.

I had a Muslim Ph.D. student Neena Abraham from Sudan. After completing her Ph.D., she left for Abu Dhabi to join a faculty position. She gifted me a copy of the Holy Quran. I enjoyed exploring Quran, too. I always fail to understand why there is so much violence, unrest, and terrorism in the Muslim countries when their Holy Quran teaches nonviolence. I was consoled by the expression of Bertrand Russell, a great British Philosopher expressed very deeply, "The whole problem with the world is that fools and fanatics are always so certain of themselves, and wiser people so full of doubts." After going through most of the religions and their philosophies, I found that the essence of all the religions is virtually the same. Though, these differ in their practice and way of belief system but convey the same message. God is one, self-created, shapeless, birthless, ageless, deathless, omnipresent, self-illuminated whose perception is ineffable. All religions lead finally to one destination, as all rivers merge into one big ocean. All the scriptures of the world whether they be the Upanishad of the Hindus, the Bible of the Christians, the

4

Quran of the Muslims or the Dhammapada of the Buddhist— in all of them run the same nectar of knowledge and guidelines to reform the humanity.

Why do people fight for different religions? Why do they hate each other by religion? In fact, God has no religion. Religion is the concept of human beings and has been changing continuously with the mist of time. Religion is a belief or faith in any dogma or philosophy. Religion divides the society where spirituality unites it. One can believe in anything whatever he feels comfortable but should not criticize or curse any other religion or belief. Robert F. Kennedy articulated very precisely, "What is objectionable, what is dangerous about extremists is not that they are extreme, but that they are intolerant. The evil is not what they say about their cause, but what they say about their opponents."

Extreme belief or dogma in any concept generates anger, prejudice, and hate. Likewise, fanaticism in religion and discrimination in any race can adversely affect an individual, the society and the entire nation in general. Very well enunciated by Martin Luther King, "I look to a day when people will not be judged by the color of their skin, but by the content of their character."

Throughout the world, there are many religions. Each one preaches and claims that his religion is the right and the best one. Spirituality is above the religions and sees the truth in all of them. It unites them because the truth is the same for all the human beings despite their differences and uniqueness. It focuses on the quality of the divine message they share. Moreover, spirituality is related to soul where religious is to mind. Religion is the belief in someone's experience where spirituality is having its own experience. Religion creates fear and spirituality gives you freedom. Religion is a cult and spirituality is meditation. Religion lives in thoughts and spirituality lives in consciousness. Moreover, religion lives in the past and future: spirituality lives in the present. Above all, spirituality begins where religion ends.

Thus, spirituality is above the religion. I started practicing spirituality instead of following one religion. I do not support any dogma or any theology. People should change with time. To practice spirituality, there is a need to develop the discipline of meditation. The term and concept of Meditation baffles many people. They want to know the right technique or process of meditation. I was also curious to figure out the right technique of meditation. During my search of right meditation, I met many mystics and asked them about meditation. Everybody has a different concept of meditation as per his or her belief and experience. I could not get any satisfactory solution from any of them, rather they confused me. Finally, I carried out my own research on the concept of meditation and explored the teachings of well-known mystics such as Osho, Maharishi Mahesh, Sri Raman Maharishi, Paramhansa Yogananda, Swami Rama Krishna, Swami Vivekananda, Swami Sivananda, Nisargadatta Maharaj, Lord Buddha, Bhagavan Krishna's Gita, Guru Nanak Devji, Saint Kabir or many other truly enlightened Gurus. I have been practicing meditation over the last three decades and it has helped me in various walks of my life. I thought I should share my findings on meditation in the form of this text to help people who are inquisitive to know the art of meditation, its techniques, and its scientifically validated benefits. I hope it will be beneficial to all of them who are interested to tread this path.

> "All religions, arts and sciences are the branches of the same tree. All these aspirations are directed toward ennobling man's life, lifting it from the sphere of mere physical existence and leading the individual toward freedom."
>
> —Albert Einstein

Chapter Two:
Quest for Meditation

"Each soul is infinitely divine. The goal of life is to manifest this divinity within, by monitoring thought processes through meditation which leads to freedom from sufferings." —Ravi K. Puri

Today, the world is passing through a revolution of high technology. Life is moving amazingly fast. State of the art electronic devices such as smart wrist watches, iPods, iPads, Kindle, high-speed internet, artificial intelligence, sophisticated mobile phone, minicomputers, robots, and supersonic jets, have made life amazingly comfortable. Thus, the distance between the planets has overcome. Communication has become easy and rapid through this modern technology.

Despite the dramatic advances in high technology medicine such as gene therapy, laser, and plastic surgery, anti-aging devices, high-resolution body scanning and scientific miracles like vital organ transplantation, it is incredible that human beings know extraordinarily little about their true selves. We have enough knowledge of the various objects and have made tremendous progress in high tech, artificial intelligence, and trying hard to explore the universe. We have also achieved success in these areas to a great extent and even enhanced life expectancy by prolonging the aging process.

On the other hand, the advancement in technology has resulted in a rat race of developing superior nuclear weapons throughout the world. Every country, big or small, rich, or poor, wants to be ahead in this race. This competition, unfortunately is causing a tremendous amount of physical, emotional, and mental stress. In other words, a revolution in technology has screwed up humanity.

All over the world, intolerance, crime, corruption, and terrorism are thriving, and many nations feel insecure among the others. Thus, we are capturing the *outer world* at the cost of the *inner world*. It is very pertinent to maintain a balance between the *outer* and *inner* worlds to keep peace in the universe. It is not out of the way to cite Terrence McKenna, an American ethnobotanist, mystic, and author, "We have been to the moon, we have charted the depth of the ocean and heart of the atom, but we have a fear of looking inward to ourselves because we sense that is where all the contradictions flow together."

Each individual must find the cause of sorrows in his inner world. Man has become unconsciously cruel, selfish, arrogant, often behaves sadistically and hysterically. He is uncouth in his thoughts, low in his morals and traumatized all round in his individual capacity to face his personal life and its problems. He lost his self-control. Like an abondon garden, the inner world has grown into a jungle. Man lives the outer world, from within. If he controls the inner world, the external world cannot influence how strong it may be. "An individual who has mastered himself is a master of the external world," is an old saying.

The sufferings of the present age are because of one's own weaknesses, within. Everyone is a slave to his own passion, lust, greed, anger, false pride and intellectual bankruptcy. He is striving hard to gain materialistic comforts at the cost of his inner peace, moral and ethics. Shattered and confused, he cannot face the challenge of the external world. He is like a neglected boat at the mercy of the waves. That is no life.

Among the world's chaos, intolerance, terrorism, corruption on the rise and countries at war, if we train ourselves by any technique to live a more definite life of self-mastery that can control our inner world, our external world problems can be mitigated to a great extent. How to control this mental turmoil? The practice of Meditation is the answer. Mediation is one of the techniques that brings change in consciousness of the people, which results in the transformation of the entire world. Very nicely expressed by Dalai Lama, "If every 8-year-old in the world is taught meditation, we will eliminate violence from the world within one generation." The change in our thinking is very essential if we want to change the modern world. By changing the inner attitude of minds, we can change the outer aspects of our lives. The outer world reflects the inner world. The all is mind: universal is mental. Mental transmutation changes the personality of an individual. We need strong motivation and determination to manifest this expression. The question arises, how to do this? The answer is simple, by meditation.

In this modern age, people require spiritual discipline through meditation to calm their shattering nerves and thus freedom from all sufferings instead of depending upon antidepressants. Meditation introduces to the spiritual part what is missing in most of the people. Spiritual growth comes from meditation. Through meditation, one knows himself. *Meditation is not to control your thoughts, but it is the way to prevent these thoughts to control you.* Very nicely articulated by Swami Paramahansa Yogananda, an Indian mystic and celebrated author of the book, *Autobiography of a Yogi,* States, "Meditation is like giving a hug to ourselves, getting in touch with that awesome reality in us. While meditating, we feel a deep sense of intimacy with God, a love that is inexplicable."

Since antiquity, man has been seeking something beyond himself. First, he struggles for survival, and after that, he fulfills his ambitions and dreams. When all his materialistic comforts are fulfilled, he starts longing for meaning of life, something unknown, the real truth or God or reality. He focuses on Meditation and wants to know about it. It is not out of the way to refer that "Meditation is the inexpressible longing of the Inner Self for the Infinite." Stated by Helena P. Blavatsky, a Russian occultist, philosopher, and author who co-founded the Theosophical Society in 1875.

Nevertheless, all the renowned Nobel Laureate like Newton (1642-1726), Max Planck (1858-1947), Albert Einstein (1879-1955), Nikola Tesla (1856 –1943), Arthur Compton (1892-1962), and many more, during their exemplary discoveries were also searching the truth or ultimate reality. In one way or the other most of them believed in *that* unknown power running the universe. They could not discover the mystery since they were part of that mystery. Search for the reality leads to some doctrine or philosophy or some faith or religion which finally results in some devotion or meditation to the unknown. The truth or reality cannot be found by books, through priests, philosophers, or saviors. Nobody can teach you meditation. The seeker has to seek by himself or herself only. Meditation is the path which the person follows for himself while trying to get beyond the limitation of the mind. Thus, it is very pertinent to know thyself. To understand the self through meditation is the beginning of wisdom. Once you find God within, you will find Him without, in all the entire creation.

There are many questions which arise in the mind of an individual who is interested in meditation. These are as follows:

Should everyone meditate? What is meditation? What is its concept? What is its experience? What do we feel during meditation? Do we see lights or images? Why is it required? Why people do meditation in the Temples, Churches, Gurudwara and Mosques? Do they please their chosen God by meditation? Is God listening to each and everybody's prayers? Is meditation beneficial to health and happiness? Is it hype? Is it a myth or reality? Is it a sheer waste of time? Is there any logic behind it? Or is it a charade? Are the so-called benefits mentioned in the literature scientifically proved? Is it a placebo for our problems? Do we gain anything, or it is sheer for passing time? If not, how should we do it? What is the correct and efficient technique?

In the middle of some curiosity about meditation, someone asked Gautama Buddha, a sage, philosopher, and founder of Buddhism.

"What have you gained from meditation all these years?" He replied, "Nothing. But I lost some anger, anxiety, depression, insecurity, fear of old age and death."

Why do people meditate? Some of the common responses from people to this question, are as follow:

For religious purposes.
For protection from ill-fate.
To search the unknown.
For Fear of losing possessions and loved one.
To gain lost health.
For prosperity in business or job.
For a better future.
To feel inner peace.
To get rid of bad habits.
To get rid of bad karmas.
Asking God to fulfil some desires.
To get rid of the cycle of birth and death.

All kinds of fears, disappointments, and sufferings lead to the practice of meditation. Out of frustrations, ill health, failures and letdowns in life, some people get to meditation. They are upset when it does not help them. Most people would like to meditate, only if they understood its value and experienced its benefits. A very few people adopt meditation practice from the early life due to their inner quest or craving to know the truth or reality of life. One of the burning examples is Prince Siddhartha, who left his wealth, wife, son, and luxury for searching the ultimate reality for eternal happiness. Finally, he was successful to achieve his goal and attained enlightenment at the age of 77. Later, he was known as Buddha. Similarly, many mystics who became known to the world started their journey to meditation quite early in their life and tread the path of spirituality throughout their life.

Meditation is not a hasty remedy. It is a slow process that needs guidance, consistency, and discipline. Like any other practice, the result usually follows a great devotion. To acquire any inspiration in life, one must strive hard with honesty, hard work and persistence. It is a holistic approach to cure and needs time with dedication. Regular practice is required. *Meditation is a lot like a physical exercise doing reps at a gym. It strengthens your attention muscles.* The purpose of meditation is to train your brain just like you do the rest of your muscles. To develop six packs, it takes regular exercise and discipline diet with devotion for a length of time. Similar is the case of meditation which requires regularity and devotion to bring results.

It is also not easy to define the purpose of meditation since every meditator has his own reasoning to practice meditation. Moreover, it also depends upon family background, bringing up, mental temperament, inborn qualities, and conscious progression of an individual. There should be a burning desire to tread the path of spirituality.

The goal of meditation is to revive the lost self and to bring it in touch with the Higher Self. Thus, making it aware of its divinity. Meditation is the direct experience of pure consciousness. People who meditate consistently and systematically must believe that behind the physical world, there is a latent spiritual world of unconceivable brilliance. To get there one has to lose himself. As they say, "when I was there, He was not there. When He was there, I was not there."

Likewise, Christ illustrated meditation as, "He who would lose his life, for my sake, shall find it." In other words, it can be expressed, "He who would find the *Eternal* has first to lose the 'me'. It cannot be achieved at once, but every effort in the right direction has its consequences. Helena Blavatsky, a Russian occultist, philosopher, author and co-founder of the Theosophical Society described in her book, *The Voice of the Silence*, "Learn that no efforts, not the smallest—whether in right or wrong direction—can vanish from the world of causes. Even wasted smoke remains not traceless. In the

Great Journey, causes sown each hour bear each its harvest of effects, for rigid Justice Rules the World. With mighty sweep of never erring action, it brings to mortals' lives of weal or woe, the Karmic progeny of all our former thoughts and deeds."

Byron Katie is an American speaker and author who teaches a method of self-inquiry says, "Meditation means questioning the stressful thoughts that cause all the suffering in the world. The whole world is an effect of mind inside and outside always match – they are reflection of each other. After the mind deeply questions and sees its own thoughts, it surrenders to itself and experiences a world that is kind and absolutely saves, the benevolent mind projecting a benevolent world."

Jiddu Krishna Murti, an Indian spiritual philosopher enunciated, "The more you know the self, the more clarity is. Self-knowledge has no end—you don't come to an achievement, and you don't come to a conclusion. It is an endless river."

As per Father Thomas Keating, one of the great spiritual leaders of present time, who started centering prayer, a method of meditation used by Christians placing a strong emphasis on interior silence, articulated, "Meditation is non-conceptual prayer, a relationship with God that emphasizes the heart rather than the mind. It is the search for the higher states of consciousness."

Spiritual knowledge regarding the invisible elusive worlds cannot be acquired by ordinary mental activity. It can be achieved with mental stability. It is necessary to go into the deeper levels of mind and consciousness by means of well-defined techniques of meditation that can shape and transform our minds.

Ajahn Amaro, a Theravada Buddhist monk, articulated about meditation. "If you have time to breathe you have time to meditate. You breathe when you walk. You breathe when you stand. You breathe when you lie down."

The term of *meditation* has been used since antiquity. But its real meaning is still ambiguous. Meditation is a word that has come to be used loosely and inaccurately in the modern world. That is why there is so much confusion about its practice. Meditation is not a mystic experience. If some mystics believe it as mystic experience, they are exploiting the innocent people. No mystic can give you any divinity, one has to attain it by himself only through self-analysis and self-experience. Meditation is a conscious phenomenon. The ultimate object of meditation is to attain conscious awareness of God, and of the soul's eternal oneness of God.

Some people use the word *meditate* when they mean thinking or contemplating; others use it to refer to daydreaming or fantasizing. Some think it is a kind of concentration. Meditation is the first stage of a process which gradually develops into concentration. In concentration there is no movement of the mind. In meditation, the mind moves from one relevant idea to another. Any concentration will involve consistent mental effort to build up the ability to focus without submitting to distraction. Meditation does not require effort. It should be spontaneous, simple of fun and a cool thing to do. It is an important technique to transform the mind. Persons with a lack of concentration must begin with meditation, whereas for those who have the capacity of intense concentration, meditation is redundant. They should concentrate on *"I am neither the gross body nor the subtle mind, I am a pure soul."*

Meditation is not any assignment. It should be considered as fun. It is not to be done to achieve some goal. When you play to win, then the play becomes work and focus is on results. You may not succeed. *"I can't meditate since I am not going to achieve anything,"* it is a business-like attitude. Meditation is nonbusiness. It is the capacity to enjoy moment to moment, all that comes to you. The moment you allow the whole existence to go in, you become one with it. If you become discontinuous with your past, then that very moment is enjoyable. In that very moment you are centered, in your being, and then you know all that has always been yours, all that has just been waiting for you.

Some people hear sounds, voices, visualize colors or feel involuntary sensations after closing eyes, and think that they have attained some level of enlightenment. These symptoms are due to a loss of awareness and control and have nothing to do with enlightenment. Colors in the eyes-- one can visualize different types of colors such as blue, yellow, green, brown, indigo, black, too during the mundane Retinal examination. Frankly speaking, any mystic or transcendental experience through meditation is nothing but merely a self-hypnosis.

There is also an old concept of meditation that we must control our thoughts during meditation. Some believe they can't stop thoughts and hence could not focus, so they are unable to perform meditation. It is not possible to control thoughts. About 50,000 -60,000 thoughts do come across in the mind per day. Rather, mental efforts such as *"I must stop thinking"* are detrimental to the mind. It causes more problems. The idea of resisting thinking can not do meditation. The efforts to control thoughts result in more disturbances. The world-renowned founding father of analytical psychology, Carl Jung, put it best, "What you resist, persists." This monkey mind creates a stress-based downward spiral, opening the door up to anxiety, depression, addiction, and diseases. *"To the mind that is still, the whole universe surrenders."* Expressed by Lao Tzu. Meditation is an effortless phenomenon that leads to "thoughtless awareness." It should be achieved effortlessly. The Zen teachers are saying, "No effort is needed: it is effortless."

However, meditation is above all this. Jiddu. Krishnamurti, one of the great spiritual leaders of the 20th century who was a well-known writer and speaker on philosophical and spiritual subjects, articulated, "If there is no meditation, then you are like a blind man in a world of great beauty, light and color." He further emphasized, "So, to meditate is to purge the mind of its self-centered activity.

And if you have come this far in meditation, you will find there is silence, a total emptiness. The mind is uncontaminated by society; it is no longer subject to any influence, to the pressure of any desire. It is completely alone, and being alone, untouched, it is innocent. Therefore, there is a possibility for the timeless, eternal, to come into being. This whole process is meditation."

As per Osho, a controversial Indian Philosopher and mystic said, "Meditation is nothing but a device to make you aware of your real self—which is not created by you, which need not be created by you, which you already are. You are born with it. You are it!"

As per Maharishi Mahesh Yogi, an Indian mystic, and founder of Transcendental Meditation, believed, "Meditation is the sharp tool to dig out the great treasure hidden within everybody's inner personality." Meditation is the ineffable desire of the Inner Self to seek the unknown or God. The art of meditation is the art of being within yourself, to know the self deeply. It is the art of getting to know one's mind, mental and emotional states. The path of meditation leads to the door of awareness and loving kindness of limitless expansion.

People have been showing love for God since the time immemorial. King, Sultan, and wealthy people have made beautiful temples, mosques, and churches to express their love for God. Some people pilgrimage famous Temples, Shrines and related religious places to emphasize their appreciation while donating money and gifts to please God. Some love him conditionally, and some worship him unconditionally. Conditionally means while giving gifts and donating the money, they ask Him to fulfill their wants. Unconditionally means, thank Him for imparting them wealth, health, and happiness. Some sing songs of His praise, too. Some read literature about His existence to search Him in any form. But He is formless and unknown. His perception is the way of belief. Different beliefs took the shape of various religions. Some pine for Him and adopt meditation to adore

Him. A section of people are still confused about the existence of God. They say, if there is no God, why should they meditate?

In the last four decades, meditation has entered the mainstream of modern medicine, and contemporary culture, too, as complementary medicine. It is being practiced by almost everyone such as business executives, professionals, scientists, physicians, politicians, and actors.

There are many techniques available for meditation. The method and practice of meditation vary according to one's faith. Present books limit to the discussion of a few interesting aspects of meditation, which are not generally understood, but are of vital interest to those who are serious about the problems of the inner life and do not want to go through their meditation as a mere routine.

However, before selecting any practice of meditation, an individual should ask himself. *What am I trying to do? Why do I need to do meditation? Whom should I meditate? Which dogma, theory or religion should I follow?*

Meditation is not merely sitting down in a lotus posture and making the mind bring up a connected series of *mantras* on a chosen religion. Neither is the common practice of allowing the mind to move in accustomed and well-worn grooves created by repetition of religious texts or *mantras,* be considered as meditation, though this is what most religious people do when they "meditate" during their daily religious regime.

Meditation is a part of all religions and every religion preaches it. It is a science that follows an order, a principle, and produces tested results. It is a specific technique for calming the mind and attaining a state of consciousness which is entirely different from the usual waking state of consciousness. It is the art of getting to know one 's self deeply, particularly mind and emotional state. In simple expression, it is the technique to calm the thoughts that controls the body. Meditation is to dissolve the thoughts in eternal pure consciousness.

During meditation, the mind is clear, relaxed, and inwardly engrossed. An individual is fully awake and alert. His mind is not focused on the external world. Meditation requires an inner state that is still and one-pointed so that the mind becomes silent. When the mind is calm and no longer sidetracks, and free from thoughts, meditation deepens. Meditation is a direct approach to the mind. Plenty of thoughts, emotions, sensations, perceptions, illusions, expectations, egos, anxieties, fears, disappointments, frustrations, reactions, conversations, ambitions, pleasant and painful memories and fantasies etc. are being displayed continuously by the mind. The mind is restless like a drunk monkey bitten by the wasp. Meditation is a direct approach to calm the mind - where a person watches his mind directly as a seer, a witness, an observer but do not get attached to it. As per Eknath Eswaran, an India-born spiritual leader, "Having come to realize in the first stage of meditation that we are not our bodies, in the second stage we make an even more astounding discovery; we are not our minds either."

The goal of meditation is to go beyond the mind and experience the essential inner nature, which is peaceful, and blissful. The Mind itself is the chief obstacle standing between the self and the awareness. It is unmanageable, disruptive, and it resists any effort to guide it on a particular path. The mind is full of fantasies, fears, daydreams, or hallucinations. It is challenging to achieve the tranquility or calmness required for deep meditation. As gold purified in a furnace loses its impurities and achieves its own true nature, the mind gets rid of the impurities of the attributes of delusion, attachment, and purity through meditation and attains reality.

During our early life, we learn all the etiquettes of the outer world such as how to walk, talk, eat and behave but we never learn how to know our inner world. Nobody has taught us how to look within, to find within and verify within. All our life, we remain strangers

18

to ourselves while trying to know others. All stress, anxiety, and depression are caused when we ignore ourselves and start living to please others. To know thyself is only possible through meditation which can bestow permanent bliss, *Sat Chit Anand*, an everlasting joy. It is the truth supported by sages and celebrated masters.

Nowadays, meditation is in vogue. Search any engine on the internet; there are plenty of advertisements about the art of meditation. Lots of meditation centers have been opened. People are being lured with false promises to cure them of all kinds of diseases through meditation. In other words, meditation has entered the mainstream of medicine. Retired rich people are lonely and have money to get into this. It can solve their social and mental problems, too. Posh residential rooms with all kinds of facilities such as spa, swimming, sports, massage, yoga, beautiful rooms for meditation, and delicious food attract these people in a natural resort with beautiful sceneries such as snowy mountain lakes and waterfalls. They are away from the hustle and bustle of the crowded cities, and thus 50 percent of the problems are mitigated in such a panoramic view with a calm and quiet environment.

True meditation is a state of no-mind, meaning, and a state of pure consciousness with no content. Generally, an individual's mind is too much full of rubbish, just like a mirror covered with dust. The mind is a constant traffic: thoughts are moving, desires are moving, memories are moving, ambitions are moving – it is a constant traffic! Day in, day out. Even when you are asleep the mind is functioning, it is dreaming. It is still thinking; it is still in worries and anxieties. It is preparing for the next day; an underground preparation is going on in the subconscious mind. This is the state of no meditation – just the opposite of it, is meditation. When there is no traffic and thinking has ceased, no thought moves, no desire stirs, you are utterly silent – that silence is meditation. And in that silence truth is known, and never otherwise. Meditation is a state of no-mind. Meditation imparts us inner peace and solace, even in the presence of chaotic or stressful outer world. Meditation is the means that takes us from the surface of life to its depths. True meditation is unifying. It awakens the Inner-Self and rejuvenates and harmonizes the person. Burn down the forest of ignorance with the fire of understanding that "*I am the pure consciousness,*" and be happy and free from distress. Meditate on yourself as pure consciousness.

> "*Meditation is painful in the beginning, but it bestows immortal bliss and supreme joy in the end.*"
>
> —*Swami Sivananda*

Chapter Three:
Meditation and its Forms

"Meditation is being in tune with our inner energy source,"

Meditation has been the part of spiritual and religious practices since time immemorial. The English word 'meditation' derives from *meditatum,* a Latin term meaning 'to ponder.' Monk Guigo II, a Carthusian Monk, introduced the terminology in the 12th century AD.

The exact time of initiation of meditation is unknown. It has been in practice even before the birth of modern civilization. However, most scholars agree that practice of meditation started about 5,000 years ago in India. The earliest documented records of meditation were cited in Vedas, Hindu sacred texts in India, around 1500 BCE. However, historians believe that origin of worship or meditation was practiced before this time, as early as 3000 BCE.

Mann (2011), an American Journalist and author, described in his article, *The Birth of Religion,* in the National Geography magazine about the world's first temple in Turkey. Scientists have excavated a site in Turkey enough to convey the reverence. Pillars at the temple of Gobekli Tepe, in Southern Turkey were 11,600 years old and up to 18 feet tall reflect a surprising new theory about the origin of worship. .

The *Yoga Sutras of Patanjali,* by Saint Patanjali, comprising many aspects of meditation was published between 400-100 BCE. The Yoga Sūtras of Patañjali was the most translated ancient Indian text in the medieval era.

During the same period, the *Bhagavad Gita* was written, which discourses the philosophy of yoga, meditation and the ways of living a spiritual life. Chapters six and thirteen are particularly focused on meditation and its philosophy. Soon, the practice of meditation was accepted by neighboring countries such as China and surrounding areas and slowly became a part of their religions.

Progress in meditation was also observed in Taoist (Chinese religion) between 600-500 BC. A Japanese monk, Dosho, explored Zen during his visit to China in 653 BC and introduced the practice of meditation on his return to Japan.

During the 18th century, the other cultures in the West also accepted the practice of meditation. Later, "Tibetan Book of the Dead" published in the year 1927, also captivated most of the Westerners and awakened them about the process of meditation. Slowly and steadily, it came into the mainstream of every religion.

Swami Vivekananda, an Indian Monk, visited Chicago in 1883. He was a pioneer in the introduction of the Indian philosophies of Vedanta and Yoga to the Western world. As per Vivekananda, "Meditation means the mind is turned back upon itself. The mind stops all the thought-waves, and the world stops. Your consciousness expands. Every time you meditate, you keep your growth." His visit to the USA also lured the western towards meditation.

Paramahansa Yogananda, an Indian mystic and celebrated father of Kriya Yoga, founded his commune in California in 1920 to teach scientific methods of meditation and principles of spiritual living through *Kriya Yoga*. According to him meditation utilizes concentration in its higher form. Concentration consists in freeing the attention from distractions, restlessness and in focusing it on God.

Later, the *Vipassana* meditation started in Burma in the 1950s. Vipassana is a self-transformation through self-observation. It connects the mind and the body by focusing on breathing that form the lifeforce of the body. Repeated focus on breathing interconnect and conditioning the mind. It is thus an observation-based, self-exploratory journey to the common root of mind and body. The process dissolves negative thoughts, resulting in a balanced mind full of love and compassion. Thus, life becomes more enjoyable, peaceful, devoid of delusion, and gains self-control.

Maharishi Mahesh Yogi introduced transcendental meditation to the West and became famous in the 1960s as the spiritual Guru to the Beatles. The Transcendental Meditation is a form of silent mantra meditation and is practiced for 20 minutes twice per day while sitting with one's eyes closed. It is one of the most widely practiced, and researched meditation techniques, with over 300 peer-reviewed studies published. At present, TM is extremely popular meditation in the USA and abroad.

In 1979, the Mindfulness-Based Stress Reduction (MBSR) program was instituted in the United States. Meditative techniques were applied as complementary medicines in the treatment plan for patients with chronic diseases. Meditation became increasingly more common. A survey in 2007 found that almost 1 in 10 Americans has meditated. It plays a significant role in many religious traditions and rituals, in addition to helping individuals to manage stress and improve overall well-being. Mindfulness is a concept of 2,500-year-old Buddhist practice Vipassana or Insight Meditation. People of every religion and faith including agnostics and atheists have been using Vipassana technique since the time immemorial.

Forms of Meditation:
Many forms of meditation have been developed. Most of the people are baffled and do not understand which forms of meditation to follow. Some of the techniques are simple and, where most of them are difficult and monotonous, each method of meditation is simply a training to strengthen the wavering mind that ultimately helps to manifest the divinity within. Peace comes from within. Meditation is being in tune with our inner universe and to strengthen the outer universe. In other words, the technique of meditation involves focusing the awareness inwards. The focus of inward attention could be on a mantra, or on the breathing process. It could be on a vision, or an emotion. Some scan areas of the body where some ponder on some

image or statue of their idol. The focus is to improve concentration on any object and get rid of redundant negative thoughts and stabilize the mind. In short, *quiet the mind and the soul will whisper.*

Moreover, no single technique is suitable to everyone. One should select any technique as per his or her liking and comfort zone. Whatever technique one follows as per his or her likings and prejudices, the result would be the same.

There is no hard and fast rule or any restriction to perform meditation, anyone can practice. One does not have to be a hippie or a yogi or a saint or a priest or a mystic to practice meditation. There is no need of wearing saffron color clothes, shave the head and applying sandalwood paste on the forehead. However, in order to get the benefits, a proper technique and particular type of meditation which suits an individual is required since each type of meditation affects the brain in a unique way.

Meditation is only beneficial with consistency. Regular practice at the same place and same time in a calm and quite environment is required. The more regularly and more deeply you meditate, the sooner you will find yourself acting always from a center of inner peace. Although some people may follow several types of meditation, mastering the one type will yield more significant brain adaptations instead of practicing different techniques. The neural adaptations in the brain will be stronger while picking and sticking to one technique since neurons are fired and wired together and repeating the same form of meditation would have significant effect on the brain.

There are many different techniques and forms of meditation depending upon a specific religion. Christian, Hindus, Buddhist, Chinese, and Sufi all follow their own techniques as per their belief system and teachings as outline in the figures. The common element in these techniques is the skill in concentrating, studying the mind and not paying attention to thoughts. The person has to set aside some time from the daily pace of busy schedule and sit quietly with closed eyes to reflect on thoughts or images that create internal feelings of peace and relaxation.

It is redundant to describe each technique of meditation in detail with their pros and cons since ample information is available in the literature about them. So, a bird's eye view of the commonly practiced meditations is depicted as follows.

1. Guided Meditations:

It is also called a universal meditation devoid of any religion. Guided meditation is a technique by which one or more participants meditate under the guidance of a trained teacher, either in person or via a written text on website, sound recording, video, or audiovisual media comprising of music or verbal instructions, or a combination of both. The instructions are very comprehensive and easy to follow through the entire process. With regular practice, an individual gets use to guided practice and does not require any further help. It's one of the easiest ways to enter into a state of deep relaxation and inner stillness.

There are plenty of guided meditations available for free online, YouTube, and even in the App Store on iPhone such as Headspace, Trixie, MindFi, Timeless Meditation and Sonus Island. Then, there are specific commune or meditation centers like Ananda Meditation, Chopra Meditation Center, Mind Valley and Maharishi University of Management who have courses on meditation. No doubt, these courses are expensive, but at least one can learn directly from an experienced teacher.

1.2 Guided Imagery:

Guided imagery is based on the concept that the body and the mind are connected. Using all the senses, the body seems to respond as its imagination is real. This is a type of meditation that involves focusing attention on an image. It can be anything, a waterfall, nature view or any pleasing scene.

1.3 Visual Imagery: Visual imagery means perceiving information through sight, smell, sound, and touch when in fact, none of these stimuli are happening.

Many people are good at imagination. For them, it is possible to perceive a very real scene inside the mind. For example, one might imagine a sound of waterfall from the mountain, sunset on the ocean and hear the noise of waves, smell some particular essence in a beautiful garden, feel a cool breeze or good time spent with his or her beloved. All this imagery is going inside the mind. This also helps to deviate negative thoughts in the mind.

1.4 Affirmation Meditation:
Affirmation Meditation is the practice of positive thoughts to focus, relax and enhance overall feelings of happiness. An affirmation can be anything, repeated out loud or in thoughts. Affirmations should be positive, personal, specific, and in the present tense. The goal is for thoughts to consume the awareness to manifests goals or changes in behavior of an individual.

This type of affirmation meditation is to inoculate a particular way of thinking within the mind. Meditator goes into a relaxed state. Thus, the message sinks in a better way to the brain. During this relaxation, positive affirmations relating to a particular focus are stated such as:

I release all anger ....and accept complete serenity.
I give away all guilt ...... and receive bliss.
I exhale bitterness .... and inhale peace.
I breathe out hate ... .and breathe in love.
I exhale fear......... ....and breathe in courage.
I give away attachment... and accept freedom.
I release tension ....and accept relaxation.
I forget the past ....and focus on the present.
I forgive all .... and be forgiven.

There are many websites comprising affirmations. Meditators can select some affirmations as per their likings.

2. Body Scan Meditation:

The body scan is a powerful and healing form of meditation. It is also known as *New Age Meditation.* It comprises increasing awareness of any stress and pain in certain parts of the body. It can be performed while seated or lying down in a comfortable position. The various regions of the body are scanned through the mind systematically and intentionally. The mind is focused anywhere on the body: starting from the left side toes, foot, leg including the shin, calf, knee, kneecap, thigh, entire pelvic region, hip and the genitals. Similarly, scan the right side. Then focus successively and slowly whole body, the abdomen, and the upper and lower back, the chest, and the ribs, breasts, heart, lungs, shoulder blades, all the way up to the collarbones and shoulders. From here attention is moved to both the arms, starting from the tips of the fingers and thumbs, and scanning through the fingers, the palms, and backs of the hands, the wrists, forearms, elbows, upper arms, armpits, and shoulders again. Finally, it moves into the neck and throat, and lastly, the face and the head. During mind scanning, positive thoughts are required to heal the various regions. Breathing technique is especially important during scanning of each part of the body. In each scan area, bring the awareness and gentle curiosity to the bodily sensations present. While scanning any major area, "breathe in" to it on the in breath and let go of that region on the outbreath. Continue slowly to the next part of the body. In case there is a tension, or of other intense sensations in a particular part of the body, "breathe in" to them—using the in breath gently to bring awareness right into the sensations, and, have a sense of their letting go, or releasing, on the outbreath. In thoughts one can say in silence, *"Heal the area and let the toxins go away with the breath."*

3. Brainwave Meditation:

Of late, science has begun to uncover the merits of meditation using state of the art techniques such as neuroimaging, functional magnetic resonance imaging, and brain mapping technology by scanning the brain of the meditators. Following these techniques, scientists found that certain brainwaves at appropriate frequency work better than the other. At the root of our thoughts, emotions and behaviors is the communication between neurons within our brain. Brain waves are produced by synchronized electrical pulses from millions of neurons communicating with each other.

Some meditations involve the use of brainwaves. These meditations incorporate some relaxing music or sound specific wave frequencies. There are five major types of brain waves, each corresponding to different activities as per the state of consciousness. If one of the waves is overproduced or under produced in the brain, it can cause health problems. During meditation, brain waves move from a higher frequency to a lower frequency and activate the different regions of the brain. Slower wavelengths impart more time between thoughts and more opportunity to skillfully selected thoughts.

The brain is an electrochemical organ and is comprised of billions of neurons (brain cells), firing and wiring at the same time and communicating with each other by way of electric impulses. This combination of neurons signals can produce an incredible amount of electrical movement in the brain, detected by EEG (Electroencephalograph). All electrical activity that occurs in the brain is known as brainwave patterns, due to wave-like characteristics. These patterns are intricately connected to thoughts, emotions, moods, biological chemistry and basically functioning of the entire body system. Brain waves change with emotional activities such as injury, medications, alcohol, fatigue, emotional distress, pain, and stress. Brain waves are divided into band width to describe their function. It is a continuous spectrum of consciousness.

Brain waves are measured in Hertz, cycle per second. *Heart also has a system of neurons that have both short and long memories, and the signal they send to the brain can affect one's emotions. In fact, heart can send comparatively more information to brain than brain sends to the heart.*

3.1 Gama Waves:

Gamma waves' frequency range is 27 Hz to 100 Hz. This is the state of hyperactivity and active learning. The gamma state is the most appropriate time to retain information. At 27 Hz Gamma waves are vital for learning, formation of ideas, memory processing. Gamma waves at 40 Hz are more important for awareness and learning new things. It has been revealed that individuals who have learning infirmities tend to have lower gamma activity than average. Too much gamma activity results in anxiety, and stress. Too little gamma waves lead to ADHD (Attention Deficit Hyperactivity Disorder), depression and learning disabilities. The activity of gamma rays in the brain region can be increased or balanced by meditation.

3.2 Beta Waves:

Beta waves' frequency range is 12 Hz to 40 Hz. Beta waves occur when the brain is working on goal-oriented tasks, such as planning a program, writing a proposal, or reacting actively over a particular issue. EEG showed few beta waves during meditation and resting. Beta brain waves are linked with the waking state of consciousness and an intensified state of alertness, logic and critical reasoning. Thus, Beta waves are known as high frequency low amplitude brain waves that are observed during waking state of consciousness. The right amount of beta waves in the system are responsible for the activities of waking state. Too much beta waves activities in the brain lead to stress and anxiety. The higher beta frequencies are associated with high levels of arousal. Too little activity leads to ADHD (Attention Deficit and Hyperactivity Disorder) and ADD (Attention Deficit Disorder), daydreaming, depression, poor cognition, and insomnia. Low beta activity between12 Hz - 15 Hz can be related to insomnia.

Beta waves are exhibited in the people throughout the day while thinking, writing, reading, and socialization. By stimulating the right beta waves activity, a person can improve their energy levels, concentration, emotional stability, and attentiveness. Beta waves are linked with logic, whereas Alpha waves relate to creativity. In fact, a healthy mind is one that has a healthy balance of Alpha and Beta waves.

3.3 Alpha Waves:

Alpha waves frequency is between 8 Hz - 12 Hz. The person is awake but in a relaxed state the brain is not processing too much information. This natural state usually occurs just before falling into sleep or the first few minutes getting up each morning. Studies have shown that alpha waves are more active in meditators. People who meditate regularly revealed more activity of alpha waves. The activity of the alpha waves has been attributed to relaxation of the mind and the reduction of pain, discomfort, anxiety and stress. Meditation induces alpha activity. Alpha brain waves are present during deep relaxation in the dreaming and sleeping state of consciousness. Meditation brings that state of mind, improves imagination, visualization, memory, learning and concentration. Alpha waves revive conscious awareness and are deeper and more effective about 7.5Hz. The brain starts to slow down out of thinking mind. Feelings more calm, peaceful, and grounded. An "alpha state" is followed a yoga class, a walk in the woods, a pleasurable sexual encounter or during any activity that helps relax the body and mind. Alpha state is lucid, reflective, has a slightly diffused awareness. The hemispheres of the brain are more balanced (neural integration). Alpha waves are more abundant in the posterior parts of the brain during meditation than during simple relaxation and are characteristic of wakeful rest.

As per Øyvind Ellingsen, cellular cardiologist, at the Norwegian University of Science and Technology, "Alpha waves have been used as a universal sign of relaxation during meditation and other types of rest. The number of alpha waves increases when the brain relaxes from intentional, goal-oriented tasks. This is a sign of deep relaxation, -- but it does not mean that the mind is void."

According to Ellingsen, "Spontaneous wandering of the mind is something you become more aware of and familiar with when you meditate, this, default activity of the brain is often underestimated. It probably represents a kind of mental processing that connects various experiences and emotional residues, puts them into perspective and lays them to rest."

"These findings indicate that you step away from problem solving both when relaxing and during meditation," says Ellingsen (Ellingsen 2010).

However, neuroimaging studies by Malia F. Mason, Professor at the Columbia University, suggests that the normal resting state of the brain is a silent current of thoughts, images and memories that is not induced by sensory input or intentional reasoning but emerges spontaneously "from within."

3.4 Theta Waves:

Theta waves have frequency 3 Hz - 8 Hz when exceptionally relaxed or in a light sleep or dream state of consciousness. This is the point where the verbal/thinking mind transitions to the meditative/visual mind. It is a move from the planning mind to a deeper state of awareness (often felt as drowsy), with stronger intuition, more capacity for wholeness and complicated problem-solving. The Theta state is associated with visualization. The theta waves are a receptive mental state proven especially useful for hypnotherapy and self-hypnosis by way of recorded suggestions and affirmations. During meditation, theta waves were most abundant in the frontal and middle parts of the brain. "These types of waves likely originate from relaxed attention that monitors our inner experiences. "Here lies a significant difference between meditation and relaxing without any specific technique," says Professor Jim Lagopoulos (2009) of Sydney University, Australia. Lagopoulos is the principal investigator of a joint study between his university and researchers from the Norwegian University of Science and Technology (NTNU) on changes in electrical brain activity during nondirective meditation.

3.5 Delta Waves:

The Delta frequency (0.5 - 4.5HZ) is the slowest of the frequencies and is experienced in deep, dreamless sleep and in very deep, transcendental meditation where awareness is fully detached. Delta waves are characteristic of sleep. Healing of the degenerating cells of the brain can be achieved by playing delta waves. Among many things, deep sleep is important for the healing process — as it's linked with deep healing and regeneration. Hence, not having enough deep sleep is detrimental to the health of an individual.

Delta waves frequency is 0.2 Hz - 3 Hz during a very deep and dreamless sleep are considered the slowest of the brainwaves, registering when the brainwave is dormant and healing itself by way of resetting internal clocks. This is unconscious state, devoid of dreams. Delta waves are reported to reduce cortisol hormone level and delay aging, too.

The brain can be stimulated into achieving target frequencies by playing tones or beats at a specific rhythm. One can achieve high focus, relaxation, deep relaxation or sleep by simply listening to the tones known as brainwave entrainment.

3.6 Binaural Beats:

One of the most popular forms of sound technology used for brain is known as binaural beats. Binaural beat is an auditory illusion perceived when two different pure-tone sine waves, both with frequencies lower than 1500 Hz, with less than a 40 Hz difference between them, are presented to a listener dichotically (one through each ear). These binaural beats have definite frequency combinations and are among the many states that brainwave entrainment can induce. In the past 50 years, technologies have been developed that can induce the same brainwave state as meditation by simply listening to certain sounds. The binaural beats can also induce the same mental state associated with traditional meditation practice. Binaural beats influence the mind by being in-sync with Beta Wave frequencies. Listening to binaural beats track for fitness keep the mind focused and calm. The brain has been known as *random thought generator,*" and produce 50,000 - 60,000 thoughts per day. About 90% of those are assumed to be negative. Negative thoughts cause chronic stress and produce stress hormones which changes the function and structure of the brain. Every thought changes neural pathways and the output of brain chemicals, creating a cascade of effects on health and emotional well-being. The best way by far to limit negative thoughts and reduce stress is through meditation. Over 1,000 studies have shown that meditation can make an individual smarter, happier, and healthier. Regular meditation can reduce stress, stimulate new brain cell formation, and slow down the rate of brain cell aging. However, experienced traditional meditators revealed that quieting the mind is not easy. It can take years to master.

Humans can generally hear sound frequencies in the range of 20 Hz to 20,000 Hz. This means that our brainwave frequencies mostly fall below our audible range. So how can we get our brains to entrain to sounds we can't hear? The binaural beats phenomenon is the key. (Binaural means, two ears.).

When two tones that are slightly dissimilar in frequency are processed by the brain, it registers a beat at the difference of the frequencies. For example, if you listen to a 125 Hz sound in your left ear, and a 115 Hz sound in the right, your brain entrains to the difference — in this case to 10 Hz, which is in the alpha brain wave frequency range.

Since each ear has to perceive a different frequency for binaural beats to be created, binaural beats are best experienced when the two tones are heard through stereo headphones. Binaural beats are for people who cannot perform traditional meditation. They cannot focus their restless mind. By binaural techniques, the results are quick as compared to traditional meditation. So, this technique provides an easy shortcut. All one has to do is put on a set of headphones or earbuds, relax, and listen. For many people, this brings their brains into the same state as deep meditation quickly. There are binaural beats audio programs designed to induce sleep, reduce anxiety, and increase weight loss, concentration, or study skills available in the markets.

One of the most unusual uses of binaural beats technology is to encourage lucid dreaming, a state of consciousness in which dreamers are aware that they are dreaming, to achieve various cognitive and emotional benefits. Brady and Stevens (2000) have shown that binaural beat induced theta EEG (Electroencephalogram) activity and hypnotic susceptibility.

4. Nondirective Meditation:

Relaxation and stress management meditation known as nondirective technique. The technique does not involve a specific experience or state of mind. Meditator nurtures the skill to endure the spontaneous wandering of the mind without getting involved in them and allows these wandering thoughts pass without any judgement.

Also, nondirective meditation produces significant changes in electrical brain wave activity. Theta brain waves are present during nondirective meditation. Several studies indicate that brain wave activity is better in nondirective meditation technique.

5. Concentration Meditation:

Meditations that involve concentration are classified as "focused attention" technique. These practices comprise focusing attention on a selective object for the entire duration. The latent idea is to cultivating laser-like focus. Any concentration meditation will involve steady mental effort to build up the ability to focus without acquiescing to interruption.

Certain practices may comprise focusing on an external object, waterfall or candle flame, while others will involve focusing on the breath. In any regard, the goal is to direct 100% focus on one thing for the entire session. When the mind wanders, the focus is calmly brought back to the object. Over time, the mind wanders less and the capacity to focus the attention improves for longer durations.

5.1 Vipassana:

Vipassanā is a Pali word from the Sanskrit. It has two parts- the prefix 'Vi' and the suffix 'paśsana'. The 'Vi' means as an intensive, and passanā meaning to see through. The combined meaning of the two words- 'Vipassana' means "seeing profoundly or intensively without judgment. It is an insight experienced before one's eyes, to see things as they are and having nothing to do with reasoning or thinking. It is one of India's most ancient techniques of meditation and was taught by Gautama Buddha over 2500 years ago. The main focus of meditation is on breathing to increase awareness. The word Vipassana literally translates to "insight into reality" which is why many people refer to it as "insight meditation." The basic meaning is of the word Vipasana is "in a special way." But there also is the connotation of both "into" and "through." The whole meaning of the word is looking into the object with clarity and precision, seeing each component as distinct, and passing all the way through to perceive the most fundamental reality of that object. This process leads to insight into the basic reality of whatever is being inspected, one must begin by focusing the attention on the breathing and then go on observing all physical and mental phenomena which arise during the process. Just sit, watching the air going in and out of the noses. Siddhartha Gautama describes, "Mindfulness" as entering the forest and sitting beneath a tree to watch the breath. If the breath is "long," notice that it is long and if the breath is "short," notice that it is short. By observing your breathing, perceptual changes take place in the brain, creating new insights.

The concept of Vipassana meditation is focused on "mindfulness" of breathing and is mentioned to as "Mindfulness, meaning a clear awareness of exactly what is happening in the present. Just stay in the present, no past, and no future. Mindful Meditation is a gentle and comprehensive technique that proceeds slowly creeping from one point to the other and it takes years to achieve Nirvana (liberation) through this. It comprises attentive listening, mindful seeing and careful testing-- a system of training the mind through self-analysis including senses such as smell, touch, hearing while paying attention to the changes taking place in all these sensory experiences. One learns to listen to his own thoughts without being caught up in them. The object of Vipassana meditation practice is to learn to search the truth within not without. To know thyself, search inside instead of looking outside in the materialistic world. This mind purifying technique does not require external help of a god, spirit or any guru or master, but depends upon one's own efforts and experience. Kabir, a 15th century Indian mystic and saint revered by Hindus, Muslims and Sikhs expressed, "If you want the truth, I will tell you the truth. I listen to the secret sound, the real sound, which is inside you."

6. Mindfulness-Based Stress Reduction:

"Mindfulness" meditation is synonymous to Vipassana meditation, however, there is a slight difference. Vipassana comes under religion aspect. Mindfulness is beyond religion. This practice is also known as MBSR (Mindfulness-Based Stress Reduction). The western world used this technique to reduce anxiety and stress. Basically, they put an old wine in a new bottle. If someone does not want any sort of religious dogma attached to his meditative practice, this is the best one to try.

The MBSR program was founded in 1979 at the University of Massachusetts by John Kabat-Zinn. The program is supported by science as being beneficial for reducing stress. Many consider mindfulness meditation (MBSR) to be among the most effective non-drug therapies for improving stress levels and became a part of complementary system of medicines.

To practice mindfulness meditation, one simply focuses on the present moment or life circumstance and pay attention to all emotions, physical sensations, and thoughts that an individual experiences, without getting attached to them. The efficacy of mindfulness stanches from non-judgment and non-attachment. Like many forms of meditation, one sits comfortably, close his eyes, and focus on his breathing. As one focuses on breathing, he becomes distracted with sensations, thoughts, emotion and feelings. Whenever one gets disturbed again with thoughts, simply redirect focus back to the breathing without getting frustrated. With practice, it helps cope with stress because the brain is trained to avoid attachment and judgment to sensations feelings, emotions via thoughts.

There is no need to sit with eyes closed to be "mindful." There is no need of going to the forest or in the mountain. One can practice mindfulness anywhere, such as in a traffic jam, walking, jogging out at the park, or doing mundane assignments. Regular practice helps the meditator become increasingly aware and non-reactive to thoughts and emotions.

During Mindful meditation there is no focusing on one specific object. In this case, the attention is flowing freely without judgment or attachment. In other words, one is simply observing all perceptions, thoughts, memories, and senses that he experiences during the practice. With mindfulness – one is "mindful" of his own experience.

Being mindful of one's perception allows one to observe his experience almost from a third-person perspective rather than first-person attachment. An individual notices all sensations such as feelings, but merely observes them rather than judge them or react positively or negatively. In summary, it is just like watching a movie without getting involved in the movie. Most people start crying watching a tragic scene because they get involved.

Meditation is designed to develop the skill of paying attention to our inner and outer experiences. It establishes a connection between the mind and the body. Mindfulness is the awareness that is not thinking but which is aware of thinking, as well as conscious of seeing, hearing, tasting, smelling, and feeling through the body and mind. All sports are mindful meditation if one is playing the sports freely. Working out or doing physical exercise is also mindful meditation. conscious cooking, washing dishes, sweeping, painting and related things are also part of mindful meditation.

Thus, Mindfulness is non-discriminated, open-hearted, lenient and welcoming of whatever arises in awareness. Regularly paying attention to purpose, genuinely, and without judgment to whatever comes in the present moment, either inside or outside of us, make the technique perfect. By practicing mindfulness, intentionally paying more careful moment-to-moment attention, an individual can live a more relaxed life. An individual is not worried about the past and the future since he is living in the present. We are here owing to our past Karmas, and our future depends on our present Karmas. So, rightful actions in the present are significant.

Susan Albers, a psychologist and mindfulness expert at the Cleveland Clinic, says about mindful meditation, "It is concentrating on what's happening at the moment, without dwelling, judging, or trying to change anything." Very well expressed by Ralph Waldo Emerson, an American philosopher, and poet, "In the past, I have nothing to do; nor with the future. I live now."

In other words, no overthinking or over-analyzing—or the opposite, expelling all thoughts. Unlike many forms of meditation, which involve entirely clearing your mind, mindfulness means letting your thoughts come and go without analyzing them. Maharishi C.V. Raman an Indian mystic explained it in a quite simple way. "I am the body is a thought. I am the mind is a thought. I am the doer is a though. Worry is only a thought. Fear is only a thought." If we deviate our thoughts by meditation, that can mitigate all our problems to a great extent.

7. Transcendental Meditation:
Transcendental meditation is classified as "effortless" because it requires no mental effort or concentration. It is also known as

"pure being" or "transcendental" because it involves emptiness, introspection, and tranquility. The objective of this meditation is to mainly help the meditator recognize their "Pure Self" or the true nature of the self by eliminating all thoughts. TM is taught by certified teachers through a standard four-day course of instructions. It is practiced 20 minutes per day.

The mind becomes a blank slate with consistent practice. The transcendental process helps the individual silence their mind and become aware of deep state of consciousness. Regular practice leads to experience of emptiness or nothingness and finally provides a solace to mind. This meditation was initiated by Maharishi Mahesh Yogi in 1955 and was introduced to pop-icons like The Beatles and The Beach Boys in the 1970s. Due to celebrity supplication, it has become one of the most popular meditations practiced throughout the world.

However, TM is not free but quite expensive. There are significant fees to be paid to get initiated. What distinguishes TM from other forms of mantra meditation is that it is considered "effortlessly transcending" without concentration and focusing as compared to other meditations.

The TM center at the Maharishi Mahesh University, Fairfield, Iowa, has scientifically proved that TM is greatly beneficial for health and happiness and can help to get rid of many diseases. It increases alpha waves in the prefrontal cortex, resulting in relaxation, increasing creativity and concentration.

8. Mantra Meditation (AUM):

Nama Japa, Japa of the holy name in India goes back to the ancient times of the Rishis of the Vedas. *Japa* is the repetition of a mantra, a potent syllable or syllables, a word or a combination of words, done with the object of realizing the truth embodied in the Mantra. Some of the mantras are short and simple where others are lengthy and complicated. Many of them are in Sanskrit language and are in praise of the God or to attain health, power and wisdom. Mantra for

Jappa should be short and easy to pronounce. Ashley-Farrand (1999) described the Sanskrit mantras in English with their meaning and benefits in his book *Healing Mantras: Using Sound Affirmations for Personal Power.* In the Hindus Buddhists, Jains and Sikh religions, mantra meditation is popular and involves repeating sound, syllable, or word with the intention of focusing the mind.

It is not easy to focus the mind on anything. However, the same mantra repeatedly done can hold the mind for some time. The sound repeated can be anything but pertaining to the part of their religion whether one knows the meaning of that mantra does not matter. The objective of mantra is to deviate the thought process, nothing else.

One can select any mantra suitable to his or her liking and suits to one's pronunciation. In guided meditation, normally mantras are assigned by an advanced meditative teacher called Guru. Although, one does not need a Guru. Mantra can be the Guru. Since the body is not the Guru but *Shabad* (Mantra) *is the Guru*, very well said by an Indian mystic Sajjan ji Maharaj (personal communication with the author).

While sitting in a comfortable position with closed eyes, mantra is being repeated for specific time. Repeat the mantra softly to enable it to sink in. Then stop speaking your mantra and repeat it silently over and over in your mind for a specific period. When the thoughts are drifting away bring them back to the mantra.

The main object of the mantra is to enhance both relaxation and concentration. It is comparatively easy to focus on a repeated sound than breath. The Gayatri mantra is the most powerful hymn in the world. Howard Steingeril, an American scientist collected mantras hymens and invocations from all over the world and tested for their strength in his physiology laboratory. Hindu's Gayatri mantra produced 110,000 sound waves/second. This was the highest among all the mantras and was found to be the most powerful hymn in the world. The Gayatri Mantra is commonly used by the Hindus all over the world in their rituals. Through the combination of sound or sound waves of a particular frequency, this Mantra is claimed to be capable of developing specific spiritual potentialities. Gayatri mantra is highly sacred and considered as mother of the Vedas. There is no need to chant any other mantra if you chant Gayatri mantra.

The *Gayatri Mantra* is broadcasted daily for 15 minutes from 7 P.M. onwards over Radio Paramaribo, Surinam, South America for the past two years, and in Amsterdam, Holland, for the last six months. Mantra in *Sanskrit* language is as follow:

"Aum Bhur Bhuvah Sah ... Tat Savitur Varenyam ... Bhargo Devasyu Dheemahi, Dhiyo Yo Nah Pra-chodayaat"

"It precisely means ....

God is dear to me like my own breath… He is the dispeller of my pains … and giver of happiness … I meditate on the supremely adorable Light of the Divine Creator… that it may inspire my thought and understanding."

The mantra comprises five faces. *Aum* is the first face: *Bhur Bhuvah Suva*ha is the second; *Tat Savitur Varenyam* is the third: *Bhargo Devasya Dheemahi* is the fourth and *Dhiyo Yo Nah Prachodayat* is the fifth. It has three parts. First, the divine is praised, then meditated upon in reverence. Finally, an appeal is made to the divine to dispel the darkness of ignorance and to awaken and strengthen the intellect. Chanting of the *Gayatri mantra* sanctifies life.

8.1 Kirtan Meditation:

It is done in a group of people and mantra is chanted loudly. Like *"Hare Krishna, Hare Krishna, Krishna Krishna, Hare Hare.* This kirtan is the common practice of ISKCON (International Society of Krishna Consciousness). ISKCON was founded in 1966 in New York City by A. C. Bhaktivedanta Swami Prabhupada. Head quarter in Mayapur, India. Iskcon believes in Kirtan. They perform kirtan in group at the Iskcon temples and wandering in the streets or on roads while chanting the mantras and beating drums and playing some musical instruments. Purpose of this practice is to deviate the thoughts to kirtan and relax the stressful mind.

9. Dynamic Meditation:

Dynamic meditation was initiated in 1970 by OSHO, an incredibly famous and controversial Indian mystic. Dynamic meditation is one of his most popular active meditations. This one-hour meditation consists of five stages. Each stage is demarked by special music meant for dynamic meditation. Deep fast chaotic breathing 10 minutes, followed by 10 minutes catharsis, 10 minutes of jumping and shouting a mantra "Hoo", 15 minutes of silence, and finally 15 minutes of slow dancing. Eyes closed; a blindfold is recommended. Osho believed, "while doing the meditation, remain a witness, observe what is happening as if you are just a spectator, as if the whole thing is happening to somebody else." It can be done in a group or alone, but the energy will be more powerful if it is done with others.

Dynamic means effort, much activity and meditation means silence, no effort, no activity. In a way it is a dialectical meditation. The process allows meditation to emerge through active movement. In this meditation chaos is expressed (dynamic movement/activity) prior to feeling relaxed (meditation/inactivity). Once the junk is thrown out, meditation is easy. Bansal *et al.* (2016) observed that Osho dynamic meditation causes decrease in several psychopathological variables such as aggressive behavior, anxiety and depression. It also reduces cortisol.

9.1. Walking Meditation:

This is a type of meditation that involves walking and is practiced between periods of the sitting (Zen) meditation. It is also called Walking Zen meditation. This type involves walking in a clockwise pattern around a room. Generally, one hand is in a "fist" (or closed) while the opposite hand is covering the fist. During the walking meditation, one step is taken after each full breath. The speed of this form of meditation can be extremely slow or quicker (rivaling a slow jog) depending upon the liking of the meditator. It is recommended for people who have problems with sitting for some time. The focus is on breathing while walking. Let the thought come and go but the focusing should be on breath.

9.2. Sexual Meditation:

It is a kind of mindful and dynamic meditation. To stay in the present and focus on your activities. Most of the partners are distracted during the sexual act. Mental distraction is the main sex drive killer. Their mind is wandering somewhere else. One is focused, the other is somewhere else. Both the partners are not at the same wavelength. If they vibrate with the same frequency in thoughts and actions, they can have powerful sex. Sex leads to super consciousness if performed with mindfulness. Lori Brotto (2018) professor of Obstetrics and Gynecology in University of British Columbia, Vancouver, described significance of mindfulness in sex in her book, entitled "Better Sex through Mindfulness."

9.3. Shower Meditation:

It is a kind of dynamic meditation. During taking shower, imagine washing away the stress and anxiety. Focus on the feel of water on the skin. Observe the power of water washing away the negative thoughts, stress, anxiety, regrets, sadness, anger and guilt from the body. Enjoy the lightness of the body and clarity of the mind. Start the day with fresh and positive feelings.

10. Compassionate Meditation (Loving-Kindness):

This meditation encompasses unconditional love and kindness towards other human beings. It is also known as Metta Meditation or "compassion" meditation. Matta comes from Pali language which means friendship. *Mettā or maitrī* in Sanskrit, meaning benevolence, loving-kindness, friendliness, amity, good will, and active interest in others Metta is considered "love" without any sort of attachment and the goal is to increase "good will" towards others. The meditation starts by loving first yourself unconditionally then extend this unconditional love for others.

Metta meditation is performed while sitting in a comfortable position with eyes closed. Mind and heart are focused to create feelings of unconditional kindness and good-will towards yourself and repeat the affirmation, "May I be happy, healthy and fearless? May I be strong? May I be peaceful? Loving-kindness meditation is a simple repetition of these kind phrases, but also directing them at different people. After a few repetitions, the phrases are used for others. "May you be healthy and fearless? May you be happy? May you be peaceful?"

Next, direct the *metta* towards someone you feel thankful for or someone who has helped you. Repeat the same affirmation. Now visualize someone you feel neutral about—people you neither like nor dislike. Repeat the same affirmation. Next, one is to visualize the people he does not like or who is hard to deal with. Direct the *metta* on him. Finally, direct the *metta* towards everyone universally: "May all beings everywhere be happy." The ultimate goal is to wish genuine "good-will," peace, and happiness towards all beings. *"Sarve Mangal Mangley, Shivey savartha sadhke....*It is Sanskrit shloka means I demand from God Almighty happiness, prosperity for all human beings on the earth.

When regularly practiced, feelings of pure "joy" will arise. Those who suffer from depression, negative thinking, and anger outbursts will significantly benefit from this type of meditation.

11. Yoga Meditation:

Many people practice yogic forms of meditation to achieve mental freedom, self-knowledge, and self-realization (moksha). Yoga is considered an integrated form of physical, mental, and spiritual practices and is used mostly in Hinduism, Buddhism, and Jainism. Yoga dates back to pre-Vedic Indian tradition, but is hypothesized to have emerged between the 6th century B.C. and the 5th century B.C.

Now, it is practiced in the entire world by all religions. Practicing yoga typically consists of the following:

The eight limbs as *yama* (abstinences), *niyama* (observances), *asana* (postures), *pranayama* (breathing), *pratyahara* (withdrawal), dharana (concentration), dhyana (meditation) and *samadhi* (absorption). The eight limbs form a sequence from the outer to the inner. Conduct is (yamas and niyamas), postures are (asanas), breathing techniques (pranayama), and meditation. The last four limbs of yoga include: *pratyahara, dharana, dhyana, and samadhi.* These four limbs comprise the meditative practice in yoga. The specific type of meditation that one uses to enhance yoga practice depends upon an individual's choice. Various types of yoga meditation are described as follows.

11.1. Chakra Meditation:

This type of meditation is based on the 7 main energy centers throughout the body called "Chakras." To perform chakra meditation, one would specifically focus on one of these centers and use a specific mantra pertaining to that center to open or expand energy flow in this area. Each Chakra has a specific mantra and color correlate as shown below. For example, focusing on the root center, the mantra would be Lum. Similarly, for concentrating on Sacral center, the mantra would be Vum and so on. One can start from the Root Chakra and proceed to Crown Chakras. Give 3 minutes chanting on each Chakra. Total time is 21 minutes.

Chakras	Mantras	Color of Chakras
Crown	Mmm	Pink
Third Eye	Ooo	Purple
Throat	Hum	Blue
Heart	Yum	Green
Solar Plexus	Rum	Yellow
Sacral	Vum	Orange
Root	Lum	Red

11.2. Gazing Meditation:

This type of yogic meditation involves gazing on an external object or symbol. Most commonly a candle will be utilized as the object of focus, and a person starts by focusing on it with eyes open. After the person has boosted their concentration ability with eyes open, they then move on to focusing on the object (e.g., candle) with eyes closed to boost their visualization ability. The goal is for those practicing this form of meditation to be able to maintain the image of the candle within their *mind*.

11.3. Kundalini Meditation:

Originally known as "laya yoga," kundalini translates to "serpent" or snake. This form of meditation is practiced with the intention of unleashing "kundalini energy" that lies dormant at the base of the spine. Those practicing Kundalini Meditation generally experience drastic changes in the functioning of their body, nervous system, and physiology as the "kundalini" energy rises from the spine. This energy rises from "lower" energy centers to "higher" energy centers in the body. It typically involves a specific breathing technique that involves "alternate nostril" inhalation. In other words, you'd close your right nostril on the first inhale, and your left nostril on the second. The thought behind the technique is to "cleanse" certain energy channels to help awaken the Kundalini or "serpent" energy. It is very pertinent to learn this technique from an expert or Guru of Kundalini Meditation. Please do no start by yourself. It can cause adverse effect.

11.4 Sahaja Yoga Meditation:

The technique was founded in 1970 in India and now its branches are almost all over the world. The idea behind this practice is to bring about "a breakthrough in human awareness" and self-realization through mental stillness, rather than through sequences of active postures on a mat. During meditation, the aspirant keeps his or her left hand on the lap, palm up, and place the right palm on various parts of the body as directed by the instructor. Shoes are kept off for meditation, so that negative energy can be sucked out through the feet.

Practitioners claim that with Sahaja Yoga, unlike other forms of meditation, it is possible to reach self-realization and "Thoughtless Awareness" almost immediately -- sometimes during a person's first session. The act of achieving self-realization is sometimes referred to as having the Kundalini -- the inner energy coiled inside each of us -- released, or awakened, and the word Sahaja means "in-born," to refer to this inner energy.

Sahaja Yoga focuses on a network of energy channels within the body known as the Subtle System, which starts in the sacrum, at the base of the spine, and rises through the crown of the head. When a person's inner energy is activated and begins to travel through the Subtle System, according to Sahaja Yoga philosophy, practitioner will feel it being released "in the form of a cool, or sometimes warm, breeze."

11.5. Kriya Yoga:

This is an ancient type of yoga that gained popularity with an Indian mystic Mahavatar Babaji. It also was popularized in the West through the book "Autobiography of a Yogi," by Yogananda. This type of yoga consists of different levels of Pranayama and is geared towards someone intending to enhance their spiritual development. It consists of not only meditation, but energy working and breathing exercises to increase tranquility and spiritual connection. Yogananda, an Indian mystic and founder of commune "Self-Realization Center" in California, has described "kriya" yoga as mentally directing energy vertically, up and down the spinal chakras. In other words, "Kriya Yoga" is a simple, psycho-physiological method by which the human blood is decarbonized and recharged with oxygen. The atoms of this extra oxygen are transmuted into life current to rejuvenate the brain and spinal centers.

11.6. Nada Yoga:

This is considered a metaphysical type of yoga that is based on the idea that the entire universe consists of sound vibrations "nada." The central idea is that sound energy is in wave motion rather than in particles and is responsible for creating the entire universe. The meditations in nada yoga involve utilizing sound in multiple ways including internal music (called "anahata") and external music (called "ahata"). As a person continues, the sound will eventually open the "Chakras" (energy centers) with their internal sound. This type of yogic meditation may seem a bit "New Age" for most but incorporates sounds.

11.7. Third-Eye Meditation:

This involves directing attention to the "Third eye" or "Anja chakra," an area located on forehead between the eyebrows. When the attention shifts away from the "Third eye" chakra, one simply refocuses and maintains attention. Eventually the mental gossip quiets and the focus on this area improves. The fast-paced, stressful thoughts subside, and one feels a sense of inner peace.

11.8. Tantra:

Tantric meditation is also yoga meditation that awakens consciousness. This meditative practice has been in India since 5th century. Tantra emerged as a rebellion against organized religion which held that sexuality should be avoided to reach enlightenment. The word Tantra consists of "tan" which means "expands" and "tra" which means "liberates."

There are enormous numbers of Tantra meditations. Traditional Tantric meditation expands the mind and activates consciousness in conjunction with Kriya yoga. Through Tantra meditation, the yogi activates the chakras, freeing the dormant kundalini *shakti* (energy) to flow from the Muladhara (root) chakra up the spine to the Sahasrara (crown) chakra, which is the connection to spirituality. By freeing this energy through Tantric meditation, the yogi awakens the entire body and consciousness through seven chakras.

The yogi then directs the energy from 7th chakra to form a body of energy and light in front of him. It is to this body of energy that the meditating yogi can direct love. He then can invite the energy to return through his head and down through the chakras to the Root chakras.

Tantra meditation has been interpreted with spiritual sexuality. A famous and controversial Indian mystic and philosopher Osho believed that sexuality was a doorway to super consciousness. He wrote a book also "From Sex to Super-consciousness." Some interpret the word Tantra as "to manifest, to expand, to show and to weave." In this context, sex is thought to expand consciousness and weave together the polarities of male, represented by Hindu God, Shiva and female embodied by the Hindu Goddess, Shakti into a harmonious whole.

In the many books, websites and related advertisements of spiritual dimension. Tantra is also health enhancing. Sexual energy is one of the most powerful energies for creating health, says Christian Northrup, in her book "Women's Bodies, Women's Wisdom." Some fundamentalists of Tantra practice condemn this concept and believe that it is a misinterpretation, and exploitation of Tantra meditation in order to make money.

11.9 Superbrain Yoga Meditation:

This technique maximizes brain power specially developed for patients with attention deficit disorder (ADD), attention deficit hyperactivity disorder (ADHD), Down Syndrome, Alzheimer's or other cognitive problems. Joie P. Jones, Professor at the department of Radiological Sciences, University of California introduced this technique. Though the technique goes back to India. Sui (2005) revealed in his book SuperBrain Yoga (SBY), "It's an ancient Indian technique that utilizes acupressure and breathing techniques that are apparently supposed to balance the two hemispheres of the brain and increase energy." It is also claimed that the actions of SuperBrain Yoga (SBY) were once used as punishment in India's schools. The author himself had gone through this punishment in school.

Since Super Brain Yoga consumes both acupressure and breathing techniques, it is possible these are responsible for the energizing effects. The benefits of proper breathing are well documented. *"Deep abdominal breathing encourages full oxygen exchange—that is, the beneficial trade of incoming oxygen for outgoing carbon dioxide. Not surprisingly, it can slow the heartbeat and lower or stabilize blood pressure."*

Of course, breathing practices can do much more, such as improve focus and mental alertness, build cardiac strength, and even potentially lead to some superhuman abilities according as per Wim Hoff Method. When done correctly Superbrain Yoga technique helps the energy trapped in the lower energy centers move up through the physical body's other major centers. At lower centers, it regulates the sex drive. As the energy travels upwards, it passes through the heart center and fills it with feelings of calm and inner peace. Then it moves up in the throat and beyond to the brain and improves intelligence and creativity. Technique is as follows:

*Stand up straight, facing to east. Connect your tongue on the roof of your mouth, directly behind your teeth. Keep it there throughout the activity.

*Take your left hand, across your upper body to take hold of your right earlobe with thumb and forefinger. Make sure that the thumb is in front.

*Likewise, take right hand across your upper body. Reach for left earlobe with your thumb and forefinger, keeping your thumb in front. At this point, you should now be gently pressing both earlobes simultaneously. Make sure your left arm is close to your chest and tucked inside your right arm.

*Inhale deeply through your nose and slowly squat down to the ground. Hold your breath for three to six counts. Exhale, while moving back up to a standing position.

*Repeat this process from 15 to 20 times. Assess your position every so often and continue holding your earlobes. Make sure your tongue is still touching the roof of your mouth throughout the entire exercise. Your focus should be on breathing.

12. Self-inquiry Meditation:

The goal with this meditation practice is to constantly pay attention to the inner awareness of "I" or the "Self." It was founded by Raman Maharishi who declared it as the single most effective way to discover the nature of the "I"-thinking. He suggested that the "I"-thought will eventually disappear and then the individual is left with true self-realization or liberation. The goal is for those practicing self-inquiry meditation to discover their authentic "Self."

Those starting out with this form of meditation are instructed to focus attention on feelings of "I" and to maintain the focus for as long as they can. Whenever getting distracted by thoughts or sensations, simply bring the focus back to "I" and continue. Those practicing self-inquiry meditation also will ask questions such as: "Who am I?" to better understand their true nature.

Maharishi Raman encouraged the practitioner not to spend extensive periods of time in meditation. Rather he suggested that it could be performed for limited periods of time in formal meditation until the individual understands it. He discouraged those from devoting significant amounts of time to an actual meditative practice.

To practice this type of meditation, one starts by asking himself about "Who am I?" The objective of this practice is to realize that the "I" often gets identified with physical sensations like the body, our friends, and family etc. Some people consider it a futile exercise, where others achieve an expanded sense of awareness.

13. Zen Meditation:

The name "Zen" meditation translates to "Seated meditation" and originated in Chinese Zen Buddhism. Historians trace the practice back to the 6th Century Indian monk "Bodhidharma." The practice generally involves sitting in the Lotus Position and observing the breath. To tame the mind, awareness is generally focused on counting or watching the breath. Many individuals that practice this specific type of meditation sit on a cushion, chair, or padded mat.

In the "Soto" teachings of Zen, observing the mind is the primary focus. In the Soto-subtype, there is no focus on any object and the goal is for the meditator to become aware of their thoughts without judgment. This could be compared to "mindfulness" in that the individual acts as an observer. In some cultures, intensive "group meditations" are practiced in a process called "Sesshin."

This type of meditation also uses what are referred to as "koans" which help the Zen student gain insight from the Zen master. They are also commonly used to test the progress of a Zen meditator. Koans may be solved through sitting meditation (Zen), but are sometimes solved during walking meditation (Kinhin).

14. Qigong (Chi Gong) Meditation:

Qigong is also known as Chi Gang and stands for "life energy cultivation." It is one of the spiritual techniques that is considered to unify the body, breath, and mind. It is traditionally used in Chinese medicine to cultivate and balance "qi" (chi) energy. It has been accepted by various religions such as Buddhism, Confucianism, and Taoism. Qi gong therapy, as well as other branches of Chinese medicine, are based on two simple principles: the cleansing of meridians to achieve harmonious energy flow and the restoration of yin-yang balance. Qigong is performed while moving slowly, with coordination and specific breathing to elicit a calm state of awareness. It is also called moving meditation.

Many people practice Qigong for recreation and/or relaxation benefit as opposed to spiritual enlightenment. It is considered a form of exercise as well as alternative medicine and has been practiced for thousands of years.

Qigong meditation could be practiced in a seated format. Be comfortable and balance your body, maintaining a sense of centeredness. Focus on breathing and relaxing the entire body as deeply as possible. After a while the mind becomes calm when the breathing is softened. After this, one can direct focus towards the *lower dantien* (energy center) which has been described as the body's "root." Think of it as the center of gravity of the body. As one focuses on the *lower dantien* (located three finger widths below the navel and two finger widths behind the navel), one builds up more "qi" (energy). By focusing on this exact spot, more "energy" is accumulated in the body. Simply feel the energy circulating throughout the body as it builds up and maintain focus on the *lower dantien* (energy center).

15. Taoist Meditation:

Taoist meditation is also known as Daoist Meditation since it comes from the traditions of Daoism, the religion of China. Taoism is derived from Lao Tzu in China and those subscribing to this practice attempt to live in harmony with "Tao" meaning nature. Taoist meditation incorporates, concentration, mindfulness, contemplation, as well as various forms of visualization. Spiritual masters in Asia have used Taoist meditation techniques for thousands of years as a gateway to higher consciousness, health and peace of mind.

The very first requirement for the inner stillness and calmness for practicing deep Tao meditation techniques is to sit in half lotus position with the spine straight for at least twenty minutes. Start with five and then extend the time as per comfort. One can also sit on the edge of a chair with feet flat on the floor and lay his hands palms up on his thighs. It is important not to fall or fiddle while practicing the Tao meditation techniques, but at the same time not to hold the body too rigidly. While breathing correctly in Taoist Meditation — from the belly, filling the lungs from the bottom up, helps diaphragm muscle, rubbing the digestive system and promoting the flow of blood and lymph to that region. Above the abdominal cavity is the diaphragm that affects the esophagus, the aorta, and the vagus nerve. Breathing slowly and deeply, also imparts a sense of peacefulness and centeredness. Thus, by simply breathing correctly, the meditation provides peacefulness and a sense of grounded and centeredness, and at the same time promote digestion and respiration.

Tao meditation techniques or other chi gong practices are based on natural breathing or prenatal breathing. The idea is to breathe into the belly or the lower dentin as babies breathing in their mother's womb — not through lungs but through the umbilical cord. During breathe in, the abdomen expands; during exhale, abdomen contracts. All Taoist breathing is done through the nose, which is specifically designed to warm and filter the air before it gets to lungs.

This is a very calming type of Taoist breathing. If one practices breathing in this way for even fifteen minutes a day, he or she will eventually begin breathing this way all of the time, even while sleeping, and the benefits will be enormous.

Extensive literature in the Taoist meditation describes various breathing practices, some are extremely difficult and require the guidance of an experienced teacher. However, daily practice of basic Taoist meditation can give amazing effects.

16. Sufi Meditation:

Sufi meditation is a part of Islamic spirituality. The Sufi tradition focuses on developing a personal relationship with God through self-knowledge and self-inquiry. It uses chanting (Zikr) and meditation (Muraqba) to empty the mind and heart of spiritual pollutants. The core of Sufi meditation is to be always conscious of the Divine, until there is no longer a sense of separation between meditation, God, and daily life. This is called oneness (*ekatmata*)—that is, the complete merging with the Beloved and cessation of duality. In Arabic, the word for meditation is *muraqabah* (also *murakebe*), and the literal meaning is to *watch over*, to *wait* or to *protect*. The essence of Sufi meditation is twofold:

*Keep your attention engrossed on God and awaken love in your heart to enable it to merge with the Divine.

*Continuously watch your mind, no other thought except that of God enters the mind.

Watching over the mind, focusing the thoughts on God, and an awakening of love in the heart. This practice is done as a formal meditation, and also should be followed during all moments of one's day. Irrelevant thoughts are considered harmful, and one keeps a watch on the mind to make sure they don't sprout. There are different types of Sufi meditations. *Sufi Mantra, Heart meditation, Sufi breathing meditation, Bond of love, Gazing meditation, Sufi walking meditation and Sufi whirling meditation.* These all comprises focusing and concentration on mantra or breathing to deviate thoughts. Needless to go into the details of these Sufi meditations since plenty of information is available on any search engine.

Conclusion:
A quite common inquiry from the aspirants of meditation is which technique is more suitable, easy, and simple for daily practice. It totally depends upon an individual who wants to meditate in the first place. First, the belief system of a meditator is very pertinent. If the person does not believe in meditation or does not have any faith in this technique, he or she should refrain from this. Faith is like Wi-Fi. It is invisible, but it has the power to connect you to what you need. Faith is to believe what we do not see, and the reward of this faith is to see what we believe.

Modern Indian mystics like Osho and Sri Nisargadatta Maharaj preached to forget about dogmas, belief system, faith, theories, and conventional concepts and listen to your inner self. They suggested to approach with a clean slate and come out of the box of your programmed mind. Our minds have been programmed from the early stages of life by parents, schoolteachers, relatives, and friends. Empty all your mental contents comprising all imaginations and dogmas, this will lead you to reality.

Osho, a controversial Indian mystic used to say quite often, "If you can get out of the mind, you will get out of Christianity, Hinduism, Jainism, Buddhism, and all kinds of rubbish will be just finished. You can come to a full stop. Meditation simply says how to go with inward: whether there is a soul or not doesn't matter; whether there is a God or not doesn't matter."

As per Sri Nisargadatta, an Indian mystic. "In the mirror of your mind all kinds of pictures appear and disappear. Knowing that they are entirely your own creations, watch them silently come and go. Be alert, but not perturbed. This attitude of silent observation is the very foundation of yoga. You see the picture, but you are not the picture."

Bhante Henepola Gunaratana, a Buddhist monk from Sri Lanka and the author of the book entitled, *Mindfulness in Plain English*, articulated, "Never mind, prejudices and stereotypes. I want to understand the true nature of life. I want to know what this experience of being alive really is. I want to apprehend the true and deepest qualities of life, and I don't want to just accept somebody else's explanation. I want to see it for myself."

If one pursues his meditation practice with this attitude, he will succeed. He will find himself observing things objectively, exactly as they are --flowing and changing from moment to moment. Life then takes on an unbelievable richness which cannot be explained but has to be experienced. Direct experience is the only confirmation. You are the consciousness in which the entire universe appears.

In view of the above discussion, different types of meditation produce specific neural and physiological changes. One should select the techniques which is enjoyable and helps to achieve his or her goal. One can try three or four types and see his or her comfort zone. A simple technique where there is **no** religious, subjective, "spiritual" hocus pocus, mumbo jumbo, and witchcraft, non-scientific voodoo, would be more suitable. The author has described such a technique in the next chapter and explained the various factors involved in detail.

> *"There is no being or non-being, no unity or dualism.*
> *What more is to say? There is nothing outside of me."*
> —*Ashtavakra Gita*

Chapter Four:
Modest Practice of Meditation

"Meditation is a way to fall in love with yourself and blossoming the divinity within you." —Ravi K. Puri

There are different schools of thought on the art of meditation. Each belief system has its own technique of meditation but there are some basic requirements common in all practices of meditation. The most practical and simplest method of meditation is being described as per the experience of the author. The main purpose of meditation is to deviate the thoughts which are controlling the mind, emotions, and actions. It is exceedingly difficult to control the mind which is constantly running in the past or in the future. There is no point in dwelling in the past or building castles in the air for future or to fear the future.

The three most important components of meditation are silence, solitude, and stillness. Preparation for meditation is all about managing the external environment to keep the meditator silent, still, and alone. During meditation, a silent mind is especially important but silent does not mean closed. The silent mind is an alert awakened mind: a mind seeking the very nature of reality. Also, the joy of silent wisdom comes from within and is always there. Constantly, wherever you go, you can experience the joyful wisdom energy of silence.

Although techniques of meditation differ in each religion or commune, there are some basic guidelines that remain the same. There is no religious, subjective, "spiritual" hocus pocus, mumbo jumbo, witchcraft, non-scientific voodoo. Present technique described below simply guides you through the meditation process at a slow, safe pace.

The following steps are mostly common to all traditional forms of meditation:

1. Find a suitable time of day and an isolated place without interruption. It is better to meditate at the same time each day. Early morning is recommended between 4-5 am.

2. It is better to practice meditation on an empty stomach to achieve concentration. The power of concentration is more during an empty stomach.

3. Sit comfortably in a chair with closed or half-closed eyes and straight back if possible. Do not stoop in the chair.

4. Take a few moments to relax the body and release any tension from the arms, legs, or the neck. Take a few slow, deep breaths. Slowly withdraw the attention from the outer world of sounds, sights, and other sensory stimuli and move to the inner world. The breath and mind work in tandem, so as breath begins to lengthen, brain waves begin to slow down.

Thoughts of the past and future will come in the mind. Do not get attached to them. Just *Watch without judgement, without attachments. Watch with panoramic attention. Whenever awareness drifts, come back. If it dims rekindle. Watch the thoughts, they will come and go. Awareness will stay in the present. If it wanders, bring it back.* In time and with practice, it may become easier to quiet your mind. You become the center of cyclone where there is always silence,

Feel the breath flowing in and out. Don't try to change it in any way. Just notice. Silently repeat the mantra of your choice: *while Breathing In. Breathing Out.* As the mind begins to wander, draw it back to the breath or to the mantra. Notice as the breath begins to lengthen and fill the body, the mind begins to calm.

Consistency is the key. Try to do this breath meditation first thing in the morning and/or at night. Be consistent with meditation. Shorter meditations on a regular basis are more productive than long sessions every few weeks. Each session of meditation should be between 15-20 minutes.

Important Precautions:

Coming Out of Meditation:
Coming out of meditation is an extremely sensitive phase. There is no hurry to plunge too quickly into everyday activities or encounter a tense situation or energy exchange with someone else. This will deplete energy gained during the meditation. Take at least five minutes to gather your energy. Relax while sitting comfortably and drink a glass of water or do some gentle stretching. Avoid talking with other people too.

Concentration in Meditation:
The first question comes to mind, why is concentration in meditation essential? The main purpose is to attain awareness. Why not just sit down and be aware of whatever happens to be present in the mind? Without any aim, one cannot achieve any target. Concentration means wholeness, unity, and equilibrium. Body and mind must be unified and independent of external circumstances.

The subconscious must be brought into complete subjection to the conscious and the conscious must be expanded into the super consciousness. When the mind has gained its full strength through singleness, it naturally becomes meditative. Often, the mind is compared to a lake. If the surface is smooth without ripples, then the sub-surface is clear. One can see his reflection in clear and still water. Similarly, when the mind becomes calm, then the image of one's true nature is clear and reveals his relationship with the Supreme Consciousness.

The mind is always busy. Thinking is a basically complex process. The mind is trapped, wrapped and stuck in the thought chain. One thought leads to another which leads to another, and another, and another, and so on. It is an endless process. For 15-20 minutes duration of meditation, it is realized that the entire time is spent in a daydream or sexual fantasy or a set of worries about bills household problems. Sometimes goes back in childhood or puberty in the memories. It travels 10,000 miles away to different countries or places of your past visits. It is very pertinent to focus on some object such as breath or mantra. It serves as that vital reference point from which the mind wanders and is drawn back.

Meditation technique is just like taming a wild horse. A newly captured animal is tied to a post with a strong rope. The wild horse is not happy and wants his freedom. The horse screams and tramples and pulls against the rope in frustration for days. Finally, he realizes that he cannot get away, and he gives in. At this point, one can feed him and handle him with safety. One can train him or ride him as per his or her needs. Eventually, the rope and the post are not required. Now the tamed horse can be put to useful work.

In this example, the wild horse is mind, the rope is mindfulness, and the post is the object of meditation, breathing. The tamed horse who emerges from this process is a well-trained concentrated mind, it can be used for the exceedingly tough job of piercing the layers of illusion that obscure reality. Meditation tames the mind. When meditation is mastered, the mind is unwavering like the flame of a candle in a windless place.

Posture in Meditation:
Most people ask the importance of the posture in meditation. Lotus posture is not essential. One can do in any posture or sit comfortably anywhere. The idea of the posture is to stabilize the body.

Focus on Breathing:
The next question is: Why choose breathing as the primary object of meditation? Why not something a bit more interesting? A useful object of meditation should be one that promotes mindfulness. *It should signify the present. It should be portable, easily available, and cheap.* Breathing satisfies these criteria. It is common to every living

being and never ceasing from birth till death. Moreover, breathing signifies a present-time process. Furthermore, breathing is a non-conceptual process, a thing that can be experienced directly without a need for thought. It is a very living process, an aspect of life that is in constant change. The breath moves in cycles-inhalation, exhalation, breathing in, and breathing out. Thus, it is a symbolic representation of life.

During the start of meditation, there are some obstacles. The mind wanders everywhere in the past and future. Do not bother about this phenomenon which is quite common. It is something that every meditator has to pass through. Focus on the breath. When mind starts wondering again by thinking, daydreaming in the past, worrying about the future, without getting upset, simply return to the sensation of the breath. Then do it again the next time, and again, and again, and again. With constant practice the mind would be tamed.

To be mindful of the present moment is to stay in the ultimate now, to be acutely aware of what is happening in body and mind at the present instant. At such times do not remember past events or anticipate the future. Frankly speaking, the last breath is in the past. It is gone. The next breath has not happened yet. Only the present breath is real. Stay in the present.

Forget the Past:
To take the practice of insight meditation to the next stage, see the ultimate reality clearly. Forget the memories of the past. Not only memories from childhood, or yesterday, or one minute ago; not only the memory of our last breath. Stay in the present moment. Memories will not be permanently erased. These can be called back again. During meditation, the more you train the mind to stay in the present moment, the more you will realize that clinging to the past and living in the future cause suffering. The past is painful, and the future is fantasy. Attachment to pleasant memories makes the person long for something that is gone, and this longing is painful. What disappears in meditation practice are not the memories themselves,

but the distress that comes from attaching to the memories of the past and fear of the future.

Ultimate Reality in Meditation:

Meditation is only concerned with ultimate reality, not conventional truth. Conventional truth is relative, conceptual, and dynamic. It changes from person to person. But ultimate truth is the same for all. It is true in the absolute sense.

A name is a concept; it is not real. It is a false identity. It is only a convention that imposes on something. Remembering the name of a thing, referring to a sight, sound, smell, taste, touch, feeling or some other form, is not the same as directly experiencing it.

Ultimate reality refers to the raw sense-data of moment-to-moment experience: the actual instances of color, sound waves, tactile sensation, fragrance, and so on, that the brain continually registers. Ultimate reality is to stay in the present moment.

Forget "I" in Meditation:

During meditation, the term of self is not required. The expression of **I** is not used. When observing the body, for instance, you would not think, "I feel pain in my body" You would only be aware of the feeling of pain. The physical body is comprised of matter. We are not the body or the mind. We are pure consciousness.

The mind is not a self either. The mind is the faculty that knows the activities of the body. But this consciousness is not equivalent to a self. It is merely an impersonal awareness that arises and passes away from moment to moment.

Meditation Object:

In any type of meditation, we have to give the mind something to focus on. This "something" is called the "meditation object." Mantra or breathing or any idol are the options.

Dedication in Meditation:

Another requirement in meditation is dedication. In practicing meditation, keeping the mind in the present is not easy. The mind always wanders away. The mind produces thoughts after thoughts, good ones and bad ones. One subject leads to another, and on and on. It takes perseverance to change the habit of a lifetime. It is important not to get upset but keep on doing.

When the mind wanders away from the meditation object, simply not "thinking," saying the manta silently in the mind, then bring your attention back to the meditation object. As soon as you notice the mind slipping into the past or dreaming about the future, sweep it back to the present moment where a new object, a new sound, thought, or movement is already erupting.

Dedication is the key because you will have to bring the mind back again and again— literally thousands of times, until it becomes habitual. Do not try to suppress any emotions or thoughts that may arise. Allow these phenomena to appear naturally. Simply be aware of them when they occur.

Separate Your Physical Body:

Meditate on yourself as pure consciousness free from duality. Give up your false identity. Physical body is an identity. During meditation it is possible to make any phenomenon into an object of mindfulness instead of identifying with it. You can separate yourself from the show of sensation that is continually arising and passing by in form of thoughts. By doing this you protect the mind from suffering. It becomes apparent that thoughts, emotions, and feelings are not in fact parts of the knower. Since they are impersonal objects, not the subject, you can turn the beam of awareness around and look at them as if they were "outside" of you.

So, whenever you will feel that some phenomenon is inseparably part of the knower, is too close to observe because it is part of yourself, turn your awareness around one-hundred-eighty degrees and observe that very thing. This is another way of saying, "don't become the object."

The more you progress in meditation, the more you'll run out of things in the "self" category; the more you will see that everything can be known, even the mind. And when you know an object with impartial awareness you are separate from it. You are not involved in it. You have taken yourself out of it.

Even the mind is not ours. It is modified consciousness. It is impersonal because it does not follow our wishes. That is one meaning of no self. We can keep turning awareness back onto itself to observe the knower more and more, one instant after the next. In this way mindfulness sweeps every form of distress out of the mind.

But normally we mistake objects— especially thoughts, emotions, or feelings— for aspects of our selves. We think, "*I'm* sleepy" or, "*I'm* bored." Note the "I" here. It is a necessary convention of everyday speech. The problem is that we believe in the fictitious self that "I" denotes. If only you will remain resting in consciousness, seeing yourself as distinct from the body, then even now you will become happy, peaceful, and free from bond.

Wheel of Birth and Rebirth:
Although the benefits of meditation can result in the present, the efforts are also focused on improving the future life, too. According to Hindu Vedic teachings, every being is reborn over and over again into various realms according to his Karmas (actions). Until a person's mind is completely purified, there is no end to the cycle. The goal of meditation is to achieve salvation or Nirvana from the cycle of birth and death. Birth and death (and the time in between) always involve some degree of *sufferings*. Although we might be relatively happy now, our existence is tainted at the most basic level because its components, mind, and matter, are unstable and transitory, continually arising and vanishing. Any satisfaction gained from them is temporary and tinted with fear about its loss. Even at

its best, mundane happiness is a mixture of pleasure and anxiety. Happiness and unhappiness are inseparable, just as the head of a coin is inseparable from the tail. Thus, we remain in duality. Nirvana leads us to non-duality which transcends birth and death, is superior, pure happiness, *free of any anxiety*, devoid of greed, hatred, and illusion. This phase is permanent bliss called *Sat Chit Annand.*

As per the Vedas, all beings have accumulated some degree of unpleasant karmas from past performance of harmful or imprudent actions including some actions performed during previous lifetimes. Those past actions can give a result at any unpredictable time and there is always the possibility of rebirth of that individual into an unpleasant state or must endure painful conditions such as severe illness, poverty, misfortune at some future time. According to the Vedas, the practice of meditation may stop the cycle of birth-death-rebirth. Since desire, disillusion, hatred, and ignorance are the necessary conditions for rebirth. Meditation gradually removes desire, hatred and delusion from the mind and thus ends the cycle of birth and death, though there is no scientific evidence to support this statement.

Source of Sufferings:
External events are not the real source of sufferings. They are just the circumstances. The root source lies within not without. The purpose of meditation practice is to eliminate the *root* source of suffering, not merely to make us feel good temporarily. The question is, how does suffering arise in the first place? Every form of suffering is the result of a *thought* process, generated in the mind that depends upon cause and effect.

For example, if you see a beautiful statue or a painting that you cannot buy. You like it so desperately that you want to get it by hook or crook. The idea of getting that product leads to action. Intentional thoughts are considered a form of action. The physical act of stealing this product is also an action. Intentional mental, verbal, and physical actions are called karmas. Good or Bad Karmas always give back a result to the one who performed it. The act of stealing will result into a bad Karmas. If by chance that person escapes while stealing and does not get into any kind of trouble. He or she will get into trouble later or sooner. Repeated actions become habit and habit leads to the character of a person. Bad actions lead to bad Karmas. Likewise, good actions lead to good Karmas.

When these mental and physical actions— i.e., these karmas— are rooted in desire, hatred, and delusion, they give an unpleasant result. This result takes the form of sensation: unpleasant sights, sounds, smells, tastes, tactile sensations, or mental phenomena. Our various actions, when rooted in delusion, also result in rebirth. Reborn into samsara, the wheel of birth and death, one must endure various kinds of suffering.

Conclusion:
Meditation is not a quick fix to the problems. It requires patience and regularity. The practice of meditation daily regularly with dedication, faith and compassion will show some results in the form of excellent health, bright fortune, and blissful pleasure. Once you know with absolute certainty that nothing can trouble you but your own imagination, you come to disregard your desires and fears, concepts and ideas and live by truth alone. Imagination can vanish slowly by meditation. It is always the false that makes us suffer, the false values, and ideas, the false love relationship between people. If we abandon the false, we are free of pain. Truth makes us happy and set us free.

Chapter Five:
Meditation over Medication

"Do not dwell in the past, do not dream of the future, concentrate the mind on the present moment." *—Buddha*

S urvey of the literature revealed several benefits of meditation on the body starting from cardiovascular diseases, Alzheimer, arthritis, stress, migraine, pain, cancer and many more. Search on Google search engine turns up almost 700,000 research documents on meditation. Some of the studies are contradictory but the majority of them are in favor of meditation. The benefits of meditation are not imaginary. According to the NCCIH (National Center for Complimentary and Integrative Health), *"Some researchers suggest that meditation may physically change the brain and body and could potentially help to improve many health problems and promote healthy behaviors".*

A recent report comprised on the data from the 2017 National Health Interview Survey (NHIS) found that U.S. adults' use of meditation in the past 12 months tripled between 2012 and 2017 (from 4.1 percent to 14.2 percent). The use of meditation by U.S. children (aged 4 to 17 years) also increased significantly (from 0.6 percent in 2012 to 5.4 percent in 2017). No doubt, meditation has myriad benefits but science is just now catching up to speed.

Regular practice of meditation helps to mitigate the sufferings caused by negative thinking. Published findings have documented many physical and mental health benefits of meditation, including decreased pain, better immune function, less anxiety and depression, a sense of well-being, happiness, and emotional self-control. Moreover, some of the imaging studies show increased activity in brain regions associated with attention, a higher volume of grey matter, and lessened amygdala response to emotional stimuli.

There is cascade of scientific studies on meditation on the various parts of the body and it is a herculean task to describe them all in this chapter. However, some significant studies to articulate the benefits of meditation with validated scientific data are being discussed in this chapter.

Benefits of Meditation:
Meditation imparts physical, mental, and spiritual benefits to the meditators as summarized below:

Meditation lowers cardiovascular diseases (CVD):
Despite numerous advances in the prevention and treatment of atherosclerosis, cardiovascular diseases (CVD) remain a leading cause of morbidity and mortality not only in the United States but around the entire world. Although educational, lifestyle modifying, and pharmacological interventions have lowered the prevalence of cardiovascular risk factors, most Americans still have at least one major risk factor. More than $200 billion are being spent on care of patients with CVD in the United States annually, and this is expected to increase 2- to 3-fold over the next several decades.

According to the American Stroke Association (ASA) and American Heart Association (AHA), cardiovascular disease (CVD), principally heart attacks and strokes, accounts for more than 800,000 deaths or 40 percent of total mortality in the U.S. each year and more than 17 million deaths worldwide. In the U.S., CVD is projected to remain the single leading cause of mortality and is rapidly becoming so worldwide. Stroke alone ranks fifth in all-cause mortality in the U.S., killing nearly 133,000 people annually as well as more than 11 percent of the population worldwide. Consequently, novel and inexpensive interventions that are of benefit to patients and can contribute to the primary and secondary prevention of CVD are of interest. Meditation is considered as one of them. The 2017

American Heart Association Scientific Statement on meditation and cardiovascular risk suggested that meditation may be considered as an adjunct to guideline-directed cardiovascular risk-reduction interventions. Meditation could potentially increase physical and mental relaxation, leading to improved outcomes after a major cardiovascular event.

Many scientific studies have been conducted to investigate the effect of meditation on cardiovascular diseases. Most of the studies are in favor of meditation and a few are contradictory. Meditation **may** decrease the risk of heart disease, according to a first-ever statement on the practice issued by the American Heart Association. But the key word to highlight is **"may."**

A recent review by Krittanawong *et al.* (2020) on meditation and cardiovascular health in the US revealed the significance of meditation. They analyzed the data from the 2012 - 2017 of National Health Interview Survey. They identified all patients with hypercholesterolemia, systemic hypertension (SH), diabetes mellitus (DM), stroke, and coronary artery disease (CAD), as well as those who reported that they meditate. Multivariable logistic regression analyses were performed to evaluate the association between meditation and risk of hypercholesterolemia, SH, DM, stroke, and CAD, adjusting for potential confounders. Of 61,267 the National Health Interview Survey participants, 5,851 (9.6%) participated in some form of meditation. After adjusting for age, gender, body mass index, race, marital status, cigarette smoking, sleeping duration, and depression, meditation was independently associated with a lower prevalence of hypercholesterolemia compared with those who did not meditate. In conclusion, using a large national database, they found that meditation is associated with a lower prevalence of cardiovascular risks factors and disease.

Levine *et al.* (2017) have carried out investigations on meditation. Levin is a professor of medicine at Baylor College of Medicine in Houston, found a potential benefit of meditation to the heart.

They looked at 57 studies that researched common types of "sitting meditation" and whether the practice had any impact on heart disease. Overall, studies of meditation suggested a possible benefit on cardiovascular risk, although the overall quality and in some cases quantity of study data was modest. Various types of meditation included in the research were: Samantha; Vipassana (Insight Meditation); Mindful Meditation; Zen Meditation (Zazen); Raja Yoga; Loving-Kindness (Metta); Transcendental Meditation; and Relaxation Response. The group excluded the studies of meditation that incorporated physical activity – such as yoga or Tai Chi – because physical activity itself has been proven to help the heart. Levine said, 'there is a good deal of research on the effects of meditation on stress, mental health and conditions such as post-traumatic stress disorder. But research is more limited on meditation and heart health. Certainly, it would be desirable to have larger trials that follow patients for a longer period." According to Levine, the research is suggestive, but not definitive. Meditation should be considered as a potential lifestyle modification, but should not be used to replace standard and proven treatments such as smoking cessation, blood pressure control and treatment of high cholesterol levels.

Katie (2016) described the condition of Jeff Breece of Columbus, Ohio, who has been meditating about 20 to 30 minutes each day and uses it as an adjunct therapy to help calm the panic attacks he suffered after having a heart attack in 2015. He said, he found that it helped him to feel calmer and allowed him to observe his anxiety without reacting to it. In his own words, "After my heart attack, I felt like it defined me, Meditating helped me to get my life back. It helps me observe the moments."

John Denninger, Director of Research at the Harvard-affiliated Benson-Henry Institute for Mind Body Medicine at Massachusetts General Hospital, says, "Not only can meditation improve how your heart functions, but a regular practice can enhance your outlook on life and motivate you to maintain many heart-healthy behaviors, like following a proper diet, getting adequate sleep, and keeping up regular exercise." Research has found that meditation can positively affect a measure of heart health known as heart rate variability (HRV). HRV reflects how quickly the heart makes small changes in the time interval between each heartbeat. A high HRV is a sign of a healthier heart. Low HRV is associated with a 32% to 45% increased risk of heart attack or stroke among people without cardiovascular disease. Regular meditation may be able to raise HRV. The study found that people who did five minutes of meditation daily for 10 days had a better HRV compared with those who did not meditate. "Set up a schedule to help establish a routine. Try to meditate at the same time each day. If you have trouble sticking to a set time, plan to do your meditation after a regular activity like brushing your teeth. If you miss a day or two, don't feel you have lost any progress and have to start over, simply pick up where you left off and keep going." Says Denninger. (Harvard Health, 2018)

Dean Ornish, leader in Healthcare and Preventive medicine, first established that a holistic lifestyle program that included meditation could reverse the fatty plaques blocking a person's coronary arteries, the chief cause of heart disease. Such a comprehensive program covers exercise, diet, and stress management as well. The latest rescarch by Morris *et al.* (2001) confirms that people who practice meditation are significantly less likely to have a heart attack or stroke or die within five years.

"Meditation can be a useful part of cardiovascular risk reduction," says cardiologist Deepak Bhatt, a professor at Harvard Medical School. "I do recommend it, along with diet and exercise. It can also help decrease the sense of stress and anxiety. It appears to produce changes in brain activity. It also can lower heart rate, blood pressure, breathing rate, oxygen consumption, adrenaline levels, and levels of cortisol, a hormone released in response to stress."

There are many types of meditation that can result in physiological benefits, such as guided meditation, which uses mental images to relax; Transcendental Meditation, which uses a repeated sound or phrase to empty the mind; and mindfulness meditation, which focuses on the present moment to accept it without judgment. To get in on the benefits, follow the advice of Harvard Medical School professor Herbert Benson, a world-renowned expert in mind-body medicine. "Getting started is easy. You can learn in one minute. But you will have to do it for at least 10 minutes a day to get the physiological effects," he says (Harvard Health, 2013).

Schnaubelt *et al.* (2019) provided an overview of currently available evidence in the literature and the potential impact of meditation on cardiovascular health. However, the data cannot render with certainty directly reproducible effects of meditation on patients' cardiovascular disease profiles. Meditation may be suggested only as an additional link in the chain of primary and secondary prevention until future research provides sufficient data on this topic.

Eight percent of U.S. adults practice some form of meditation, according to a National Health Interview Survey, a division of the National Institutes of Health done in 2012. In addition, 17 percent of all cardiovascular disease patients surveyed expressed interest in participating in a clinical trial of meditation. But until more research does come, patients should adhere to proven cardiovascular disease therapies and use meditation only as an additional boost toward cardiovascular diseases.

Meditation Lowers Blood Pressure:
One in three U.S. adults has high blood pressure, according to the Centers for Disease Control and Prevention. The National Heart, Lung, and Blood Institute considers 140/90 millimeters of mercury (mm Hg) and above to be high blood pressure. Different types of meditation are incorporated to control blood pressure particularly in those people whose blood pressure could not be controlled by allopathic medicines. Systematic studies were funded by government and private agencies to study the effect of meditation to control blood pressure. Regarding prevalence of hypertension in the US, however, there are racial and ethnic disparities, too. Hypertension prevalence

is 48% higher in African Americans than in white Americans, which may contribute to the 50% higher mortality rate from CVD in African Americans, compared with white Americans. Almost same findings can be assumed in case of Asian Americans. According to the American Stroke Association (ASA) and the American Heart Association (AHA), more than 100 million Americans have high blood pressure. Elevated blood pressure is a major avoidable cause of premature morbidity and mortality in the United States and worldwide due primarily to increased risks of stroke and heart attacks. Elevated blood pressure is the most important major and modifiable risk factor to reduce stroke. In fact, small but sustained reductions in blood pressure reduce risks of stroke and heart attacks. Therapeutic lifestyle changes of weight loss and salt reduction as well as adjunctive drug therapies, are beneficial to treat and prevent high blood pressure. Sometimes, conventional methods of controlling BP do not work in certain people owing to their stress related problems. So, alternative, or complementary medicine is another option.

Meditation is better than blood pressure medication as per Randy Zusman, Director of the Division of Hypertension at the Massachusetts General Hospital Heart Center and Consultant in Cardiology, who asked patients suffering from high blood pressure to try a meditation-based relaxation program for three months. Relaxation results in the formation of nitric oxide which opens blood vessels (Aubrey 2008). The "relaxation response" technique was first described 30 years ago by cardiologist Herbert Benson. The Study of Zusman was conducted under his guidance by Dusek et al. (2008). These were patients whose blood pressure had not been controlled with medication. After meditating regularly for three months, 40 of the 60 patients showed significant drops in blood pressure levels and were able to reduce some of their medication.

Moreover, meditation also increases conscious awareness, which make lifestyle changes such as quitting smoking, drinking, and enjoying a healthy diet.

Several high-quality studies also show that meditation can modestly lower blood pressure, according to a 2013 American Heart Association scientific statement published in *Hypertension*. One analysis pooled results from nine studies and found that, on average, meditation lowered systolic blood pressure by 4.7 mm of mercury and diastolic blood pressure by 3.2 mm Hg.

Research from Yale University suggests that the best meditation to lower blood pressure is mindful breathing with paced breathing. We usually breathe at a rate of around 12 to 14 breaths per minute. Slowing this down to a pace of five to seven breaths per minute may help balance blood pressure, according to Yale. Brenner *et al.* (2020) have found that mindfulness meditation with paced breathing reduces blood pressure. Paced breathing is deep diaphragmatic breathing with typical rates equal to or less than 5–7 breaths per minute compared with the usual rate of 12–14. One plausible mechanism of benefit is that paced breathing stimulates the parasympathetic nervous system which alters neuronal function in specific areas of the brain and reduces stress chemicals and increase vascular relaxation that may lead to lower blood pressure.

Another study by Pramanik *et al.* (2009) revealed that slow-paced *bhastrika* pranayama breathing balances blood pressure and that a respiratory rate of six breaths per minute for five minutes can significantly decrease systolic and diastolic blood pressure. Bhastrika pranayama is derived from the Sanskrit word *bhastrika* which is the *bellows* mostly used by blacksmiths to melt metal. Like the bellows fan the fire, similarly, *Bhastrika Pranayama* surges the flow of air into the body to produce heat at both the physical and subtle level– stoking the inner fire of mind and body.

Numerous scientific studies have been conducted on the benefits of the Transcendental Meditation program at more than 200 independent universities and research institutions worldwide over the past 40 years. The National Institutes of Health have awarded over $26 million to research the effectiveness of TM for reducing stress and stress related illness with a focus on cardiovascular disease. Findings have been published in leading peer-reviewed scientific journals, including the American Journal of Cardiology and the American Heart Association's Hypertension and stroke.

Some studies reveal that Transcendental Meditation (TM) lowers blood pressure by stimulating genes that produce telomerase – an enzyme linked with reduced blood pressure and mortality. These studies were conducted with a pilot trial involving 48 black men and women with high blood pressure, who were recruited and studied at Howard University Medical Center in Washington, DC. Of the participants, half were assigned to a group that learned the TM technique and received a basic health education course, and the other half were assigned to a group that focused on achieving lifestyle modifications, including weight reduction, reducing salt intake, taking up regular physical activity and moderating alcohol intake. Results show that after 16 weeks, both groups exhibited significant increases in telomerase gene expression and reductions in blood pressure. Furthermore, there were no major differences between the changes in the two groups. "The finding that telomerase gene expression is increased, and that this is associated with a reduction in blood pressure in a high-risk population, suggests that this may be a mechanism by which stress reduction improves cardiovascular health,

Transcendental Meditation improves blood pressure and insulin resistance in heart patients according to a placebo-controlled study carried out at an academic medical center in California. Researchers studied 84 patients with coronary artery disease, randomly dividing them into two groups. The first received a 16-week course of health education; the second was enrolled in a course in transcendental meditation. Both groups continued to receive conventional medical care and advice. By the end of the study, the participants in the meditation group had significantly lower blood pressure compared with participants in the control group. They also had significantly improved in measures of insulin resistance, the ability of the body to properly process insulin and blood sugar. The scientists suggest that transcendental meditation causes improvements in certain elements of the metabolic syndrome, the group of related symptoms that increase the risk of coronary heart disease and other cardiovascular problems. "The good thing about meditation is that it has a very nice quality-of-life component," said the senior author of the study, Bairey Merz, Professor of medicine at the University of California, at Los Angeles. "There's no ongoing financial cost, no side effects and a lot of data to demonstrate that it has a beneficial effect." (Bakalar 2006).

Robert Schneider Head of the Centre of Natural Medicine and Prevention at the Maharishi University of Management in Iowa who led the research, said: "The study found that in older people with mild high blood pressure, those practicing transcendental meditation had a 23% lower risk of death from all causes." The study was funded by the US government. The study pooled the findings of two previous trials that followed 202 elderly people in the US over 18 years. Some practiced transcendental meditation, while others tried different techniques, such as progressive muscle relaxation. The transcendental meditation group had 30% fewer deaths from heart disease and 49% fewer from cancer. Although the sample [size] was relatively modest, these preliminary results suggest that an effective stress reducing intervention may decrease mortality. Schneider is a respectable physician of international repute. He has been investigating the effects of TM on various ailments for the last 25 years and published his findings in prestigious journals of international repute. Recently, he wrapped up a 10-year study (Jayadevappa 2007) of African-American men which found that the incidents of death from heart attack or stroke for those patients who regularly practiced the Transcendental Meditation technique were cut by a stunning 60%.

Previous research has found that transcendental meditation can lower stress hormone levels and blood pressure. According to Schneider, "This study builds on that and shows the outcome of these physiological and psychological changes is a longer life span.

These findings are very encouraging for prevention. They show that both the Transcendental Meditation technique and active lifestyle modification can contribute to heart health. Nidich *et al.* (2009) under the guidance of Schneider conducted a randomized controlled trial on effects of TM program on blood pressure, psychological distress and coping in young adults. TM program decreased BP in association with decreased psychological distress, and increased coping in young adults at risk for hypertension. This mind-body program may reduce the risk for future development of hypertension in young adults.

Results of a 2009 NCCIH-funded (National Center for Complementary and Integrative Health) trial involving 298 university students suggest that practicing Transcendental Meditation may lower the blood pressure of people at increased risk of developing high blood pressure. The findings also suggested, meditation can help with psychological distress, anxiety, depression, anger/hostility, and coping ability.

A literature review and scientific statement from the American Heart Association suggest that evidence supports the use of Transcendental Meditation (TM) to lower blood pressure. However, the review indicates that it is uncertain whether TM is truly superior to other meditation techniques in terms of blood-pressure lowering because there are few head-to-head studies.

Hughes (2013), and Fresco, associate professors of psychology in the College of Arts and Sciences at Kent State, reported that MBSR (Mindfulness-Based Stress Reduction) "may be an appropriate complementary treatment" for patients who prefer lifestyle changes and stress-management approaches to treating high blood pressure, or hypertension. This was the first scientific study in the U.S. to document that MBSR, an increasing popular practice, can influence high blood pressure, he said. The study was funded by a $545,000 grant from the National Institutes of Health. Hughes and Fresco were co-principal investigators. They are preparing to follow up with a longer study involving 180 adults to find out whether the effects of MBSR practice on blood pressure are lasting.

A study conducted by Blom *et al.* (2014) under the leadership of Sheldon Tobe, Chair in Aboriginal and Rural Health Research at Sunnybrook Health Sciences Centre in Toronto, found eight weeks of mindfulness meditation had no effect on people with slightly elevated blood pressure who were not yet taking medication. "This doesn't mean that meditation is bad. It just simply doesn't lower blood pressure," senior author Sheldon Tobe was expecting to see an effect on blood pressure based on past studies showing benefits with mindfulness meditation. But when he looked back over those earlier trials, he found most participants had been taking blood pressure-lowering drugs. In those studies, mindfulness therapy could have worked by helping people take their medicine more consistently.

A 2007 summary report published by the U.S. Agency for Healthcare Research and Quality found Zen Buddhist meditation and Qi Gong significantly reduced blood pressure.

More recently Marquez *et al.* (2019) studied the benefits of mindful meditation in reducing blood pressure and stress in patient with arterial hypertension and found encouraging results. Blood pressure was considerably reduced by mindfulness meditation.

Since scientists have yet to prove that meditation can significantly lower blood pressure, it is pertinent not to rely solely on meditation as a means of keeping the blood pressure in check. To achieve and maintain normal blood pressure levels, one should follow a healthy diet, limit intake of sodium and alcohol, exercise regularly, maintain a healthy weight, and avoid smoking and too much sex.

Meditation slows Aging:
The quest for the fountain of youth has been ongoing since time immemorial. Many efforts have been done to slow aging, too. Aging is inevitable. We cannot prevent aging but may slow it down. Aging is a complex process. "While many of the body's genes begin to break

down starting at age 40, science shows we aren't completely at the mercy of genetics," says longevity expert Farid Wassef (Torkos and Wassef, 2003). Genes play a role, but the rest is up to an individual.

During recent years, the life expectancy has also risen dramatically. But on the other hand, when middle age hits, people start experiencing mental fogs. The brain begins to wither — its volume and weight begin to decrease. As this occurs, the brain can begin to lose some of its functional abilities. Although people might be living longer, the years they gain often come with increased risks for mental illness and neurodegenerative disease like dementia. Over 35 million people were suffering from dementia worldwide in 2010, and this number is expected to triple by 2050 as per World Health Organization report. Thus, currently in the absence of a general cure for age-related pathological conditions or disease-modifying treatments for dementia, it is very pertinent to develop effective preventative approaches to brain aging and neurodegeneration. Scientists are trying to find the way out of this problem with complementary medicines, too.

A new study shows meditation could be one way to minimize those risks. Researchers at UCLA have been studying the effects meditation has on brain aging. Most recently, they examined how longtime meditators at age 50 fare in cognitive tests compared to other 50-year-olds who do not meditate. They found a big difference: meditators have brains that are about seven-and-a-half years younger than those who do not meditate. The researchers found among those who meditated, the volume of gray matter did not decline as much as it did among those who did not. Kurth *et al.* (2017) studied the effect of meditation on aging. The researchers were surprised by the magnitude of the difference. The researchers however, cautioned that they cannot draw a direct, causal connection between meditation and preserving gray matter in the brain. Too many other factors may come into play, including lifestyle choices, personality traits, and genetic brain differences.

Meditation Stimulates Glutathione:

Aging occurs by the attacks of free radicals on the cells and cause cellular aging. Free radicles are also produced under stress and a chain reaction called 'oxidative stress' begins. Early signs are skin spots, sagging, wrinkles, hardening of arteries resulting in strokes and heart diseases. It also damages DNA that leads to arthritis, Alzheimer's disease, diabetes, and cancer. Free radical is the main cause of cancer, too. It is truly relevant to prevent free radical oxidation occurring in the human body.

Glutathione naturally produced in the body is an antioxidant. There are about 90,000 medical articles published on glutathione. It is known as the master detoxifier and maestro of the immune system (Hyman 2011). Since glutathione is naturally found in the body, it can protect. However, the poor diet, pollution, toxins, medications, stress, trauma, aging, infections and radiation reduce the concentration of glutathione in the body. Glutathione deficiency results in chronic fatigue syndrome, heart disease, cancer, chronic infections, autoimmune disease, diabetes, autism, Alzheimer's disease, Parkinson's disease, arthritis, asthma, kidney problems, liver disease and many more. Glutathione is a combination of three simple building blocks of amino acids — cysteine, glycine, and glutamine. Due to the sulfur (SH) chemical groups which comes from cysteine in the molecule of glutathione, it gives awful smell.

During too much oxidative stress or too many toxins, the concentration of glutathione is reduced in the body and it is unable to protect the body from free radicals, infections, and toxins. Glutathione also supports the immune system to fight infections and prevent diseases.

Glutathione is an integral part of the detoxification system, too. All the toxins stick onto glutathione molecules and carried into the bile and excreted to the stool. Gutman (2019) has written a comprehensive guide to glutathione covering all its aspects in human body.

Research has shown that glutathione decreases muscle damage, reduce recovery time, increase strength and endurance and shift metabolism from fat production to muscle development. The highest glutathione levels are found in healthy young people and lower levels in healthy elderly. The lowest level is found in the elderly sick people. Somersall and Bounous (1999) gave a comprehensive description of the role of glutathione as the key element for immune system in their book "Breakthrough in cell-Defense." About 117,000 scientific studies on meditation have shown that regular practice of meditation increases 'glutathione' (GSH), known as *mother of all oxidants*, as cited in the Huffington Post. According to Bounous (2003) retired professor of McGill University, *"It's the body's most important antioxidant because it's within the cell, which is prime position to neutralize free radicals."*

Appleton, the Chairman of the Department of Nutrition at the National College of Medicine in Naturopathic Portland, Oregon, a naturopathic physician and celebrated author, recently illustrated about the importance of Glutathione: *"If you look in a hospital situation at people who have cancer, AIDS, or another very serious disease, almost invariably they are depleted in glutathione. The reasons for this are not completely understood, but we do know that glutathione is extremely important for maintaining intracellular health."*

Glutathione not only neutralizes oxidative stress but also plays a significant role for many critical enzymes, fights cancer by slowing apoptosis (programmed cell death), boosts t-cells, shields environmental toxin damage, and guards against drug resistance, while enhancing immunity.

Meditation power up the body with glutathione. Sinha *et al*, (2007) study showed that mediation increased the concentration of glutathione in the body. Fifty- one person were participated in this study which showed that meditation boosts this powerhouse peptide glutathione by a whopping 41%.

Mahagita (2010) studied the role of meditation on alleviated oxidative stress and found that meditation diminishes oxidative stress and therefore raises glutathione.

It's also important to note that people who are chronically ill often have low glutathione. While many things may contribute to low glutathione, a state of chronic stress depletes glutathione. Some guidelines are also given below to improve glutathione levels, improve health, adjust performance, and live a long, healthy life with meditation.

In addition to Meditation, some tips to increase Glutathione level in the body:

Regular Exercise boosts glutathione levels. Thirty minutes a day of vigorous aerobic exercise and strength training for 20 minutes, 3 times a week is also helpful.

Eat Foods Rich in Glutathione: Sulphur-rich foods include garlic, onions, broccoli, kale, collards, cabbage, cauliflower, watercress, horseradish, and wasabi. Broccoli and broccoli sprouts contain the largest amounts of glutathione-stimulating sulforaphane which are rapidly absorbed in our small intestine, then is distributed throughout the body, providing powerful health benefits to many vulnerable tissues. However, if the broccoli is cooked for more than a four-minute steam, it rapidly loses the compound, along with it many of the health benefits.

Selenium: This important mineral selenium helps the body recycle and produce more glutathione.

Vitamin C: recycles glutathione.

Alpha lipoic acid: helps in energy production, blood sugar control, brain health and detoxification.

Meditation Increases Nitric Oxide and Extends Life:

Nitric Oxide helps to extend life to 130 Years through meditation. Our brain, arteries, immune system, liver, pancreas, and lungs would quickly shut down without nitric oxide. The aging is directly proportional to the concentration of nitric oxide in the body. It is known as the natural elixir of life. It also increases libido and improves erectile dysfunction. In other words, meditation improves sex life, too.

Kim *et al.* (2005) studied the Zen Meditation on serum nitric oxide activity and lipid peroxidation. The experimental group included 20 subjects who had practiced the Zen Meditation program in Meditation Center located in Seoul, South Korea. The control group included 20 subjects who did not practice any formal stress management technique and were age and sex matched with experimental group. To provide an assessment of nitric oxide production, the serum level of nitrate/nitrite was determined. Meditation group showed a significant higher level of serum nitrate/nitrite concentration than control group.

In 2007, researchers from the Cleveland Clinic and Case Western Reserve University took blood samples from 88 Tibetans. They found mind bowing results that Meditation Boosts Nitric Oxide dramatically. When compared to non-meditating persons, the Tibetans had more than ten times the amount of nitric oxide in their systems. Hence, it was called the Zen molecule. Some claim the fantastic results from this study were due to the Tibetans 15,000ft altitude. Kemper *et al.* (2015) at the Ohio State University have shown "amateur" low elevation meditators to have a colossal 213% nitric oxide boost thorough meditation.

Meditation Alters Gene Expression:

A new study (Kaliman *et al.* 2014) conducted in collaboration with researchers from Wisconsin, Spain, and France shows that mindfulness meditation can even affect our genes. Specifically, the study shows that mindfulness can limit the "expression" of genes associated with inflammation. "The changes were rough observed in genes that are the current targets of anti-inflammatory and analgesic drugs," study co-author Kaliman, a researcher at the Institute of Biomedical Research of Barcelona in Spain, said, "Our findings set the foundation for future studies to further assess meditation strategies for the treatment of chronic inflammatory conditions." For the study, a group of experienced meditators practiced mindfulness over the course of an eight-hour period. During that same period, another group of people simply engaged in quiet non-meditative activities. After the sessions, they noticed a "down-regulation," or a suppression, of inflammatory genes in the meditators compared to the other group. There was no difference in the tested genes between the two groups at the start of the study.

Study coauthor Richard Davidson, Psychology Professor and founder of the Center for Investigating Healthy Minds at the University of Wisconsin in Madison, articulated, "The product of genes, e.g., the proteins that they manufacture, will vary with the extent to which the gene is turned on or off, We can think of genes possessing a molecular volume control that ranges from low to high that will govern the extent to which the gene produces the protein for which it is designed. The genes that we found to be down-regulated with mindfulness mediation practice are those implicated in inflammation." According to Davidson, this new research is the first of its kind to show changes in gene expression within mindfulness meditators.

Benson (2010) studied the effect of relaxation techniques on gene expression by comparing 16 people who have regularly evoked "the relaxation response" for an average of 9 years to 19 people who did not use these techniques.

The human body has about 30,000 genes. Benson's experiment found that roughly 2,000 genes differed in expression between groups. Many genes that triggered inflammation and cell death were turned off in the group that regularly practiced relaxation techniques. However, this deactivation does not appear to be permanent. The daily practice of relaxation techniques such as meditation is necessary to sustain benefits.

When controls were taught techniques to evoke the relaxation response, about 1,500 genes changed their expression within 8 weeks. These were many of the same genes seen in the group that have been practicing these relaxation techniques for years.

Meditation Improves Telomerase and Extends life:
Serving as the protective layer over the human chromosomes, telomerase extend life. There have been some amazing studies showing meditation's telomere lengthening capabilities, with far reaching implications.

A study by Jacobs *et al.* (2011) at the University of California-Davis, observed the white blood cells of 30 people before and after a three-month meditation retreat. The scientists revealed that the meditators activated about 40% more "telomerase units per 10,000 cells" versus the control group. Saron, neuroscientist at the University of California Davis Center, recently said, *"We have found that meditation promotes positive psychological changes, and that meditators showing the greatest improvement on various psychological measures had the highest levels of telomerase."* Meditation's proven anti-aging properties are unbelievably encouraging, with life extension and longevity. Saron, is also a coauthor of the study for mind and brain, and the Principal Investigator of Shamatha Project, the most comprehensive study to date investigating the effects of long-term intensive meditation practice on physiological and psychological processes central to well-being, attention, emotion regulation and health.

Carlson *et al.* (2014) measured the telomere length of 88 stage I to III breast cancer survivors, with mindfulness meditation. The meditating cancer survivors had managed to maintain their telomere length while the non-meditators' telomeres shortened significantly.

Another study by Dean Ornish and his colleagues at the University of California (UCSF) examined prostate cancer survivors practicing a deep breathing meditation routine. Amazingly, after 3 months, the subjects had "molecularly mitigated" and "silenced" the processes which play a role in developing cancer,

This is a landmark finding because, according to Dean Ornish, "So often people think 'Oh, I have bad genes, there's nothing I can do about it.' But these findings indicate that telomeres may lengthen to the degree that people change how they live [practicing meditation]. Our genes, and our telomeres, are not necessarily our fate."

Rathore and Abraham (2018) studied the implication of Asana, Pranayama and Meditation on Telomere Stability and found that practice of asana, pranayama, and meditation can help to maintain genomic integrity and are of key importance to human health and lifestyle disorders. Asana and Pranayama are parts of yoga meditation.

Meditation Slows Rate of Cellular Aging:
Understanding the pliable factors of cellular aging is critical to understanding human longevity. Telomeres may provide a pathway for exploring this issue. Telomeres are the protective caps at the ends of chromosomes. The length of telomeres offers insight into mitotic cell and possibly organismal longevity. Telomere length has now been linked to chronic stress exposure and depression. This raises the question of mechanism: How might cellular aging be modulated by psychological functioning? Epel *et al.* (2009) consider two psychological processes or states that are in opposition to one another-threat, cognition and mindfulness-and their effects on cellular aging. Psychological stress cognitions, particularly appraisals of threat and ruminative thoughts, can lead to prolonged states of reactivity. In contrast, mindfulness meditation techniques appear to shift cognitive appraisals from threat to challenge, decrease ruminative thought, and reduce stress arousal. Mindfulness may also directly increase positive arousal states. They review data linking telomere length to cognitive stress and stress arousal and present new

data linking cognitive appraisal to telomere length. Given the pattern of associations revealed so far, they propose that some forms of meditation may have salutary effects on telomere length by reducing cognitive stress and stress arousal and increasing positive states of mind and hormonal factors that may promote telomere maintenance. Aspects of this model are currently being tested in ongoing trials of mindfulness meditation.

Meditation and Cancer:

Breast cancer is the cancer most frequently diagnosed in women worldwide. Even though survival rates are continually increasing, breast cancer is often associated with long-term psychological distress, chronic pain, fatigue, and impaired quality of life. Yoga comprises advice for an ethical lifestyle, spiritual practice, physical activity, breathing exercises and meditation. It is a complementary therapy that is commonly recommended for breast cancer-related impairments and has been shown to improve physical and mental health in people with different types of cancer.

Cancer-related cognitive impairment has been acknowledged as a substantial limiting factor in quality of life among cancer patients and survivors. In addition to deficits on behavioral measures, abnormalities in neurologic structure and function have been reported. Biegler *et al.* (2009) review the findings from the literature on cognitive impairment and cancer, potential interventions, meditation and cognitive function, meditation, and cancer. With the increasing success of cancer treatment and the ability to return to previous family, social, and work activities, symptom management and quality of life are an essential part of survivorship. They propose that meditation may help to improve cancer-related cognitive dysfunction, alleviate other cancer-related sequelae, and should be fully investigated as an adjuvant to cancer treatment.

Chemotherapy-induced peripheral neuropathy (CIPN) syndrome causes significant pain as an adverse effect of treatment, with few nonpharmacological interventions tested. A somatic yoga and meditation (SYM) intervention on functional outcomes and quality of life (QOL) was investigated by Galantino *et al*. (2019). Preliminary data suggest SYM may improve QOL, flexibility, and balance in cancer survivors with CIPN, with a fully powered randomized controlled trial indicated.

Meditation Increases Sirtuins to Extend life:
It is well-known that resveratrol extends life. There are two main reasons that resveratrol extends human life. The first one is, resveratrol is a strong antioxidant. Second, resveratrol activates an immensely powerful longevity family of genes and proteins known as 'Sirtuins.'. Meditation extends human life while increasing sirtuins level *without* taking red wine. Sirtuins are a family of seven proteins that play a role in cellular health, metabolic regulation, cardiovascular health, DNA expression, and healthy aging. In fact, when Sirtuins were discovered, they were quickly nicknamed "the longevity genes." Sirtuins can only function in the presence of NAD+, nicotinamide adenine dinucleotide, a coenzyme found in all living cells. NAD+ is vital to cellular metabolism and hundreds of other biological processes.

David Sinclair, world famous molecular geneticist at Harvard University, one of TIME Magazine's *"100 Most Influential People In The World."* found that, by activating a prominent member of the 'Sirtuin' gene family (SIRT1), resveratrol increased cell survival in yeast and mice by nearly 30%. Sirtuins and the proteins they encode have received loads of financial investment from heavy hitting pharmaceutical companies looking to isolate the compound for formulating the drug (Cameron 2014).

A study by Tolahuanase *et al*. (2017) examined the cellular aging of 96 meditators over 12 weeks. After measuring a variety of key "metabotropic" cellular aging biomarkers, the researchers found that meditation had "significantly *reduced the rate of cellular aging* in apparently healthy population." Included among their many intriguing test results was the most prominent member of the red wine/resveratrol linked 'Sirtuin' family of proteins. According to the researchers, the meditators' Sirtuin 1 levels were boosted by a massive 52%. This is the same Sirtuin found in red wine. Meditation imparts the same life extending benefits of red wine without drinking red wine. Subsequent work from Sinclair and colleagues showed that *caloric restriction,* known for many decades to have life-prolonging effects in certain organisms, works by activating two other sirtuins called *SIRT3* and *SIRT4.* Thus, caloric restriction and meditation both prolong aging (Longo *et al.* 2015)

Meditation Improves Dementia and Alzheimer's Disease:
As there is currently no cure for Alzheimer's disease and other neurodegenerating diseases, many are seeking non-pharmacological treatment options. Moreover, with the high prevalence and cost of these diseases care worldwide, a need exists to develop cost-effective and evidence-based treatment. Meditation, which has been demonstrated to have positive effects on brain health, may be a viable intervention option.

Hoffman *et al.* (2020) reviewed the meditation-based intervention for adults with dementia and found encouraging results. The data published between 1997-2018 was reviewed. Their findings suggest that incorporating meditation into interventions for people with dementia can have beneficial effects. Meditation-based interventions for people with dementia are associated with improved quality of life and cognition and may be viable treatment options for occupational therapists to implement in their practice.

The effects of meditation on grey matter atrophy and neurodegeneration were reviewed by Last *et al.* (2016). Thirteen studies were considered eligible for review and involved a wide variety of meditation techniques and included participants with and without cognitive impairment. All studies reported significant increases in grey matter volume in the meditators/intervention group, albeit in assorted regions of the brain.

Cahn *et al.* (2017) at University of Southern California (USC) tested 38 people before and after a three-month meditation retreat. They found that neurotrophins BDNF (Brain Derived Neutrophic Factor) levels was boosted by 280 percent preventing old age brain degenerating diseases like dementia, Alzheimer's etc. Brain-derived neurotrophic factor abrineurin, is a protein that, in humans, is encoded by BDNFgene. BDNF is a member of the neurotrophin family of growth factors, which are related to the canonical nerve growth factor. Neurotrophic factors are found in the brain and the periphery.

Khalsa (2015) reported the effects of Kirtan Kriya meditation on Alzheimer disease. Kirtan Kriya is basically chanting some mantras in group or alone as per the choice of meditators. According to him, stress and lifestyle are the possible factors contributing to Alzheimer Disease (AD). Meditation helps on cognition and well-being for reduction of neurodegeneration and prevention of AD. His focus is on Kirtan Kriya (KK), an easy, cost effective meditation technique requiring only 12 minutes a day, which has been successfully employed to improve memory in studies of people with subjective cognitive decline, mild cognitive impairment, and highly stressed caregivers, all of whom are at increased risk for subsequent development of AD. KK has also been shown to improve sleep, decrease depression, reduce anxiety, down regulate inflammatory genes, upregulate immune system genes, improve insulin and glucose regulatory genes, and increase telomerase by 43%; the largest ever recorded. KK also improves psycho-spiritual well-being or spiritual fitness, important for maintenance of cognitive function and prevention of AD. KK is easy to learn and practice by aging individuals. It is the premise of this review that meditation in general, and KK specifically, along with other modalities such as dietary modification, physical exercise, mental stimulation, and socialization, may be beneficial as part of an AD prevention program.

Meditation Slows Aging of Skin:

Conger (2009) reported that Chang and coworkers at Stanford University have reversed the aging of skin in mice, making it look and act just like new skin by turning off the Nf-kB, the skin gene that regulates the aging process of skin. Skin becomes thicker and wrinkle-free. Nf-kB (nuclear factor kappa-light-chain-enhancer of activated B cells) is a protein complex that controls transcription of DNA, cytokine production and cell survival. NF-κB is found in almost all animal cell types and is involved in cellular responses to stimuli such as stress, cytokines, free radicals, heavy metals, ultraviolet irradiation, oxidized LDL, and bacterial or viral antigens. According to Chang, "When you block NF-κB, when the organism is quite old," Chang said, "you can basically block the genetic program, 'aging'." He told The New Yorker magazine, "It's the most difficult field I've ever worked in, and I didn't want to define my scientific life with all these fights." Luckily, meditation picked up where Chang left off. Researchers at the UCLA had 45 family dementia caregivers practice meditation for 8 weeks, Meditation turns this key age accelerating gene off and rejuvenated the skin. Elastin is a highly elastic protein which keeps our skin stretchy and able to bounce back. Collagen keep the skin thick, agile, and strong. Meditators' skin often looks younger than non-practicing ones.

Meditation Reduces Cortisol Level:

People who practice meditation look younger. During non-stop stress, brain pumps out stress hormones cortisol through amygdala over activity. A high concentration of cortisol in the body can suppress immunity, raise blood pressure, reduce libido, increase obesity and blood sugar levels. When sugar binds to proteins and lipids through "glycation," it makes the skin wrinkled.

Effects of Buddhist meditation on serum cortisol were studied by Sudsuang (1991) in 52 males 20–25 years of age practicing *Dhammakaya Buddhist* meditation, and in 30 males of the same age group not practicing meditation. It was found that after meditation, serum cortisol levels were significantly reduced, serum total protein level meaningfully increased, and systolic pressure, diastolic pressure and pulse rate considerably reduced. Results from these studies indicate that practicing *Dhammakaya Buddhist* meditation produces biochemical and physiological changes.

In a wide range of studies, including one at University of California at Davis and Rutgers University, meditation has been shown to drop cortisol levels significantly. Turakitwanakan *et al.* (2013) showed that meditation reduces cortisol levels. Mindfulness meditation lowers the cortisol levels in the blood suggesting that it can lower stress and may decrease the risk of diseases that arise from stress such as psychiatric disorder, peptic ulcer, and migraine. Brand *et al.* (2012) also confirmed that practice of mindful meditation reduces cortisol level.

Effects of mindfulness training on levels of cortisol in cancer patients were also studied by Bränström *et al* (2012), The study gives preliminary support indicating that mindful meditation can influence the hypothalamic-pituitary-adrenocortical (HPA) axis functioning. The importance of these findings for future research in the field of mindfulness and stress reduction among cancer patients are discussed.

Jacob *et al.* (2013) reported from Saron Lab at the University of California-Davis that meditation reduces cortisol levels. At an individual level, there was a correlation between a high score for mindfulness and a low score in cortisol both before and after the retreat. Individuals whose mindfulness score increased after the retreat showed a decrease in cortisol.

Recently Bansal *et al.* (2016) studied the effect of Osho Dynamic meditation on serum cortisol. Dynamic meditation is one of the most popular active meditation, introduced by an Indian mystic and philosopher Osho in 1970. This one-hour meditation consists of five stages: Deep fast chaotic breathing, catharsis, using a mantra "Hoo", silence, and dancing. A previous study observed that Osho dynamic meditation causes decrease in several psychopathological variables such as aggressive behavior, anxiety and depression. Sixteen volunteers out of the 20 completed the study while four dropped out due to their health and personal reasons. The serum cortisol levels were decreased in all the 16 participants on 21st day as compared to the baseline levels and the decline in the mean cortisol level was highly significant. It can be concluded that the Osho dynamic meditation produces anti-stress effects. The mechanism of action could primarily be attributed to the release of repressed emotions and psychological inhibitions and traumas. Thus, dynamic meditation could be recommended for the amelioration of stress and stress related physical and mental disorders.

Vincent Giampapa, a well-known longevity researcher and past president of the American Board of Anti-Aging Medicine,1943 revealed that regular deep meditation dramatically lowered cortisol levels by about half, Ross (2016). By balancing the pain sufferer's hormonal chemistry, meditation dramatically reduces pain on all fronts. High cortisol, can raise blood pressure, worsen inflammation, elevate heart rate, and contribute immensely to the never-ending pain anticipation feedback loop. Reducing this hormone by meditation solves all these problems.

Meditation Reduces Stress:
Stress is extremely dangerous for the body and destroys the body day and night beyond one's imagination. According to Bruce Lipton, an internationally recognized authority in bridging science and spirit and a leading voice in new biology, "Stress is the cause of at least 95% of all diseases." Numerous studies have proven that stress was a cause of mass destruction. It is very pertinent to get rid of this *"silent killer."* During stress the mind reacts, and hormones are released in the system that cause changes in the body such as high blood pressure, disturbed breathing and heart rate, and tightening of body muscles. Stress is exceedingly harmful and even leads to death.

Nevertheless, modern life is awfully stressful of issues such as job complications, marital problems, financial difficulties, and household snags which are silently inflating the secretion of cortisol, adrenaline and related chemicals causing severe health problems. Long-term stress can imbalance the entire nervous system, releasing more and more cortisol and adrenaline in a vicious cycle. Its results enhance aging, weakens immune system, damage vital brain tissues and leads to major depression and dementia.

Practicing meditation regularly will diminish the stress, depression, and related problems. Scientists believe that the brains generate more than 50,000 to 60,000 thoughts per day. Most of the thoughts, are useless comprising fear of the past and fantasies of the future. Though they have no effect on the present life but repeated such negatives thoughts day and night destroy health and happiness. Realizing the situation, the person tries to resist bad thoughts but in return compounds the problem. The world-renowned psychologist, Carl Jung, put it best, "what you resist, persists." The more you resist to control bad thoughts, the more they persist. So, keep the mind still, do not react. Lao Tzo founder of philosophical Taoism, articulated nicely, *"To the mind that is still, the whole universe surrenders."*

Meditation is the best and easiest technique of calming the mind. Meditation teaches to be mindful of incoming thoughts - aware of the inner epilogue. It transfers power away from the busy, "monkey mind" to the slow, deep, profound so-called "ox mind".

Meditation sessions will eliminate stress from the body like anxiety, depression or related disease. Meditation will calm the mind and decrease cortisol, adrenaline stress producing hormones. It is very well expressed by Napoleon Bonaparte, *"The best cure for the body is a quiet mind."* Swami Vivekananda also emphasized, "Let the mind be cheerful but calm. Never let it run into excesses because every excess will be followed by a reaction."

For a thousand years, people have reported feeling better by meditating but there has never been a systematic study that quantified stress and how much stress changes as a direct result of meditation until now. Very recently, U.S. Army Research Laboratory researchers spent a year collaborating with a team of scientists from the University of North Texas to develop a new data processing technique that uses heart rate variability as a sensor to monitor the state of the brain. Heart rate variability provides a window through which we can observe the heart's ability to respond to external disturbances, such as stress, said Bruce West, the Army's senior research scientist. Stress modulates the autonomic nervous system signals, which in turn disrupts normal HRV and therefore the stress level can be detected by processing HRV time series. Through a new method of processing HRV time series data, the researchers developed a way to measure the change in the level of stress provided by meditation. They found encouraging results that meditation reduces stress. (US Army 2018).

The mindful meditation does an amazing job: by staying in the present moment, the awareness of now and enjoying the present can keep the mind calm and quite. Staying in the past or worrying about the future will enhance the problems.

Communication is a big problem among people. They interpret and make a mountain of mole hills that leads to stress. It adversely affects the heart rate, stomach swirl, and can also increase weight. Stress increases cortisol production in the body and increases weight. Cortisol interferes with sleep, eats away muscles, causes anxiety and depression and triggers extensive tissue inflammation, slows the digestive, and immune system.

Roth (2018), a well-known author and meditation teacher says, *"We know if a person is stressed, he gets sick more. If they are stressed, they gain weight. A lot of this comes down to the release of cortisol in the body... [which becomes] toxic when we have too much."*

Financial worries, unhealthy relationship(s), and unfulfilling desires and ambitions pump cortisol into the body every hour. It is quite evident that the chronic stress has taken the lives of in so many people. Dunlop (2015) reports that as the pace of life increases, stress is becoming prevalent, and in the radiologic sciences, stress is keenly felt by technologists and patients. Meditation, a potential remedy to stress, is the subject of an increasing number of medical studies that often rely upon radiologic imaging scans to determine the physiological effects of meditation on brain activity. A wide range of meditation techniques have beneficial effects on the mind, body, and emotions. Radiologic technologists might find that meditation improves their quality of life as well as their level of job satisfaction, allowing them to provide improved quality of care to their patients.

A mindfulness meditation course decreases burnout and improves well-being among healthcare providers. Mindfulness meditation is reported to support mental well-being; however, findings are limited in Australian business settings. A mindful pilot study by Vella (2019) revealed that mindful meditation reduced stress and burnout in the public sector. Accordingly, this study explored the efficacy of a mindfulness meditation program tailored for an Australian public-sector workplace.

Goodman and Schorling (2012) reported that healthcare providers were under increasing stress and work-related burnout had become common. Mindfulness-based interventions have a potential role in decreasing stress and burnout. The purpose of this study was to determine if a continuing education course based on mindfulness-based stress reduction could decrease burnout and improve mental well-being among healthcare providers, from different professions.

Meditation on Brain:
Lazar (2005), a Harvard neuroscientist discovered that meditators had much more neural density, gray matter thickness, and neural activity within their left prefrontal cortex — perhaps the smartest & happiest brain region of all. Lazar found that meditation increases the size of super-beneficial prefrontal cortex with regular meditation practice.

Meditation and Neuroscience:

Research over the past two decades broadly supports the claim that mindfulness meditation - practiced widely for the reduction of stress and promotion of health - exerts beneficial effects on physical and mental health, and cognitive performance. Recent neuroimaging studies by Tang *et al.* (2015) have begun to uncover the brain areas and networks that mediate these positive effects. However, the underlying neural mechanisms remain unclear, and it is apparent that more methodologically rigorous studies are required to gain a full understanding of the neuronal and molecular bases of the changes in the brain that accompany mindfulness meditation.

The brain network governing meditation has been studied by Tomasino *et al.* (2013) using a variety of meditation practices and techniques practices eliciting different cognitive processes (e.g., silence, attention to own body, sense of joy, mantras, etc.). It is possible that different practices of meditation are subserved by largely, if not entirely, disparate brain networks. This assumption was tested by conducting an Activation Likelihood Estimation (ALE) meta-analysis of meditation neuroimaging studies, which assessed 150 activation foci from 24 experiments. Different ALE meta-analyses were carried out. One involved the subsets of studies involving meditation induced through exercising focused attention (FA). The network included clusters bilaterally in the medial gyrus, the left superior parietal lobe, the left insula and the right supramarginal gyrus (SMG). A second analysis addressed the studies involving meditation states induced by chanting or by repetition of words or phrases, known as "*mantra.*" This type of practice elicited a cluster of activity in the right SMG, the SMA bilaterally and the left postcentral gyrus. Furthermore, the last analyses addressed the effect of meditation experience (i.e., short- vs. long-term meditators). They found that frontal activation was present for short-term, as compared with long-term experience meditators, confirming that experts are better enabled to sustain attentional focus, rather recruiting the right SMG and concentrating on aspects involving disembodiment.

Meditation Shrinks the Brain's Fear Center:

The restless mind is continuously firing different types of thoughts one after the other. Some are good and some are awfully bad. Most of these thoughts do not even make any sense. Too much involvement in insignificant thoughts would make people crazy. Meditation helps and takes the mind away from the whirlpool of thoughts. Instead of repeating the past tragedies and worrying about tomorrow's troubles, mindful meditation's focus puts an end to the sufferings. When there is no fears and worries, one gets the experience of the intoxicating silence between each thought. Thus, meditation allows the mind to finally experience itself in its truest, purest, most natural state of stillness.

Desbordes *et al.* (2012) at the Boston University and Harvard Medical School fMRI brain-scanned participants before and after a series of mindfulness meditation classes — with staggering results. In only 8 weeks, along with far fewer "distress signals" transmitted throughout the brain, the meditators' brain imaging for "fear center" electrical activity had gone silent. What surprised the scientists the most, however, was that their "anxiety engine" amygdala somehow managed to physically shrink. The Culprit is Our Brain's Fear Center: Amygdala almond shaped group of nuclei buried deep within the temporal lobes of the brain.

An overactive amygdala creates ample health problems. Meditation through neuroplasticity keeps the activity of amygdala under control. Mindfulness Meditation study at the Boston University, through MRI scans showed that the brain's anxiety, depression, fear center, and the amygdala - shrunk significantly. The scientists found that the synergetic connectivity between the amygdala and the rest of the brain also weakened, while the brain areas associated with focus and higher consciousness got stronger.

Taren *et al.* (2015), a mindfulness researcher at the Center of Neuroscience, University of Pittsburgh, has done extensive research on amygdala and mindfulness meditation. According to her, the scale of these changes strongly correlated with the number of hours of meditation practice.

Meditation and Brainwaves:

Sleep or awake, brain fires electrical signals 24 hours per day, outwardly measured as "brainwaves." The brainwave state at any given time is the sum total of the thoughts, emotions, mood and overall health.

Beta brain waves has shown to be dominant under stress, anxiety, and depression. Beta waves can wreak havoc on mental, emotional, and physical health.

Meditation keeps the brain in the most healthy, advanced states in Alpha, Theta, and Delta, waves, respectively. These super-beneficial brainwaves produce amazing benefits, including super-learning, memory, creativity, releasing of good neurochemicals.

Tang *et al.* (2019) studies the effect of theta waves with mindful meditation. Both brain alpha and theta power have been examined in the mindfulness meditation literature and suggested as key biological signatures that potentially facilitate a successful meditative state. However, the exact role of how alpha and theta waves contribute to the initiation and maintenance of a meditative state remains elusive. In this investigation, they discuss the role of frontal midline theta (FMθ) activity in brain white matter plasticity following mindfulness meditation. In accordance with the previous studies in humans, they propose that FMθ activity indexes the control needed to maintain the meditation state; whereas alpha activity is related to the preparation needed to achieve the meditative state. Without enough mental preparation, one often struggles with and has difficulty achieving a meditative state. Animal work provides further evidence supporting the hypothesis that mindfulness meditation induces white matter changes through increasing FMθ activity. These studies shed light on how to effectively enhance brain plasticity through mindfulness meditation.

Desai *et al.* (2015) reviewed the effects of yoga on brain waves and structural activity of the brain. Previous research has shown the vast mental and physical health benefits associated with yoga. Yoga practice can be divided into subcategories that include posture-holding exercise (asana), breathing (pranayama, Kriya), and meditation (Sahaj) practice. Studies measuring mental health outcomes have shown decreases in anxiety and increases in cognitive performance after yoga interventions. Similar studies have also shown cognitive advantages amongst yoga practitioners versus non-practitioners. The mental health and cognitive benefits of yoga are evident, but the physiological and structural changes in the brain that lead to this remain a topic that lacks consensus. Therefore, the purpose of this study was to examine and review existing literature on the effects of yoga on brain waves and structural changes and activation. After a narrowed search through a set of specific inclusion and exclusion criteria, 15 articles were used in this review. It was concluded that breathing, meditation, and posture-based yoga increased overall brain wave activity. Increases in gray matter along with increases in amygdala and frontal cortex activation were evident after a yoga intervention. Yoga practice may be an effective adjunctive treatment for a clinical and healthy aging population.

Baijal and Narayanan (2010) investigated the brain oscillatory activity associated with different cognitive processes that plays a critical role in meditation. In this study, they investigated the temporal dynamics of oscillatory changes during Sahaj Samadhi meditation (a concentrative form of meditation that is part of Sudarshan Kriya yoga). EEG was recorded during Sudarshan Kriya yoga meditation for meditators and relaxation for controls. Spectral and coherence analysis was performed for the whole duration as well as specific blocks extracted from the initial, middle, and end portions of Sahaj Samadhi meditation or relaxation. The generation of distinct meditative states of consciousness was marked by distinct changes in spectral powers especially enhanced theta band activity during deep meditation in the frontal areas. Meditators also exhibited increased theta coherence compared to controls. The emergence of the slow frequency waves in the attention-related frontal regions provides strong support to the existing claims of frontal theta in producing meditative states along with trait effects in attentional processing. Interestingly, increased frontal theta activity was accompanied reduced activity (deactivation) in parietal-occipital areas signifying reduction in processing associated with self, space and time.

Meditation and Aphasia:

Stroke is currently the leading cause of long-term disability in adults in the entire world. There is a need for accessible, low-cost treatments of stroke-related disabilities such as aphasia. To explore an intervention for aphasia utilizing mindfulness meditation (MM). Marshall *et al.* (2018) studied the effect of mindful meditation on aphasia patient. This preliminary study examines the feasibility of teaching MM to individuals with aphasia. Since physiological measures have not been collected for those with aphasia, the study was also an exploration of the potential attention, language and physiological changes after MM in adults with aphasia during a brief, daily group training. Results were encouraging. This is an emerging area of interest due to the potential low cost of MM training. Furthermore, MM is easily taught to patients, suggesting the possibility for widespread use in clinical practice as a supplement to existing language-focused interventions.

Despite the potential behavioral and neurological benefits of Mindfulness Meditation (MM), its use in treating stroke related communication disabilities appears to be underexplored. Specifically, aphasia, a language disorder resulting from stroke, may be amenable to the benefits of MM because of the observed attention problems often underlying the language symptoms. Laures-Gore (2016) treated aphasia patient with mindful meditation. Overall, changes were observed in both psychophysiological measures (heart rate and heart rate variability) and behavioral measures (word productivity, phrase length, word generation, decreased impulsivity, and increased attention).

Orenstein *et al.* (2012) studied the effects of mindfulness meditation on three individuals with aphasia. There is evidence to suggest that people with aphasia (PWA) may have deficits in attention stemming from the inefficient allocation of resources. The inaccurate perception of task demand, or sense of effort, may underlie the misallocation of the available attention resources. Given the lack of treatment options for improving attention in aphasia, Mindfulness Meditation, shown to improve attention in neurologically intact individuals, may prove effective in increasing attention in PWA. All three participants reported that Mindfulness Meditation was easy to learn and carry out daily and reported feeling more 'relaxed' and 'peaceful' after Mindfulness Meditation training than before. With the knowledge that PWA can learn meditative practices, and with such successful findings in neurologically intact individuals, it is important to continue evaluating the benefits of Mindfulness Meditation in PWA.

Meditation Activates the Relaxation Response:
Benson (2010), a cardiologist, and founder of the Mind/Body Medical Institute at Massachusetts General Hospital (MGH) in Boston, noticed that most of the patients had stress related disorders. Benson found that meditation was the key to eliciting the body's "relaxation response". By simultaneously activating the "cool and calm" parasympathetic nervous system while deactivating "fight or flight" stress mode, in meditation, he discovered that his patients could essentially reverse countless health issues. While meditation further multiplies the relaxation response's many chemical benefits, effectively making it the body's status quo.

His research emphasized that meditation is the significant technique for the prevention and even the reversal of 100's of serious mental, emotional, and physical diseases.

Many longevity scientists believe stress is the new "biological clock" — a dominant force which can make the person old long before his time. The "telomeres" within the DNA begin to decay over time under stress and makes the person look and feel older, weakens cells, followed by vicious diseases, however, telomere damage can be slowed down and even reversed by meditation. Scientists at the University of California-Davis found meditators' white blood cells had remarkably longer and stronger telomeres than the control group, showing their vibrant health and longevity. Meditation effectively creates a stress "immunity shield", adding both quantity and quality years to life and delayed old age.

Meditation Boosts Melatonin Level:

Nagendra *et al.* (2012) suggest that meditation may boost levels of melatonin, a hormone that helps regulate sleep. Melatonin is produced by the pineal gland in the brain. The philosopher Rene Descartes called this tiny gland "the seat of the soul." In the Hindu spiritual tradition, meditation techniques are used to direct energy flow through seven energy centers in the body, or chakras, and selectively activate or suppress their associated glands. The pineal gland corresponds to a chakra located at the top of the head and is believed to influence happiness (Kumar *et al.* 2018).

Neuroscientists at Massachusetts General Hospital have shown that meditation helps to strengthen sleep brain region. The connection between melatonin and meditation was first explored in 1995 by researchers at the University of Massachusetts Medical Center's Stress Reduction and Relaxation Program. Researchers found that women who meditated had significantly higher levels of melatonin compared with women who did not. Another study by Massion *et al.* (1995) found that meditation before bedtime increased melatonin levels for that night. No increases in blood melatonin levels were noted on nights where participants did not meditate. Another study by Tooley *et al.* (2000) found that meditation before bedtime increased melatonin levels for that night. No increases in blood melatonin levels were noted on the nights where participants did not meditate.

Rutgers University researchers discovered that melatonin levels for meditation practitioners were boosted by an average of 98%, with many participants having increases by more than an incredible 300%. "Melatonin" is responsible for sleep. Stress inhibits natural sleep cycles and decreases melatonin levels. Meditation successfully re-balances all the biological markers and gently removes insomnia.

Meditation and Obesity:

Mantzios and Egan (2020) at the Birmingham University have created some tools that are designed to facilitate healthier eating, including the Mindful Construal Diary and the Mindful Chocolate Practice. They have revealed that mindfulness eating reduce obesity and reduce body fat. Around 62% of the UK population is classed as overweight and 25% as obese, according to Health Express, which can lead to potentially life-threatening conditions such as Type 2 Diabetes and strokes, as well as a decrease in quality of life and depression. The NHS spends £5.1 billion a year on treating obesity and related illnesses. Therefore, addressing behavior that leads to overeating is high priority for the healthcare sector and the government.

Meditation Reduces Belly Fat:

Ian Campbell, British weight loss expert, BBC contributor, and medical consultant for "The Biggest Loser", recently told DailyMail, "Just telling people to eat less and exercise more doesn't tend to work, we have incorporated mindfulness into our weight loss programmer and the results have been fantastic... Mindfulness could provide the 'missing link' between the biology and psychology of weight loss." (Asda Good Living 2016).

Most of the people eat food to extinguish their emotions. Emotional hunger means overeating. Natural hunger needs just the right amount of food. Meditation controls craving for food and habit of overeating is dropped through the power of neuroplasticity. Meditation enhances brain's "command and control center" prefrontal cortex. Meditation ensures a balanced state of consciousness all the livelong day. Moreover, meditation activates our body's "relaxation response." Meditation cleans our cellular toxic stress residue. By reducing the

60-70,000 thoughts per day that the human mind thinks, meditation anchors our awareness firmly into the present moment.

Hairston (2012) Professor of Endocrinology at the Wake Forest University said that visceral fat *"doesn't just sit there,"* it creates *"lots of nasty substances."* Hiding under our abdominal wall, too much of this *"bad fat"* can impact our health in big ways. So destructive, this stuff sticks to our organs, cranks up our stress hormones, sets our body ablaze with inflammation — while also being linked to high blood pressure, diabetes, heart disease, certain cancers, and even brain disorders like dementia.

Data from the 2017 Stress in America Survey conducted by the American Psychological Association (APA) found that 3 out of 4 Americans reported experiencing at least one stress symptom. Unfortunately, all of this excess stress can lead to an increase in weight. The extra weight is a result of overeating and unhealthy food choices, or body's response to increased levels of cortisol.

Linderburg (2019) has shown that stress and elevated cortisol tend to cause fat deposition in the abdominal area rather than in the hips. This fat deposition has been referred to as "toxic fat" since abdominal fat deposition is strongly correlated with the development of cardiovascular disease, including heart attacks and strokes.

Caroline Cederquist, a Bariatric Medicine Specialist and a leading expert in the field of medical weight management, founder of Cederquist Medical Wellness Center in Naples, Florida, investigated that around 90% of her obese patients suffered from insulin resistance. When the insulin receptors do not open properly, liver and muscle cells cannot store the energy need from food. This elevates blood sugar level. All this extra energy's gets converted to fat. The load of glucose circulating in insulin resistant people's blood stream becomes the visceral fat. Stress is also responsible for this. Meditation controls stress, the secret evil agent responsible for insulin resistance and reduce fat.

Paul-Labrador *et al.* (2006) at the Cedars-Sinai Medical Center in Los Angeles conducted a 16-week trial of Transcendental Meditation in patients with coronary heart disease. Fifty-two participants (average age 67.7 years) were instructed in Transcendental Meditation and 51 control patients (average age 67.1 years) received health education. Overall, of the 103 participants who were enrolled, 84 (82 percent) completed the study. At the end of the trial, patients in the Transcendental Meditation group had significantly lower blood pressure; improved fasting blood glucose and insulin levels, which signify reduced insulin resistance; and more stable functioning of the autonomic nervous system. "These physiological effects were accomplished without changes in body weight, medication or psychosocial variables and despite a marginally statistically significant increase in physical activity in the health education group," the authors write. The meditators beaten the non-meditating group's metabolic syndrome by more than 200%. *Meditation reduces tenacious visceral belly fat significantly.*

Loucks *et al* (2016) at the Brown University measured the "everyday mindfulness" levels of 400 participants via a short questionnaire (MAAS-Mindful Attention Awareness Scale). The study found that those who were highly aware of their thoughts and feelings (as measured by MAAS) actually weighed much less overall (BMI), also had significantly less abdominal fat than the control group. Dispositional mindfulness may be inversely associated with obesity and adiposity. Replication studies are needed to adequately establish whether low dispositional mindfulness is risk factor for obesity and adiposity.

Satyanarayana *et al.* (1992) studied the effect of Shanti Kriya on certain psychophysiological parameters. Santhi Kriya is a mixture of yogic practices of breathing and relaxation. Preliminary attempts were made to determine the effect of Santhi Kriya on certain psychophysiological parameters. Eight healthy male volunteers of the age group 26 years were subjected to Santhi Kriya practice daily for 50 minutes for 30 days. The volunteer's body weight, blood pressure, oral temperature, pulse rate, respiration, ECG and EEG were recorded before and after the practice on the 1st day and subsequently on 10th, 20th and 30th day of their practice. Results indicate a gradual and significant decrease in the body weight from 1st to 30th day and an increase in alpha activity of the brain during 30 days of Santhi Kriya practice. Increase of alpha activity both in occipital and pre-frontal areas of both the hemisphere of the brain denotes an increase of calmness. It is concluded that the Santhi Kriya practice for 30 days reduces body weight and increases calmness.

Meditation Minimizes Food Cravings:
Camilleri *et al* (2015) examined the link between body image and weight loss for 14,000 adults. A total of 14,400 men and 49,228 women participating in the NutriNet-Santé study were included in this cross-sectional analysis. Women with higher dispositional mindfulness scores were less likely to be overweight. They found that adults who perceived themselves as "fat" were far more likely to put on weight. As per Watkins and Wulaningsih (2016), obesity is a byproduct of trade and eating attitude of an individual. Mindful meditation helps to reduce weight.

Camilleri *et al* (2016) examined the relationship between intuitive eating (IE), which includes eating in response to hunger and satiety cues rather than emotional cues and without having forbidden foods, and weight status in a large sample of adults. A total of 11,774 men and 40,389 women aged ≥18 years participating in the NutriNet-Santé cohort were included in this cross-sectional analysis. IE is inversely associated with overweight and obesity which supports its importance. Although no causality can be inferred from the reported associations, these data suggest that IE might be relevant for obesity prevention and treatment.

University of Wisconsin neuroscientists have shown that helping and being kind to others lights up one specific part of the brain, the "right anterior dorsal insula," This transformation automatically quiets down negativity "*I hate my big fat stupid body*" self-talk. With a positive mindset capable of achieving anything, one can accept his shortcomings, and compromise with the present conditions. With this mindset, one has the strength and discipline to stick to any plan moving forward. Meditation is the perfect way to bring about this shift in consciousness to pure consciousness. Channeling the power of meditation will leads to positivity. Watkin (2016) studied the attitude of the obese people recently and concluded that their attitude and outlook have to be positive in order to lose weight and stay healthy.

A recent study by Johnston *et al.* (2014) at the University of Toronto compared the success of various weight loss programs for overweight people. Many claims have been made regarding the superiority of one diet or another for inducing weight loss. Which diet is best remaining unclear? The scientists discovered that success in losing weight was not which diet the participants followed (low carb vs low fat), it was whether they were "*extrinsically*" or "*intrinsically*" motivated to lose weight. Most of the people overeat mindlessly and quickly. If they are insulin resistant, they accumulate more fat as compared to Mindful Eaters who stay "*Effortlessly Slim.*"

Wansink *et al.* (2015) put 61 of these "*effortlessly slim*" persons to investigate the result of mindful eating. Wansink told Science Daily, "*We wanted to find this group's small or simple behaviors that might have a big impact on why they so easily stay slim.*" In other words, whether they knew it or not, the effortlessly slim folks were mindful eaters.

Kristeller and Hallet (1999) studied the efficacy of a 6-week meditation-based group intervention for Binge Eating Disorder (BED). It was evaluated in 18 obese women, using standard and eating-specific mindfulness meditation exercises. Results suggest that meditation training may be an effective component in treating BED.

Meditation and Dopamine:

Schulte *et al.* (2015) found that the most addictive foods of all tend to be full of calories, sugar, and saturated fat — with French fries, pizza, ice cream, cake, and cookies topping the list. Such food stimulates dopamine, chemical of addiction. Deserts increase the blood sugar and dopamine level and cause addiction to sugar. Hours after that big meal, signals are sent to the brain, and food cravings begin all over again. This vicious cycle continues. Meditation diminishes the craving for such food.

Kjaer *et al.* (2002) at the John F. Kennedy Institute found that dopamine levels were boosted by 65% during meditation, the meditators dopamine levels remained high. and their craving for sugar diminished. It is suggested that being in the conscious state of meditation causes a suppression of cortico-striatal glutamatergic transmission.

Meditation Raise Serotonin and Norepinephrine Level:

Serotonin and norepinephrine are the two most important neurotransmitters responsible for causing depression. As per Andrew Weil, a physician and expert of integrating medicine, 25 percent of people taking antidepressants gain weight. The reasons for this phenomenon vary from carbohydrates cravings to slower metabolism. Studies have shown that the ancient meditation practice boosts serotonin and norepinephrine to reduce depression.

Newburg (2010), a famous neuroscientist, took brain images of Tibetan monks during meditation. He discovered that meditation cooled off the very brain region that gets overheated when we feel disconnected, isolated, and lonely — the time and space oriented "parietal lobe." Instead of emptiness and loneliness, meditation entangles us back into the quantum, making us feel connected to everyone and everything. The meditators have claimed for centuries that the powerful practice makes them feel "at one with everything."

Perreau-Linck *et al.* (2007) at the University of Montreal have shown mindfulness activities have a direct impact on the brain's production of serotonin levels. Meditation increases the secretion of serotonin and mitigates many problems in the human body. The study by Perreau-Linck and colleagues is the first to report that self-induced changes in mood can influence serotonin synthesis. Neuroscientist Perreau-Linck also carried out a study in which she confirmed that we can alter our own brain chemistry. Perreau-Linck had professional actors self-induce a state of happiness or sadness and used a PET (Positron Emission Tomography) scan to measure the serotonin synthesis capacity (SSC) of their brains. SSC is an indicator of how efficiently the brain makes serotonin from its chemical precursor tryptophan. The cortex and deeper brain regions showed significant differences in SSC activity for those actors who self-induced happiness and those who self-induced sadness. "We found that healthy individuals are capable of consciously and voluntarily modulating SSC by transiently altering their emotional state," said Perreau-Linck. "In essence, people have the capacity to affect the electrochemical dynamics of their brains by changing the nature of their mind process. This is a kind of 'positive emotion therapy' that anyone can use to modify chemical functioning of the brain" (Perreau-Linck *et al.* 2004).

Meditation Stimulates Endorphins:
Meditation Stimulates Endorphins level in the body. Endorphins are neurotransmitters released by the pituitary. These substances also impart a sense of happiness and contentment. Endorphins reduce blood pressure and have several benefits such as reduced depression, anxiety, improved self-esteem, regulation or modulation of appetite, an enhanced immune response and reduced pain.

Harte *et al.* (1995) tested the neuro-chemical release of two groups — 11 elite runners and 12 highly trained meditators — after running and meditation, respectively. As the scientists suspected, both groups had boosted their endorphin levels. On the contrary, meditation scored higher level of endorphins than exercise.

Meditation Releases DHEA:

DHEA, dehydroepiandrosterone known as *longevity molecule*, is one of the most important hormones in the body. Meditation provides a dramatic boost in DHEA hormone levels. Vincent Giampapa, former President of the American Board of Anti-Aging Medicine, and current prominent longevity researcher discovered that meditation practitioners have an incredible 43.77% more DHEA over everybody else.

DHEA levels is decreased during old age which leads to number of diseases. In fact, a 12-year study of 240 men (50-79 years) found that DHEA levels were directly linked to mortality. The researchers' findings were simple yet impactful: the lesser the DHEA, the fewer years left in age. Karen Civello, founder of KalyaaNa Spa & Wellness Retreat, meditation can assist with anti-ageing. "Ageing occurs due to the deterioration of the endocrine system. However, people who meditate regularly produce 100 per cent more dehydroepiandrosterone (DHEA) than people who do not meditate. DHEA is produced in the adrenal glands and is said to counteract the ageing process," Civello explains. She adds meditation can cause your adrenal glands to produce less cortisol, one of the main hormones responsible for ageing. In addition, she says a study by Hoge (2013) found people who meditated daily for at least four years had longer telomeres (the protective caps at the end of chromosomes) than people who did not meditate. Relatively short telomere length may serve as a marker of accelerated aging, and shorter telomeres have been linked to chronic stress. Specific lifestyle behaviors that can mitigate the effects of stress might be associated with longer telomere lengths.

Kumar *et al* (2018) studied the effects of yoga and meditation on serum DHEA levels in medical students. His study concludes that practicing Yoga has significantly raised serum DHEAS levels in medical students and improved their immunological status as well as enhanced mood and behavior. Lai *et al* (2017) reported that long practice of Tai Chi meditation raises the level of DHEA. Glaser *et al* (1992) reported that Transcendental Meditation increases the serum DHEA level in 270 men and 153women in TM meditators.

Meditation Boosts GABA:

Gamma aminobutyric acid, known as the "calm chemical," is one of the major inhibitory neurotransmitters in a person's central nervous system. GABA, a mood stabilizer released from the body, is also released during meditation. GABA is a substance found to be low in persons suffering from food addiction. To lose weight, your body needs more GABA so you will not crave food. Lack of GABA leads to addiction on drugs, alcohol, tobacco, food and even caffeine, with side effects such as anxiety, racing thoughts, and a lack of sleep. Several studies have shown that regular meditation practice increases this chemical tremendously. A study by Streeter *et al.* (2010) at the Boston University School of Medicine found a 27% increase in GABA levels in patients after just 60 minutes of mindful meditation practice. As a result, people who practice meditation can both help addictions and keep impulsive behavior at bay.

Streeter *et al* (2007) reported that yoga asanas sessions increase brain GABA levels. They suggest that the practice of yoga should be explored as a treatment for disorders with low GABA levels such as depression and anxiety disorders.

Elias and Wilson reported (1995) that Transcendental Meditation (TM) is a stylized form of physical and mental relaxation which is associated with changes in the secretion and release of several pituitary hormones. The hormonal changes induced by TM mimic the effects of the inhibitory neurotransmitter gamma aminobutyric acid (GABA). It is hypothesized that TM produces changes in pituitary hormone secretion by enhancing hypothalamic GABAergic tone, and its anxiolytic effects by promoting GABAergic tone in specific areas of the brain. This mechanism is similar to the effects of synthetic anxiolytic and tranquilizing agents such as benzodiazepines that bind to components of the GABA-A (GABAA) receptor. TM, therefore, may produce relaxation by enhancing the effects of an endogenous neurotransmitter analogous to the effects of endorphins in runners who reportedly experience a 'runner's high'.

Meditation and Anxiety: Meditation Replaces Benzodiazepine: Platt *et al.* (2016) reviewed a nonpharmacological alternative to benzodiazepine drugs for the treatment of anxiety in outpatient populations. The overuse of benzodiazepine drugs to treat anxiety, mood, and sleep disorders is a growing problem in clinical practice. GABAergic medications (benzodiazepine drugs in particular) have side effects, drug interactions, and the potential to create tolerance and dependence in users. GABA-enhancing dietary supplements have similar and unique risks. Natural, non-chemical, anxiolytic treatments exist and can be safely recommended to patients. Three such treatments have been the focus of study in the past 20 years: mindfulness, meditation, and yoga. Growing evidence exists that these treatments can be safely recommended to patients with anxiety.

Internationally acclaimed Harvard brain researcher, Sara Lazar, discovered that one brain region responsible for the "wandering mind," the posterior cingulate cortex (PCT), becomes deactivated during meditation. Lazar (2005) also showed that meditators had significantly more neural density, cortical thickness, and overall activity within their prefrontal cortexes.

Chanting Cures Depression: An 8-week study was carried out at the Samarya Center for Integrated Movement Therapy and Ashtanga Yoga in Seattle, WA, to see the effects of chanting on general well-being and particularly respiratory functions in people suffering from mild-to-severe depression. The results showed that chanting helped participants increase control over their breath and expiratory output level. The participants claimed that chanting reduced their anxiety and improved their mood. Researchers thus concluded that if done at least once a week, chanting is an effective means of enhancing people's moods in the immediate present, as well as over an extended period (Jane Yoga 2010).

Meditation Removes Addiction:

Addiction of alcohol, smoking and drugs increasingly seek alternative interventions to assist in cessation or reduction efforts. Mindfulness meditation, which facilitates detached observation and paying attention to the present moment with openness, curiosity, and acceptance, has been studied as an addiction cessation intervention.

Goldstein and Volkow (2002) examined the role of certain brain regions in drug addiction. They found that the brain's happiness center, the prefrontal cortex, to be super stimulated during intoxication (the "fix"), and incredibly under-active during withdrawal (the "crash"). If only there was a better way to activate the prefrontal cortex!

Meditation stimulates and keeps the brain happy and "naturally high", without alcohol, prescriptions, marijuana, drugs, cigarettes, or any other addictive substance to feel good. Mindfulness meditation has a long tradition of being used to manage cravings.

Khanna and Greeson (2013) studied the effect of yoga and mindful meditation in combination on addiction. Current theoretical models suggest that the skills, insights, and self-awareness learned through yoga and mindfulness practice can target multiple psychological, neural, physiological, and behavioral processes implicated in addiction and relapse. A small but growing number of well-designed clinical trials and experimental laboratory studies on smoking, alcohol dependence, and illicit substance use support the clinical effectiveness and hypothesized mechanisms of action underlying mindfulness-based interventions for treating addiction. Very few studies have been conducted on the specific role of yoga in treating or preventing addiction, they propose a conceptual model to inform future studies on outcomes and possible mechanisms. Overall, current findings increasingly support yoga and mindfulness as promising complementary therapies for treating and preventing addictive behaviors.

More than 5 million deaths a year are attributable to tobacco smoking but attempts to help people either quit or reduce their smoking often fail, perhaps in part, because the intention to quit activates brain networks related to craving.

Tang *et al.* (2013) experimented with the use of meditation in smoking reduction. They recruited participants interested in general stress reduction and randomly assigned them to meditation training or a relaxation training control. Among smokers, 2 wk. of meditation training (5 h in total) produced a significant reduction in smoking of 60%; no reduction was found in the relaxation control. Resting-state brain scans showed increased activity for the meditation group in the anterior cingulate and prefrontal cortex, brain areas related to self-control. These results suggest that brief meditation training improves self-control capacity and reduces smoking.

The limited success of current smoking cessation therapies encourages research into new treatment strategies. Mind-body practices such as yoga and meditation have the potential to aid smoking cessation and become an alternative drug-free treatment option.

Carim-Todd *et al.* (2013) reviewed the role of yoga and meditation for smoking cessation. The aim of their review was to assess the efficacy of yoga and other meditation-based interventions for smoking cessation, to identify the challenges of clinical trials applying mind-body treatments, and to outline directions for future research on these types of therapies to assist in smoking cessation. The literature supports yoga and meditation-based therapies as candidates to assist smoking cessation. However, the small number of studies available and associated methodological problems require more clinical trials with larger sample sizes and carefully monitored interventions.

Gryffin and Chen (2013) studied the implications of t'ai chi meditation for smoking cessation. Their findings suggest, T'ai chi, is a more dynamic form of meditation, can be an effective method for enhancing mindfulness and awareness for breaking cycles of addiction and habit. Possible effects on physical cravings were also identified. As a novel and unusual form of mind/body exercise, t'ai chi may be a particularly appealing adjunct to smoking cessation programs, particularly in light of the many ancillary health benefits of t'ai chi.

The core clinical symptoms of addiction include an enhanced incentive for drug taking (craving), impaired self-control (impulsivity and compulsivity), emotional dysregulation (negative mood) and increased stress reactivity. Symptoms related to impaired self-control involve reduced activity in anterior cingulate cortex (ACC), adjacent prefrontal cortex (mPFC) and other brain areas. Tang *et al* reported (2016) that behavioral training such as mindfulness meditation can increase the function of control networks including those leading to improved emotion regulation and thus may be a promising approach for the treatment of addiction.

Tapper (2018) reviews 30 experimental studies that have examined the effects of different types of mindfulness practice on cravings for food, cigarettes, and alcohol. The findings are interpreted considering relevant theories of craving. Nevertheless, a smaller number of studies show promising results where mindfulness meditation has been repeatedly practiced over a longer period. The results of these studies suggest mindfulness practice may confer unique benefits in terms of both craving reduction and reducing the extent to which craving leads to consumption.

Scott *et al.* (2005) looked at 121 patients going through an inpatient substance abuse program. The participants were given EEG biofeedback training which, put simply, the brainwave patterns of the user into a more advanced state of consciousness by using alpha &

theta waves. Surprisingly, at a one year follow up, 77% of patients were completely drug free.

Bowen *et al.* (2006) at the University of Washington, examined 78 substance addicted prison inmates for three months. The participants were taught meditation for 10 days and given questionnaires to self-report their drug use at day 0 and again at day 90. The study found that inmates who practiced meditation for 3 months drank 87% less alcohol and used 89% less marijuana. Furthermore, meditation was found to be almost 6 times more effective than the control group's more traditional chemical dependency treatment plan. Results indicate that after release from jail, participants in the meditation course, as compared with those in a treatment-as-usual control condition, showed significant reduction in alcohol, marijuana and crack cocaine.

Maglione *et al.* (2017) reviewed the effect of mindfulness meditation on the smoking cessation. Mindfulness meditation did not differ significantly from comparator interventions in their effects on tobacco use. Low-quality evidence, variability in study design among the small number of existing studies, and publication bias suggest that additional, high-quality adequately powered RCTs (Randomized controlled Trials) should be conducted. Overall, mindfulness meditation did not have significant effects on abstinence or cigarettes per day,

In a study, mantra chanting was used as a method for treating alcoholism, wherein mantras were practiced at sunrise and sunset for six weeks. Golechha *et al.* (1991) found that mantra chanting by suppressing delta and alpha brain waves produces mental tranquility and helped subjects to curb urge for alcohol.

Alfred A. Thomas, Doctorate in Medicine from Paris School of Medicine found that chanting sounds have therapeutic effect on the body. Chanting calms the bodily system and activates the body's natural process. It also helps in getting rid of addictions like smoking, alcohol and drugs.

Meditation Diminishes Chronic Pain:

A Gallup-Healthways survey of 2012 found that 47% of US adults experienced some form of chronic pain (HuffPost 2012). Thus, numerous studies have been conducted with healthy individuals to understand meditative analgesia. Grant (2014) review focuses explicitly on experimental pain studies of meditation and attempts to draw preliminary conclusions based on the work completed in this new field over the past 6 years. Dividing meditative practices into the broad categories of focused attention (FA) and open monitoring (OM) techniques allowed several patterns to emerge. Most of the evidence for FA practices suggests they are not particularly effective in reducing pain OM, on the other hand, seems to influence both sensory and affective pain ratings depending on the tradition or on whether the practitioners were meditating. The neural pattern underlying pain modulation during OM suggests meditators actively focus on the noxious stimulation while inhibiting other mental processes, consistent with descriptions of mindfulness.

Zeidan *et al.* (2011) studied, at Wake Forest University, effect of meditation on pain.18 chronic pain participants underwent 4 days of meditation training before and after training, their brain activity was measured using advanced MRI brain imaging technology. The findings of this study were encouraging, the subjects' "brain pain centers" were 57% less active after meditation within 4 days of meditative experience.

Meditation teaches to emotionally detach from your negative thoughts and physical sensations, where there is no longer pain. By becoming a passive, impartial observer of your mind, suffering is no longer a function of pain. Meditation deviates the thought process of pain.

Meditation has been proven to release endorphins healthily and naturally, which are up to several times powerful than modern medicine's best painkiller, morphine. Research about meditation's ability to reduce pain has produced mixed results. However, in some studies scientists suggest that meditation activates certain areas of the brain in response to pain. Meditation "rewires" the brain's pain circuitry. Neuronal pathways within the brain get programmed every time you expect pain to occur — in time, less and less stimulus is needed to trigger the pain reflex. Eventually, the simple thought of pain becomes the true source of pain. Thinking of pain creates more pain.

A small 2016 study funded in part by the National Center for Complementary and Integrative Health (NCCIH) found that mindfulness meditation does help to control pain and does not use the brain's naturally occurring opiates to do so. This suggests that combining mindfulness with pain medications and other approaches that rely on the brain's opioid activity may be particularly effective for reducing pain.

In another 2016 NCCIH-funded study, adults aged 20 to 70 who had chronic low-back pain received either mindfulness-based stress reduction (MBSR) training, cognitive-behavioral therapy (CBT), or usual care. The MBSR and CBT participants had a similar level of improvement, and it was greater than those who got usual care, including long after the training ended. The researchers found that participants in the MBSR and CBT groups had greater improvement in functional limitation and back pain at 26 and 52 weeks compared with those who had usual care. There were no significant differences in outcomes between MBSR and CBT.

Hilton *et al.* (2018) reviewed the intervention of meditation to relieve chronic pain. They concluded that mindfulness meditation improves pain and depression symptoms and quality of life. Ball (2017) investigated the effect of mindful meditation on chronic pain. They found that Mindfulness meditation has a most prominent effect on psychological aspects on living with chronic pain, improving associated depression and quality of life. Survey of literature is full of evidence that meditation of any kind, if carried out regularly, reduces chronic pain.

Meditation Elevates Growth Hormone:

The major isoform of the human growth hormone is a protein of 191 amino acids and a molecular weight of 22,124 Daltons. The structure includes four helices necessary for functional interaction with the GH receptor. It appears that, in structure, GH is evolutionarily homologous to prolactin and chorionic somatomammotropin. GH stimulates growth during childhood and sustains tissues and organs of the body. During middle age the pituitary gland, at the base of the brain, produces growth hormone. Deficiency of the GH results in decrease of bones and muscles, increased body fat, poor heart contractions, bad moods, lack of motivation, and fatigue. The growth Hormone is released during delta brainwave frequency found during the deepest stage of sleep and meditation. Therefore, during meditation, the Growth Hormone is released which will help meditators stay young and healthy. That means meditation elevates growth hormone levels and delays aging.

This study by Cooper (1985) was designed to assess whether transcendental meditation (TM) could influence various endocrine responses in 10 experienced male meditators. Nine matched subjects, uninformed of the TM procedure, acted as controls. Meditators successfully practiced their technique for 40 min in the morning while controls relaxed for this period. No significant differences emerged between these 2 groups with respect to carbohydrate metabolism (plasma glucose, insulin and pancreatic glucagon concentrations), pituitary hormones (growth hormone and prolactin) or the 'stress' hormones, cortisol and total catecholamines-although meditators tended to have higher mean catecholamine levels. Plasma free fatty acids were significantly elevated in meditators 40 min after completing the period of TM. No clear evidence was thus obtained that any of the stress, or stress-related, hormones were suppressed during or after meditation in the particular setting examined.

The Transcendental Meditation (TM) and an advanced program, the TM-Sidhi program, have been reported to produce several acute and long-term metabolic and electrophysiologic changes by Werner *et al.* (1986). To investigate the possibility that the practice of these techniques may be associated with long-term endocrinologic changes, they evaluated 11 male subjects before and over a 3-year period after starting the TM-Sidhi program. A progressive decrease in serum TSH, growth hormone, and prolactin levels occurred over the 3 years while no consistent change in cortisol, T4, or T3 (Thyroid Hormones) levels was observed. These results suggest that the long-term practice of the TM and TM-Sidhi program may have effects on neuroendocrine function.

Brainwave Stimulate Growth Hormones:
One of the more enticing benefits of listening to brainwave entrainment is its ability to stimulate Human Growth Hormone (also known as HGH). HGH has been found through scientific study to benefit multiple functions of the body and has a valuable effect on every cell. It is a kind of meditation. Extensive research has been done in this field and various videos and CDs have been prepared comprising selective wavelength suitable for calming the mind. Advertisers claim brain waves are more effective than any regular meditation. Many people believe that delta brain waves provide access to God, "Infinite Intelligence", or the "Collective Unconscious" mind. It is linked with production of human growth hormone, serotonin, DHEA and related chemicals in the body. Several people have also reported having spiritual experiences and sometimes O.O.B.E. (Out-Of-Body-Experiences) while having Delta Brainwave activity. These mystical experiences are more common if a person has access to slower levels of their Brain Waves.

Meditation Increases Gray Matter:
Vestergaard-Poulsen (2009) at the Center for Functionally Integrative Neuroscience at Aarhus University in Denmark, when comparing MRI scans of the brains of meditators with the brains of non-meditators, found that meditation causes actual physical changes in the gray matter of the lower brain stem. Meditation helps the gray matter grow.

Pagnoni and Cekic (2007) from the Department of Psychiatry and Behavioral Sciences at Emory University in Atlanta, compared the volume of gray matter in the brains of people performing Zen meditations with another group of nonmeditators. The volume of gray matter normally reduces with age and this is what the scientists found in the group of non-meditators. But for the meditators, their gray matter had not reduced at all with age. According to the scientists, meditation had a 'neuroprotective' effect on the meditators: It protected the brain from some of the effects of aging.

Schwartz and Gladding (2012) have written a comprehensive view of the brain in their book entitled "You Are Not Your Brain." The brain, and how we can mold it, is fascinating and nothing short of amazing.

Meditation and Irritable Bowel Syndrome:
Kuo *et al* (2015) conducted a pilot study on IBS including relaxation meditation. They found that participating in a nine-week training program had a significant impact on clinical symptoms of the gastrointestinal disorders irritable bowel syndrome (IBS) and inflammatory bowel disease (IBD). The expression of genes related to inflammation and the body's response to stress were also affected. The report from investigators at the Benson-Henry Institute for Mind Body Medicine at Massachusetts General Hospital (MGH) and at Beth Israel Deaconess Medical Center (BIDMC), both Harvard affiliates, is the first to study the use of the relaxation response in these disorders and the first to investigate the genomic effects of the relaxation response in individuals with any disorder.

Several studies have found that stress management techniques and other psychological interventions can help patients with IBS, at least in the short term; and while the evidence for IBD is less apparent, some studies have suggested potential benefits. What is novel about their study is demonstration of the impact of a mind/body intervention on the genes controlling inflammatory factors that are known to play a major role in IBD and possibly in IBS. "Results suggest exciting possibilities for further developing and implementing this treatment in a wider group of patients with gastrointestinal illness," said Kuo the coauthor of the study.

Both IBS and IBD are chronic conditions that produce related symptoms, including abdominal pain and changes in bowel function such as diarrhea. But while IBD — which includes Crohn's disease and ulcerative colitis — is characterized by severe inflammation in all or part of the gastrointestinal tract, no inflammation or visible abnormality is present in IBS. Stress appears to aggravate both conditions, and since the symptoms themselves can increase stress in patients, finding ways to break that vicious cycle could have significant clinical benefits.

The relaxation response — a physiologic state of deep rest induced by practices such as meditation, yoga, and prayer — was first described more than 40 years ago by Herbert Benson, Director Emeritus of the Benson-Henry Institute and a co-author of the current paper. Many studies have shown that regular practice of the relaxation response not only alleviates stress and anxiety but also directly affects physiologic factors such as blood pressure, heart rate, and oxygen consumption.

Ford *et al.* (2014) from the American College of Gastroenterology stated that the few studies that have looked at mindfulness meditation training for IBS found no significant effects. But the authors noted that given the limited number of studies, they can't be sure it doesn't help.

Results of a 2011 NCCIH-funded trial that enrolled 75 women suggest that practicing mindfulness meditation for 8 weeks reduces the severity of IBS symptoms. The study found that the physical and psychological symptoms of IBS were more effectively managed by people practicing mindfulness meditation than in support group therapy.

Gaylord *et al.* (2011) evaluated mindfulness meditation as a therapeutic technique for IBS. They found very encouraging results. Mindfulness training reduces the severity of irritable bowel syndrome in women in a randomized controlled trial. In this study, 75 women between the ages of 19 and 71, participants were placed in a mindfulness meditation group or a comparison group that offered mutual support for IBS and life's problems. Each group took an eight-week course that included weekly sessions and a half-day retreat. After the end of the eight-week period, overall IBS severity was reduced more among patients in the mindfulness meditation group compared to the support group: 26.4% vs. 6.2%.

After a three-month follow-up, 38.2% of those in mindfulness meditation reported a reduction in severity of IBS symptoms, compared with only 11.8% who said that among patients who took part in the support group therapy. Changes in quality-of-life impairment, anxiety, and psychological distress were not significantly different after the eight-week period. But all were much improved at the three-month follow-up in the meditation group. "Our study indicates that mindfulness meditation is a practical, widely applicable and inexpensive method to enable irritable bowel syndrome patients to improve their clinical outcomes and gain associated improvement in well-being, says Palsson, one of the coinvestigators. This method can be learned in educational classes, without the need for clinical therapists, for long-term use."

In a small 2014 NCCIH-supported study, young adults (18 to 26 years old) reported generally feeling better and having less pain, constipation, and nausea after completing a series of yoga classes, compared with a waitlist control group. They were still feeling better at the study's 2-month follow up.

Berrill *et al.* (2014) studied the mindfulness-based therapy for inflammatory bowel disease patients with functional abdominal symptoms or high perceived stress levels. Multi-convergent therapy (MCT) is a form of psychotherapy that combines mindfulness meditation with aspects of cognitive behavioral therapy and has been used in the management of irritable bowel syndrome (IBS). This study aimed to assess the feasibility and efficacy of MCT in the management of IBD patients with either functional abdominal symptoms or high perceived stress levels. IBS-type symptoms in patients with IBD represent a potential therapeutic target to improve quality of life. This study suggests that MCT may be useful in the management of these symptoms.

Keefer *et al* (2002) investigated the effect of Relaxation Response Meditation (RRM) on IBS. Ten of thirteen original participants with Irritable Bowel Syndrome (IBS) participated in a one-year follow-up study to determine whether the effects of Relaxation Response Meditation (RRM) on IBS symptom reduction were maintained over the long-term. From pre-treatment to one-year follow-up, significant reductions were noted for the symptoms of abdominal pain, diarrhea, flatulence, and bloating. When they examined changes from the original three-month follow-up point to the one-year follow-up, they noted significant additional reductions in pain and bloating, which tended to be the most distressing symptoms of IBS. It appears that: continued use of meditation is particularly effective in reducing the symptoms of pain, bloating and RRM is a beneficial treatment for IBS in the both short- and the long-term.

Ljotsson *et al.* (2010) conducted the study based on exposure and mindfulness in the treatment of irritable bowel syndrome (IBS). Out of 49 outpatients, most of whom were referred from gastroenterological clinics, 34 entered the 10-week treatment. Patients were assessed before, immediately after and 6 months after treatment. The assessments consisted of a gastrointestinal symptom diary, self-report questionnaires covering quality of life, gastrointestinal specific anxiety, general functioning, and a psychiatric interview. At post-treatment, the mean reduction in symptoms was 41% and 50% of patients showed clinically significant improvement in symptom level. Patients also showed marked improvement on other outcome measures. Treatment gains were maintained at follow-up. The results support the use of exposure and mindfulness-based strategies in the treatment of IBS.

Ljotsson *et al.* (2011) conducted a follow-up of a previously reported study of internet-delivered cognitive behavior therapy (CBT) for IBS, based on exposure and mindfulness exercises. Internet-delivered exposure and mindfulness-based therapy for irritable bowel syndrome - a randomized controlled trial. Seventy-five participants from the original sample of 85 (88%) reported follow-up data at 15-18 months (mean 16.4 months) after completing treatment. The follow-up sample included participants from both the original study's treatment group and waiting list after it had been crossed over to treatment. Intention-to-treat analysis showed that treatment gains were maintained on all outcome measures, including IBS symptoms, quality of life, and anxiety related to gastrointestinal symptoms. A total of fifty participants reported adequate relief of symptoms. Improvements at follow-up were more pronounced for the participants that had completed the full treatment and maintenance of improvement did not seem to be dependent on further treatment seeking. This study suggests that internet-delivered CBT based on exposure and mindfulness has long-term beneficial effects for IBS-patients.

Meditation and Multiple Sclerosis (MS):

The desirability of a safe and inexpensive medical treatment that can improve a patient's health and sense of well-being has resulted in the growing use of complementary and alternative medicine (CAM) worldwide. Once considered fringe medicine, meditation, yoga, and other mind-body therapies—the most practiced form of CAM—are increasingly practiced by patients with chronic neurologic disorders, such as multiple sclerosis (MS). In a recent survey, up to 67% of patients with MS reported the current use of at least one form of CAM, with most regarding their practice as complementary rather than as an alternative to conventional medicine. Despite the popularity of CAM, there is a scarcity of well-designed clinical trials evaluating its use in MS; most studies are hampered by small sample size or lack of a control arm.

Multiple sclerosis (MS) is an autoimmune, demyelinating, inflammatory disease of central nervous system (CNS) which is characterized by spasticity, fatigue, depression, anxiety, bowel and bladder dysfunction, impaired mobility, cognitive impairment etc. and affects approximately 2.5 million people worldwide. Disease modifying therapies for MS which help in preventing accumulation of lesions in white matter of CNS are costly and have significant adverse effects. Therefore, patients with MS are using complementary and alternative medicine (CAM). According to the National Institute of Neurological Disorders and Stroke, the age of disease onset is typically between 20 and 40 years, with a higher incidence in women. Individuals with MS experience a wide range of symptoms, including declining physical, emotional, and psychological symptoms (e.g., fatigue, imbalance, spasticity, chronic pain, cognitive impairment, bladder and bowel dysfunction, visual and speech impairments, depression, sensory disturbance, and mobility impairment). To date, both the cause of and cure for MS remain unknown. In recent years, more individuals with MS have been pursuing alternative methods of treatment to manage symptoms of the disease, including mind-body therapies such as yoga, meditation, breathing, and relaxation techniques. It has been suggested that the practice of yoga may be a safe and effective way of managing symptoms of MS. Yoga is one of the most popular forms of CAM which is being used immensely to reduce or overcome the symptoms of MS.

Health-related quality of life (HRQOL) is often much reduced among individuals with multiple sclerosis (MS), and incidences of depression, fatigue, and anxiety are high. Grossman *et al.* (2010) examined effects of a mindfulness-based intervention (MBI) compared to usual care (UC) upon HRQOL, depression, and fatigue among adults with relapsing-remitting or secondary progressive MS. A randomized, single-blind, controlled trial that investigated the effects of mindfulness-based meditation compared to usual care on depression and quality of life measures in 150 patients with MS. Patients with remitting-relapsing and secondary progressive MS with an Expanded Disability Status. The results were encouraging. In addition to evidence of improved HRQOL and well-being, these findings demonstrate broad feasibility and acceptance of, as well as satisfaction and adherence with, a program of mindfulness training for patients with MS.

Thakur *et al.* (2020) presented the potential impact of yoga practices on reducing MS related symptoms.

Rogers *et al.* (2015) found that Yoga is an intervention to manage multiple sclerosis symptoms. Therefore, the purpose of this studies is to summarize the most relevant literature on exercise and mind-body modalities to treat MS symptoms and, more specifically, the benefits and potential role of yoga as an alternative treatment of symptom management for individuals with MS. It has been suggested that the practice of yoga may be a safe and effective way of managing symptoms of MS.

Varied evidence shows that mindfulness-oriented meditation improves individuals' mental health, positively influencing practitioners' personality profiles as well. A limited number of studies are beginning to show that this type of meditation may also be a helpful therapeutic option for persons with multiple sclerosis (MS). Crescentini *et al.* (2018) evaluated the effects of an 8-week mindfulness-oriented meditation training on the personality profiles, anxiety and depression symptoms, and mindfulness skills of a group of patients with MS. A control group of patients with MS not enrolled in any training was also tested. After mindfulness-oriented meditation training, participants in this group showed an increase in character traits reflecting the maturity of the self at the intrapersonal (self-directedness) and interpersonal (cooperativeness) levels. Moreover, increased mindfulness and conscientiousness and decreased trait anxiety were observed in participants after the training. The data supports the utility for patients with MS of therapeutic interventions based on mindfulness meditation that may lead to enhanced character and self-maturity.

Meditation and Ulcerative Colitis:

Meditation may help people with Crohn's disease and ulcerative colitis cope with their condition and improve their overall quality of life. A regular meditation practice has been shown to reduce stress levels, lower inflammation, alleviate chronic pain and improve mood.

In a 2014 pilot study by National Center for Complementary and Integrative Health (NCCIH), 55 adults with ulcerative colitis in remission were divided into two groups. For 8 weeks, one group learned and practiced mindfulness-based stress reduction (MBSR) while the other group practiced a placebo procedure. Six and twelve months later, there were no significant differences between the two groups in the course of the disease, markers of inflammation, or any psychological measure except perceived stress during flare-ups. The researchers concluded that MBSR might help people in remission from moderate to moderately severe disease—and maybe reduce rates of flare-up from stress.

A 2015 joint-study by Gerbarg *et al* (2015) between the Jill Roberts IBD Center and researchers at the New York Medical College, Columbia University and Weill Cornell Medical College tested the effectiveness of the Breath-Body-Mind Workshop (BBMW)—breathing, movement and meditation—on 29 patients with IBD. The researchers were specifically interested in the effect that BBMW would have on the patients' psychological and physical symptoms and inflammation levels. Of the 29 participants, one group underwent BBMW training while the other group underwent an educational seminar. Using various tests, the researchers measured factors like stress, anxiety, and depression levels, as well as self-reported symptoms and C-reactive protein levels—an inflammation biomarker. At the 6-week mark, the BBMW group significantly improved their results, both in psychological symptoms (stress, anxiety, and depression) and self-reported physical symptoms compared to the seminar group. At the 26-week mark, the BBMW group showed a significant decrease in C-reactive protein levels compared to the seminar group, which saw no significant change at all. C-reactive protein (CRP) is produced by the liver. Its level rises when there is inflammation in in the body due to certain diseases like ulcerative colitis, Crohn's disease and rheumatoid arthritis. Its level should be below 350mg per liter.

The study results suggest that mind-body interventions, like meditation and breathing exercises, can potentially help IBD patients with a host of psychological symptoms, as well as make measurable improvements in physical symptoms—especially inflammation activity.

Meditation Affects Genes Associated with Inflammation:
A 2015 pilot study by Kuo *et al.* (2015) from researchers at the Benson-Henry Institute for Mind Body Medicine at Massachusetts General Hospital examined the effect of meditation in patients with inflammatory Bowel Disease (IBD) and irritable bowel syndrome (IBS). Participants—19 with IBS and 29 with IBD—underwent a nine-week relaxation response training, and researchers assessed participants' symptoms and inflammation markers before and after the training.

The results showed that patients had sustained significant improvements in their symptoms, stress levels and overall quality of life three weeks after the training. They found no significant changes in the patients' inflammation levels. However, in the IBD patients, they did observe changes in over 1,000 different gene expressions—many of which are known to contribute to stress response and inflammation. The results showed that the relaxation response training did reduce the expression of several genes that directly affect the inflammatory responses in IBD patients. In other words, the relaxation response training changed the way the patients' bodies trigger IBD inflammation.

A 2016 Australian study (Root 2021) investigated whether meditation might be more effective than conventional treatment at improving the overall quality of life of IBD patients. In the study, 60 IBD patients were divided into two groups, with one group undergoing an eight-week MBSR intervention, and the other group receiving treatment-as-usual.

The researchers compared the participants in both groups by measuring their levels of mindfulness, quality of life and anxiety and depression. Researchers measured these results in participants before intervention, immediately after intervention and then again six months post-intervention.

The results showed that patients who underwent the meditation intervention had significantly better results in all areas compared to the treatment-as-usual group. Additionally, at the six-month mark, the meditators also had sustained their mood, quality of life and mindfulness scores better than the non-meditator group. Steven Root the author of this article has healed himself from Ulcerative Colitis through systematic application of his nutrition and lifestyle principles.

Arruda *et al*. (2018) studied the effect of yoga as adjunct therapy for inflammatory bowel disease Nine adolescents with IBD participated. Eight participated in one or more yoga videos per week and all nine attended at least two in-person yoga classes. Focus group themes revealed that the intervention was well liked, with all participants reporting reduced stress, improved emotional self-awareness, and increased ability to identify and manage the physical symptoms of IBD. Participants had difficulty, however, completing the yoga videos due to time limitations and competing priorities.

A combination of in-person instructor led yoga with video-based yoga is a feasible and acceptable adjunct therapy for adolescents with IBD. Participants reported reduced stress and improved ability to identify and manage physical symptoms.

Meditation and Bipolar Disorder:

Bipolar afflicts up to 4 million people in the United States and is the fifth leading cause of disability worldwide. The suicide rate for people with bipolar disorder is 60 times higher than in the general public. Bipolar disorder was conceptualized over100 years ago by Emil Kraeplin, the founder of modern scientific psychiatry, psychopharmacology and psychiatric genetics, but its symptoms were first described as long ago as 200 A.D. Bipolar disorder is a mental illness marked by extreme changes in mood from high to low, and from low to high. Highs are periods of mania, while lows are periods of depression. The changes in mood may even become mixed, so one might feel elated and depressed at the same time. Women are more likely to receive bipolar diagnoses than men, though the reason for this remains unclear. Bipolar disorder can be hard to diagnose, but there are signs or symptoms that one can look for. Such as feeling sad or hopeless for long periods of time. Bipolar disorder has a number of types, including bipolar I and bipolar II disorder based on the severity of symptoms, and may be described as mixed or rapid cycling based on the duration and frequency of episodes. As with most other mental illnesses, bipolar disorder is not directly passed from one generation to another genetically but is thought to be due to a complex group of genetic, psychological, and environmental risk factors. The adolescent with bipolar disorder is more likely to have depression and mixed episodes, with rapid changes in mood. Treatment of bipolar disorder with medications tends to relieve already existing symptoms of mania or depression and prevent symptoms from returning. Talk therapy (psychotherapy) is an important part of helping people with bipolar disorder achieve the highest level of functioning possible. So, some scientists are investigating the role of meditation to use as alternative and complementary treatment for bipolar disorder.

Perich *et al.* (2013) carried out the study to examine the impact of quantity of mindfulness meditation practice on the outcome of psychiatric symptoms following Mindfulness-based Cognitive Therapy (MBCT) for those diagnosed with bipolar disorder. Meditation homework was collected at the beginning of each session for the MBCT program to assess quantity of meditation practice. Clinician-administered measures of hypo/mania and depression along with self-report anxiety, depression and stress symptom questionnaires were administered pre-, post-treatment and at 12-month follow-up. This study suggested that the quantity of mindfulness meditation practiced throughout an MBCT program for bipolar disorder is related to lower depression scores at 12-month follow-up. There is also some evidence to suggest that mindfulness meditation practice is associated with improvements in depression and anxiety symptoms if a certain minimum amount (3 times a week or more) is practiced weekly throughout the 8-week MBCT program.

Chadwick *et al.* (2011) explored the experiences of practicing mindfulness meditation related to living with, and managing, bipolar disorder. Qualitative methodology was used to explore the experiences of 12 people with bipolar disorder who had been practicing mindfulness for at least 18 weeks. Semi-structured interviews exploring how mindfulness practice related to living with bipolar disorder were recorded verbatim, transcribed, and analyzed using thematic analysis. Seven themes emerged: focusing on what is present; clearer awareness of mood state/change; acceptance; mindfulness practice in different mood states; reducing/stabilizing negative affect; relating differently to negative thoughts; and reducing impact of mood state. All participants reported subjective benefits and challenges of mindfulness practice and gave insights into processes of change.

Ball *et al.* (2007) reviewed the role of mindful meditation in bipolar disorder. They emphasized that mindful is particularly relevant in the treatment of bipolar patients for number of reasons. Relapse rates are extremely high, about 90 % besides medication. Anxiety and stress play major roles. Lower self-esteem is a significant issue in many patients. Lastly, bipolar patients feel difficulty in regulating thoughts and feelings are intrinsic to the conditions. These factors can be mitigated by mindful meditation.

Alidina (2010) described in his book "Mindfulness for Dummies," the role of Mindfulness for Bipolar Disorder. Mindfulness looks like a potentially effective way of managing bipolar disorder, especially the depressive pole, which may be the most difficult to treat with medication alone. Mindfulness exercises and meditations are useful for people with bipolar disorder (manic depression) because mindfulness decreases the relapse rate for depression. Reduces stress and anxiety, which contribute significantly to the onset of both mania and depression and may worsen the course of the illness. Improves a person's ability to manage thoughts and feelings and increases awareness of the way the person tends to internalize external stimuli.

There is a need to generate evidence on whether meditations can treat bipolar disorder II affected patients. A 2-year longitudinal multi-city randomized controlled trial experiment was conducted by Pandya (2019) comprising 311 bipolar disorder II affected patients in the intervention and control group respectively across eight African and Asian cities. The Bipolar Depression Rating Scale (BDRS) was administered with the intervention and control groups that were equal at baseline. Meditation had a positive impact on the intervention group. Post intervention BDRS scores were significantly lower for patients from Asian cities, men, Hindus and Buddhists, middle class, and married patients as well as those who attended all the meditation rounds and regularly self-practiced. Within the BDRS outcome measure, depressive symptoms were impacted the most as compared with mixed symptoms. Meditation helped alleviate guilt, depressed mood, and helplessness-hopelessness. The meditation program can be used as a combination therapy along with pharmacological treatment to treat mood instability and depression among patients with bipolar disorder II.

Meditation alone cannot replace traditional therapy for bipolar disorder, so check with your doctor about other treatments you may need, such as medication or psychotherapy. Even though it's not a cure for bipolar disorder, meditation can help you relax and reduce stress. It can also help the person disengage from stressful or anxious thoughts, and better control his mood. Meditation is easy and anyone can practice it, at home or in a class. It can be a helpful addition to the bipolar disorder treatment plan.

Yoga Meditation for Stroke Rehabilitation:

Stroke is a major health issue and cause of long-term disability and has a major emotional and socioeconomic impact. There is a need to explore options for long-term sustainable interventions that support stroke survivors to engage in meaningful activities to address life challenges after stroke. Rehabilitation focuses on recovery of function and cognition to the maximum level achievable and may include a wide range of complementary strategies including yoga. Yoga is a mind-body practice that originated in India, and which has become increasingly widespread in the Western world. Recent evidence highlights the positive effects of yoga for people with a range of physical and psychological health conditions. A recent non-Cochrane systematic review by Lawrence *et al.* (2017) concluded that yoga can be used as self-administered practice in stroke rehabilitation.

Meditation Overcome Loneliness:

A National Survey by Oscar (2010) of adults above 45 revealed, over one-third (35%) of the survey respondents were categorized as lonely. Older adults reported lower rates of loneliness than those who were younger (43% of those age 45-49 were lonely compared to 25% of those 70+). Married respondents were less likely to be lonely (29%) compared to never-married respondents (51%), and those with higher incomes were less likely to be lonely than those with lower incomes. Lonely respondents were less likely to be involved in activities that build social networks, such as attending religious services, volunteering, participating in a community organization or spending time on a hobby. Almost half (45%) of those who had lived in their current residence for less than 1 year reported feeling lonely.

Studies have shown that isolation causes psychological distress that can lead to mental health issues, illness, and even premature death. Experts are of the opinion that loneliness poses a health hazard as dangerous as obesity, smoking and drinking. A new survey of more than 2,000 American adults found 72 percent report having felt a sense of loneliness, with nearly a third (31 percent) experiencing loneliness at least once a week. People can also become lonely because of feeling emotionally exhausted and burnt out. Almost 50% of the American workforce is either permanently or frequently exhausted. This is a 32% increase from just 20 years ago. Chronic loneliness puts the brain into self-protect mode. It causes psychological stress that can lead to depression loneliness, can resemble depression, anxiety, boredom and many other diseases.

Not all people who are alone are lonely, just as not all people who are in the presence of others feel connected. A study published in Cambridge University Press addressed the fact that loneliness is often described as "a gap between desired and actual social connectedness, and is caused by low self-esteem, shyness, fear of negative evaluation, and poor social skills."

"If one's different, one's bound to be lonely." articulated by Aldous Huxley, an English writer and philosopher.

Loneliness increases the stress hormones and can lead to chronic inflammation. Inflammation leads to more susceptibility to illnesses such as cardiovascular disease, Alzheimer's, dementia, arthritis, Type 2 diabetes, and can increase suicidal tendencies. A recent study found that three quarters of the American population is lonely. The internet and social networks have contributed to a rise in loneliness. Young adults, for example, were brought up in the era of personal computers, the internet, and social media. For many, these platforms replaced real relationships in exchange for those on-screen. Unfortunately, these new technologies are increasing their feelings of loneliness. The millennial generation has become a very lonely one. "Loneliness can change the neurochemistry of the brain, turning off the dopamine neurons, which trigger the reward response, and causing some degeneration in the brain when the reward response is not activated," says Katherine Peters, a Neuro-oncologist, at the Duke Cancer Center Brain Tumor Clinic.

Elderly individuals who cannot easily leave their homes are also incredibly vulnerable to becoming lonely. According to the World Health Organization, as older people face additional stressors such as chronic pain, reduced mobility, even retirement, they can become lonely and isolated, and as a result can develop mental health issues. There are numerous factors that contribute to loneliness such as experiencing: Isolation, Grief, Betrayal, Jealousy, Stress, Lack and break up of a romantic partner, Pressures from social media, Relocation to a new town, A new job position, Social media, etc. etc. and in brief loneliness is a menace to public health and happiness.

Meditation has been found to be beneficial in helping to reduce feelings of loneliness. Loneliness disturbs the "parietal lobe." Meditation keeps it cool. Meditation has been found to be beneficial in helping to reduce feelings of loneliness. It assists in expanding the field of awareness, embracing practices such as loving-kindness and learning how to notice emotions without becoming attached to them.

A recent scientific report by Brash (2014) an evolutionary biologist and professor of psychology emeritus at the University of Washington suggests that Buddhist-style meditation has a discernible (and beneficial) effect on brain function, especially among elderly people suffering from various consequences of loneliness and depression. Meditation is medicine for loneliness. Meditation can be neuro therapeutic.

Nevertheless, loneliness and social isolation are a growing public health concern, yet there are few evidence-based interventions for mitigating these social risk factors. Accumulating evidence suggests that mindfulness interventions can improve social-relationship processes. However, the active ingredients of mindfulness training underlying these improvements are unclear. Lindsay *et al.* (2019) study the role of mindfulness in loneliness on 153 people. They found encouraging results. Mindfulness-based meditation continues to reveal itself as a therapeutic powerhouse, with far-reaching influence on both psychological and physical health.

Wein (2012) recommended in his publication that between solitude and loneliness, meditation is the way out.

Study of Thimmapuram *et al.* (2021) is one of the first attempts to assess loneliness and sleep problems among physicians and advance practice providers during COVID-19 pandemic in the US. A significant burden of loneliness and sleep problems was identified. An improvement of sleep and loneliness was noted with the practice of *Heartfulness meditation*. This remote intervention might be a useful tool to be explored in larger studies. Heartfulness is a simple, modern, methodical approach to meditation. Rather than focusing on your breath or repeating a mantra, you simply focus inward, on your heart, to cultivate inner strength and serenity.

Loneliness is a common phenomenon associated with several negative health outcomes. Three interventions were statistically significant for reducing loneliness, that is, *meditation/mindfulness, social cognitive training* and *social support* as investigated by Veronese *et al.* (2020).

Malaktaris *et al.* (2020) found that Compassion meditation (CM) training has demonstrated potential in improving well-being and psychosocial functioning. However, most prior studies of CM training have focused on younger adults. The generalizability of the effectiveness of CM training with older adults requires further study. This pilot study was intended to inform future randomized controlled studies of CM training in older adults. Compassion meditation (CM) training has demonstrated potential in improving well-being and psychosocial functioning. Exploratory outcome measures were administered prior to, during, and after the intervention. These findings provide preliminary support for the feasibility of CM training in community-dwelling older adults and suggest the need for future efficacy and effectiveness clinical trials.

Meditation Balances Both Brain Hemispheres:

The human brain is made up of two parts and was discovered by Sperry. He found out that both the left and right parts of the human brain have specialized functions and that the two sides can operate independently. Sperry's model suggests that left-brained people are generally more logical, practical, and analytical, often better at math and science including reading, writing, and speaking. Right-brained people are generally more imaginative, intuitive, and sensual, often excelling at philosophy and the arts. Sperry received the 1981 Nobel Prize in Physiology and Medicine for his split-brain research.

While a great deal of Sperry's "left brain / right brain" research still holds true today, certain parts of his model have been updated over the years. For example, neuroscientists have recently learned that highly creative people are actually "whole brain" thinkers rather than just "right brain" thinkers. However, his "imbalanced" brain findings have stood the test of time. Brain imaging studies have shown that phenomenally successful, massively creative people like Elon Musk, Richard Branson, Einstein, and Steve jobs, use both brain halves in a much more balanced and integrated way than the rest of us.

Luders *et al.* (2012) found that the *corpus callosum*, the grand central station-like cable of nerves cross-linking the brain hemispheres, was remarkably stronger, thicker, and better connected in meditation practitioners. Studies have shown the corpus callosum is thicker in ambidextrous people and people who meditate. Studies have shown ambidextrous people (Being ambidextrous technically means equal with both hands) to be better able to read people, see both sides of an issue, and recall details of an event and their context. Better integration and balance of the brain hemispheres allows a better kind of thinking.

Harmonizing both brain hemispheres results in better focus, deeper thought, super creativity, excellent mental health, enhanced memory, and clearer thinking just the start. Meditation balances the right and left-Brain hemispheres. Numerous electroencephalograph

(EEG) studies have relieved that greatest philosophers, thinkers, inventors, and artists use both brain hemispheres together, in unison.

Meditation works to balance both hemispheres of the brain, forcing them to work in harmony. Scientists call this "whole brain synchronization" and when achieved, the brain experiences extremely beneficial changes in hemispheric blood flow and chemistry. During meditation, the grand central station-like cable of nerves connecting the two brain hemispheres, the corpus callosum becomes deeply stimulated.

Yogi Kriya Meditation Balances Both the Hemispheres:
It is a type of breathing called Alternate Nostril Breathing (*Nadi Shodhana*). It can also balance both the hemispheres. This technique has been used by yogis throughout history to purify the nadis or energy channels in the body. The nasal cycle has been scientifically shown to be linked to the opposite hemispheric dominance. When your right nostril is dominant, the EEG (electroencephalogram) measured activity in the brain is greater in the left hemisphere of your brain – and vice versa. When the nostril dominance switches, so does the activity of the brain hemisphere. Daily practice of this yoga kriya balances both the hemispheres (thebraindoctor.pdf).

One of the easiest ways to synchronize the left and right hemispheres of the brain is through binaural beats. This involves delivering sound waves of slightly different frequencies through headphones into each ear to produce brainwave entrainment that follows the difference in hertz between each frequency. So, if one ear is hearing 100 HZ and the other is hearing 107 HZ, there is a difference of 7 HZ and your brain will entrain (or follow) the frequency of 7 HZ, thus falling into theta brainwave frequency. (Chaieb *et al.* 2015).

Music or Mantras Synchronizes Both Hemispheres:
Creative people have less marked hemispheric dominance. It was found that the right hemisphere is specialized for metaphoric

thinking, playfulness, solution finding and synthesizing. It is the center of visualization, imagination, and conceptualization, but the left hemisphere is still needed for artistic work to achieve balance. A specific functional organization of brain areas was found during visual art activities. Marked hemispheric dominance and area specialization is also very prominent for music perception. Brain can make new connections, activating new pathways and unmasking secondary roads; it is "plastic". Music is a strong stimulus for neuroplasticity. fMRI studies have shown reorganization of motor and auditory cortex in professional musicians. Other studies showed the changes in neurotransmitter and hormone serum levels in correlation to music. Listening to music or playing a musical instrument can also synchronize both the hemispheres of the brain. Various studies have been done on the effects of music on the brain. Listening to music lights up the large-scale neural networks of the brain associated with emotion (limbic system), listening, motor (movement) skills and creativity. Playing music is unique because it engages the right brain, through focus on the melody in music. The left hemisphere is responsible for the understanding of musical structure and motor skills when playing the instrument.

Listening to music and playing instruments strengthens the various areas of the brain and their connections and improves the amount of neural response to stimuli for increased coordination and sensitivity have been recommended by the review of Demarin *et al.* (2016).

Enchanting of *Mantras* has the same effects. Om or Aum is a sacred sound and a spiritual symbol in Indian Hindu religions. It signifies the essence of the ultimate reality, consciousness, or Atman. It is a syllable that is chanted either independently or before a spiritual recitation in Hinduism, Buddhism, and Jainism. The meaning and connotations of Om vary between the diverse schools within and across the various traditions. It is also part of the iconography found in ancient and medieval era manuscripts, temples, monasteries and spiritual retreats in Hinduism, Buddhism, Jainism and Sikhism.

OM Mantra Chanting at 417Hz. OM is the Primordial Sound of the Universe. It is the sound that reverberates in the entire cosmos and in every cell of our body, and 417Hz is an amazingly beautiful frequency that acts as a cleansing agent for our body, removing negativity, negative blocks and toxicity from our body and mind. It comprises AUM three syllables representing three states of consciousness.

There are various mantras. Every mantra produces a unique sound and vibration that when recited resonates with specific parts of the body and helps in natural healing. The sound vibrations and frequencies of mantras have shown enormous healing advantages as Mantras not only provide spiritual benefits but also help in psycho-physiological healing. Description of various Mantras and their powers have been described very nicely by Ashley-Farrand (1999) in his book "Healing Mantras: Using Sound Affirmations for Personal Power." Sanskrit Mantras are written in English language with their meanings.

Marian Diamond, a professor of Anatomy at the University of California, Berkeley, also confirms that chanting helps in increasing immune system (Janeyoga 2010).

Watkins, Professor of neuroscience at Imperial College London, investigated that musical structure of chanting can have a significant and positive physiological impact. The chants are said to reduce stress levels, lower blood pressure, increase performance hormones level as well as reduce anxiety and depression. Alan Watkins also confirmed that when we chant, the vibration of the sound calms the nervous system. It also reduces stress and increases memory power.

In a research done at Cleveland University USA, it is proved that the rhythmic tones produced during chanting create a soothing effect on the body and mind called Neuro-linguistic effect (NLE). When we understand the meaning of reciting mantra, that creates a Psycholinguistic effect (PLE) on the body. NLE and PLE effects in the body, produce a curative chemical in the brain.

Chanting mantras also purify the environment around us. Mantras can be used as tool to cleanse negative energies from home and even from within.

By examining effect of mantra chanting on brain, several structural and functional benefits have been seen by Tomasino *et al.* (2013) by using magnetic resonance imaging (MRI) during mantra chanting found that mantra chanting activates inferior frontal gyrus, prefrontal cortex, limbic and superior parietal areas, middle cortex, and precentral cortex. The activation of these areas increases connectivity between white matter and gray matter of the brain. This connectivity is related to higher intellection and improvement in stroke patients.

By reciting mantras, certain brain areas get activated that result in an alert state, while other areas are deactivated that induces calmness and peace. Mantra chanting can also activate the brain areas that help with language skills during memory loss. Cerebral blood flow changes during chanting mantras (Khalsa *et al.* 2009).

A study conducted by Telles *et al.* (1995) showed that practicing "OM" mantra – thought in the brain rather than vocalized-showed significant reduction in the heart rate during chanting as compared to the controls. The autonomic and respiratory variables were studied in seven experienced meditators (with experience ranging from 5 to 20 years). Each subject was studied in two types of sessions-- meditation (with a period of mental chanting of "OM") and control (with a period of non-targeted thinking). The meditators showed a statistically significant reduction in heart rate during meditation compared to the control period.

Bernardi *et al.* (2001) studied the effect of rosary prayer and yoga mantras on autonomic cardiovascular rhythms. Both prayer and mantra caused striking, powerful, and synchronous increases in existing cardiovascular rhythms when recited six times a minute. Rhythm formulas that involve breathing at six breaths per minute induce favorable psychological and possibly physiological effects.

Studies have shown that reciting mantras can slow respiratory rate to six breaths per minute. This correlates with the rhythm of circulatory system. This synchronized rhythm is important for maintaining healthy blood pressure and heart rate. Slower respiratory rate also increases sinus arrhythmia, blood oxygenation and tolerance to exercises.

Chanting Sharpens the Mind and Boosts Intellect:

Pradhan and Derle (2012) compared the effect of Gayatri Mantra and Poem Line Chanting (PL) on Digit Letter Substitution Task. Their object was that one of the components was to enhance academic excellence. Traditional techniques were included in Indian schools to develop mental faculties with a view to add value to the latter. The aim was to evaluate the effects of Gayatri mantra (GM) chanting on attention as measured by digit-letter substitution task (DLST). Both GM and PL led to improvement in performance, as assessed by DLST. But the influence of GM had significantly higher than PL in net score of female groups.

Meditation and Neuroplasticity:

Meditation leads to neuroplasticity, which is defined as the brain's ability to change, structurally and functionally, based on environmental input. Scientists believed previously that the brain essentially stopped changing after adulthood. But research by University of Wisconsin neuroscientist Davidson (2008) has shown that experienced meditators exhibit high levels of gamma wave activity and display an ability ---continuing after the meditation session has attended -- to not get stuck on a particular stimulus. Thus, they are automatically able to control their thoughts and reactiveness.

Scientific evidence suggests that meditation alters the functional and structural plasticity of the brain. In the milestone study, Lazar *et al.* (2005) demonstrated that meditation increases the cortical thickness of the brain. Since then, many studies, mostly with varying sample sizes, are conducted to identify the relationship between meditation techniques and development of cortical thickness in different brain areas. Cortical thickness is also associated with decision making, attention and memory.

Lazar *et al.* (2005) used a matched-pairs design to compare the brains of 20 meditation expert practitioners with a control group that had no yoga or meditation practice. The experts were not monks but were typical Western meditation practitioners who incorporate their practice into a daily routine involving career, family, friends and outside interests. The participants were matched for sex, age, education, and race. Using an MRI, the researchers compared the brain structures of the two groups and the results showed that there were significant differences in cortical thickness between the meditators and the controls in particular areas of the brain, including the prefrontal cortex. The differences between the groups were largest with the older participants Meditation can change the brain neuroplasticity. As per Lazar, the more meditation experiences a person had under his/her belt, the more highly developed their prefrontal cortex.

Previous studies on mindfulness had shown that this practice can have an effect of reducing the activation of the amygdala during the perception of emotional stimuli. This is measured using the common experimental paradigm of having participants in an fMRI viewing images of different types of emotional stimuli (e.g., emotional faces or other types of images) and their brain activity is measured. The earlier research has shown that when people are exposed to angry or other emotional stimuli, mindfulness can reduce their amygdala activation.

Yang *et al.* (2016) imaged in resting stage (fMRI) the brains of 13 novice meditation before and after 40 days of mindfulness training. In addition to massively reducing their anxiety and depression scores, the meditators had, in just six short weeks, significantly increased the "internal consistency" of their temporoparietal junction (TPJ). Hence, these findings suggest that mindfulness meditation might be of therapeutic use by inducing plasticity related network changes altering the neuronal basis of affective disorders such as depression. Functional magnetic resonance imaging (fMRI) is a technique for measuring and mapping brain activity that is noninvasive and safe. It is being used in many studies to better understand how the healthy brain works, and in a growing number of studies it is being applied to understand how that normal function is disrupted in disease.

Meditation Strengthen Immune System:

Davidson *et al.* (2003) studied the effects of mindful meditation and reported that meditation stimulates immune function. They performed a randomized, controlled study on the effects on brain and immune function of a well-known and widely used 8-week clinical training program in mindfulness meditation applied in a work environment with healthy employees.

Likewise, Pace *et al.* (2009) examined the effect of compassion meditation on innate immune, neuroendocrine, and behavioral responses to psychosocial stress and evaluated the degree to which engagement in meditation practice influenced stress reactivity. The data suggest that engagement in compassion meditation may reduce stress-induced immune and behavioral responses.

Meditation Improves Glaucoma:

Meditation is a unique intervention as it targets the brain and impacts multiple mechanisms of glaucoma pathogenesis, thereby having the potential to serve as 'polypill' for comprehensive glaucoma management.

Dada *et al.* (2020) evaluate the benefits of meditation practice for the glaucoma patient and support for its candidature as adjunctive therapy for glaucoma patients. It has multiple potential benefits for normal-pressure and high-pressure glaucoma patients including a reduction in intraocular pressure, increasing cerebral blood flow and oxygenation, and decreasing action of the sympathetic nervous system with a corresponding increase in parasympathetic nervous system activity. Meditation leads to a "relaxation response" mediated by nitric oxide with decrease in the stress hormone cortisol, increase in neurotrophins and mitochondrial energy production, and improves the overall quality of life of glaucoma patients. It can also benefit caregivers of glaucoma patients and health care providers. It appears that meditation can function as a multifaceted management approach for glaucoma using the natural potential of the human body and target not only the eye but the patient behind the eye to ameliorate this "sick eye in a sick body" condition.

Meditation and Menopause:

Tonob and Melby (2017) conducted a literature review—collecting, assessing and synthesizing previously published information on the subject of menopause and CAM (Complementary and Alternative Medicine). It had been about seven years since such a wide-ranging review was undertaken, said Melby, who specializes in the biological and medical aspects of anthropology. Complementary and Alternative Medicine (CAM) is widely used for menopause, although not all women disclose use to their healthcare providers. This review aims to expand providers' understanding of cross-cultural approaches to treating and managing menopause by providing an overarching framework and perspective on CAM treatments. Increased provider understanding and awareness may improve not only provider-patient communication but also effectiveness of treatments. The distinction between illness (what patients suffer) and disease (what physicians treat) highlights the gap between what patients seek and doctors provide and may help clarify why many women seek CAM at menopause. For example, CAM is often sought by women for whom biomedicine has been unsuccessful or inaccessible. Tonob and Melby review the relevance to menopause of three CAM categories: natural products, mind-body practices including meditation, and other complementary health approaches including traditional Chinese medicine (TCM) and Japanese Kampo. Assessing the effectiveness of CAM is challenging because of the individualized nature of illness patterns and associated treatments, which complicate the design of randomized controlled trials. Because many women seek CAM due to inefficacy of biomedical treatments, or cultural or economic marginalization, biomedical practitioners who try to learn about CAM and ask patients about their CAM use or interest may dramatically improve the patient-provider relationship and rapport, as well as harnessing the 'meaning response' imbued in the clinical encounter. By working with women to integrate their CAM-related health-seeking behaviors and treatments, providers may also boost the efficacy of their own biomedical treatments.

Xiao *et al.* (2019) studied the effect of mindfulness meditation training on anxiety, depression, and sleep quality in perimenopausal women. Mindfulness meditation training can effectively alleviate the symptoms of anxiety and depression and improve the quality of sleep in perimenopausal (during menopause) women, and the frequency of the exercise is positively correlated with the improvements. Menopause meditation training was delivered in 121 perimenopausal women with anxiety, depression, or sleep disorders. The remission rates of anxiety, depression and sleep disorder increased significantly.

Postmenopausal women with troublesome vasomotor symptoms (VMS) often seek alternatives to hormone-based treatment due to medication risks or personal preference. Goldstein *et al.* (2017) sought to identify the effects of meditation, mindfulness, hypnosis and relaxation on VMS and health-related quality of life in perimenopausal and postmenopausal women. Results were not encouraging.

Owing to hormonal changes, women experience various psychophysiological alterations over a wide age range, which may result in decreased quality of life as well as in increased risks of diseases, such as cardiovascular diseases. Although studies have been performed to research complementary methods, such as meditation, the research field still requires an adequate number of studies for public health guidelines. Sung *et al.* (2020) conducted a pilot cross-sectional study to investigate a potential association of meditation with menopausal symptoms and blood chemistry for healthy women.

In this study, data of 65 healthy women (age range 25-67) including 33 meditation practitioners and 32 meditation-naïve controls were analyzed. They suggested a potential association of practicing meditation with alleviations in menopausal symptoms and changes in blood chemistry.

Breast cancer survivors have only extremely limited treatment options for menopausal symptoms. The objective of Cramer *et al.* (2015) was to evaluate the effects of a 12-week traditional Hatha yoga and meditation intervention on menopausal symptoms in breast cancer survivors. In total, 40 women were randomized to yoga or to usual care. Women in the yoga group reported significantly lower total menopausal symptoms compared with the usual care group at week 12 and at week 24. At week 12, the yoga group reported less somato-vegetative (hot flushes, insomnia) psychological, and urogenital menopausal symptoms; less fatigue; and improved quality of life. At week 24, all effects persisted except for psychological menopausal symptoms. Short-term effects on menopausal symptoms remained significant when only women who were receiving antiestrogen medication were analyzed. Six minor adverse events occurred in each group. Cramer *et al.* (2015) concluded yoga combined with meditation can be considered a safe and effective complementary intervention for menopausal symptoms in breast cancer survivors. The effects seem to persist for at least 3 months.

With increased life expectancy, today, women spend one-third of their life after menopause. Thus, more attention is needed towards pre- and post-menopausal symptoms. Studies by Vaze *et al,* (2010) concluded that age old therapy, Yoga mediation is effective in managing menopausal problems. Estrogen replacement therapy is the most effective treatment; however, it has its own limitations. The present need is to explore new options for the management of menopausal symptoms. Yogic lifestyle is a way of living which aims to improve the body, mind and day to day life of individuals. The most performed Yoga practices are postures (asana), controlled breathing (pranayama), and meditation. Yoga has been utilized as a therapeutic tool to achieve positive health and control and cure diseases. The exact mechanism as to how Yoga helps in various disease states is not known. There could be neuro-hormonal pathways with a selective effect in each pathological situation. There have been multiple studies that have combined the many aspects of Yoga into a general Yoga session to investigate its effects on menopausal symptoms. Integrated approach of Yoga therapy can improve hot flushes and night sweats. There is increasing evidence suggesting that even the short-term practice of Yoga can decrease both psychological and physiological risk factors for cardiovascular disease (CVD) as described earlier in this chapter.

Meditation and Pregnancy:

Several research papers have been published on the role of meditation in pregnancy. It has been validated by scientific research that meditation has several benefits during pregnancy. Meditation can help to cope with a variety of physical and emotional stresses during pregnancy, enabling the woman to relax, reduce stress, anxiety, fatigue, insomnia, blood pressure, depression, fear of pain associated with childbirth and enhances peace of mind. Combining deep breathing (or deep belly breathing) with meditation can help to soften and relax the central nervous system during childbirth, improve labor experience and even reduce perceptions of the pain and length of labor. Moreover, meditation imparts good thoughts to the infants, too. Some of the studies are being cited for the information of the readers since it is impossible to quote all the research done in this area.

Prenatal Meditation Influences Infant Behaviors:

Prenatal meditation has positive effect on infant temperament. Pregnancy care providers should provide prenatal meditation to pregnant women. A randomized control quantitative study was carried out by PoChan (2014) at Obstetric Unit, Queen Elizabeth Hospital in Hong Kong. 64 pregnant Chinese women were recruited for intervention and 59 were for control. The study concludes the positive effects of prenatal meditation on infant behaviors and recommends that pregnancy care providers should provide prenatal meditation to pregnant women. Prenatal meditation influences infant behaviors.

Narendran *et al.* (2005) studies the efficacy of yoga on pregnancy. Three hundred thirty five women attending the antenatal clinic at Gunasheela Surgical and Maternity Hospital in Bangalore, India, were enrolled between 18 and 20 weeks of pregnancy in a prospective, matched, observational study, 169 women in the yoga group and 166 women in the control group. Women were matched for age, parity, body weight, and Doppler velocimetry scores of umbilical and uterine arteries. Yoga practices, including physical postures, breathing, and meditation were practiced by the yoga group one hour daily, from the date of entry into the study until delivery. The control group walked 30 minutes twice a day (standard obstetric advice) during the study period. Compliance in both an integrated approach to yoga during pregnancy is safe and beneficial. It improves birth weight, decreases preterm labor, and decreases IUGR (Intra Uterine Growth Retardation) either in isolation or associated with PIH (Pregnancy Induced Hypertension) with no increased complications.

Muthukrishnan (2016) studied the effect of mindfulness meditation on pregnant women. Pregnant Indian women of 12 weeks gestation were randomized to two treatment groups: Test group with Mindfulness meditation and control group with their usual obstetric care. The effect of Mindfulness meditation on perceived stress scores and cardiac sympathetic functions and parasympathetic functions (Heart rate variation with respiration, lying to standing ratio, standing to lying ratio and respiratory rate) were evaluated on pregnant Indian women. The results of this study suggest that mindfulness meditation improves parasympathetic functions in pregnant women and is a powerful modulator of the sympathetic nervous system during pregnancy.

Meditation Boosts Libido & Sex-Drive:

Both sex and meditation involve taking breaks from daily routines and responsibilities. Both include deep diaphragmatic breathing. Both encourage emptying the mind of extraneous thoughts and focusing attention on the present moment. And both help free the mind from daily hassles and impart relaxation. However, there is a big difference in both. In meditation, the energy is gained whereas in sex, it is lost.

In the 1960s and 70s, William Masters and Virginia Johnson—the original *masters of sex— brought science to the bedroom*; they were really the pioneers of applying mindfulness-based practices to the solution of men's and women's sexual difficulties. Although they never used the term "mindfulness," the cornerstone of their approach to sex therapy was to get patients to focus on being in the here and now and to pay attention to body sensations evoked from a partner's touch instead of getting lost in their heads.

Modern mindfulness practices go well beyond those developed by Masters and Virginia Johnson in the sense that they can be practiced individually or with a partner, and they involve paying attention to more than just the sense of touch—breathing, sound, taste, and other sensory input is part of what people are instructed to pay attention to as well. So far, most research on mindfulness and sexual difficulties has focused on women, and the results have been impressive. Studies have found that mindfulness training significantly increases sexual desire and arousal, vaginal lubrication, and sexual satisfaction.

Research has only just begun exploring the effects of mindfulness on male sexual difficulties, but the results suggest that it is similarly effective. Stress, anxiety and_worry triggers the fight-or-flight reflex that constricts the arteries in the central body, limiting blood flow to the gut and genitals and sending it out to the limbs for self-defense or escape. Reduced blood flow through the genitals compromises sexual responsiveness, function, and satisfaction. But deep relaxation, the kind produced by meditation, opens the arteries that supply blood to the genitals and enhances sexual function and pleasure.

In recent years, several sex researchers, outstandingly Lori Brotto at the University of British Columbia, have channeled the power of meditation to treat a broad range of sex problems: Despite their widespread prevalence, there are no existing evidence-based psychological treatments for women with sexual desire and arousal disorder. Mindfulness, the practice of relaxed wakefulness, is an ancient eastern practice with roots in Buddhist meditation which has been found to be an effective component of psychological treatments for numerous psychiatric and medical illnesses. In recent years, mindfulness has been incorporated into sex therapy and has been found effective for genital arousal disorder among women with acquired sexual complaints secondary to gynecologic cancer. Brotto *et al* (2008) investigated a mindfulness-based group psychoeducational intervention targeting sexual arousal disorder in women. There was a significant beneficial effect of the group PED (mindfulness-based psychoeducational) on sexual desire and sexual distress. Also, they found a positive effect on self-assessed genital wetness despite little or no change in actual physiological arousal, and a marginally significant improvement in subjective and self-reported physical arousal during an erotic stimulus. A follow-up comparison of women with and without a sexual abuse history revealed that women with a sexual abuse history improved significantly more than those without such history on mental sexual excitement, genital tingling/throbbing, arousal, overall sexual function, sexual distress, and on negative affect while viewing the erotic film. Moreover, there was a trend for greater improvement on depression scores among those with a sexual abuse history.

Brotto *et al.* (2012) enrolled 20 adult survivors of childhood sexual trauma in a program shown to aid recovery, CBT (cognitive behavioral therapy). CBT helped them reframe their stories away from the horror of abuse toward self-forgiveness and personal empowerment. Half the group also learned mindfulness meditation and practiced it daily. After one month, both groups reported less sexual distress, but the mindfulness group reported greater relief and better sexual functioning.

Brotto and Basson (2014) team recruited 117 low-desire women. Forty-nine were placed on a waitlist. The rest participated in three 90-minute classes over six weeks that discussed the causes of low libido and offered instruction in mindfulness meditation. Between classes, the women practiced mindfulness daily at home. After six months, the treatment group reported significantly greater desire, arousal, and lubrication, easier orgasms, and greater satisfaction.

Dascalu and Brotto (2018) studied the effects of mindfulness on women's sexual difficulties. They investigated the relationship between meditation experience and women's sexual function. 450 women answered online survey questions about meditation experience sexual function, and desire, interoceptive awareness, health and mood. Women who meditated scored higher than nonmeditators on measures of sexual function and desire, however there was no significant correlation between frequency/length of meditation experience in either of these domains. Global mental health was a significant predictor of both increased sexual function and desire in women who meditate. These findings suggest that, compared to women with no meditation experience, women who meditate to any extent have, on average, improved sexual function associated with better overall mental health.

Brotto *et al.* (2016) in their investigations found that Mindfulness-Based Sex Therapy Improves Genital-Subjective Arousal Concordance in Women with Sexual Desire/Arousal Difficulties. They examined the effects of mindfulness-based sex therapy on sexual arousal concordance in a sample of women with sexual desire/arousal difficulties (n = 79, M age 40.8 years) who participated in an in-laboratory assessment of sexual arousal using a vaginal photoplethysmography (device to determine vaginal blood flow) before and after four sessions of group mindfulness-based sex therapy. Genital-subjective sexual arousal concordance significantly increased from pre-treatment levels, with changes in subjective sexual arousal predicting contemporaneous genital sexual arousal (but not the reverse). These findings have implications for their understanding of the mechanisms by which mindfulness-based sex therapy improves sexual functioning in women and suggest that such treatment may lead to an integration of physical and subjective arousal processes. Moreover, their findings suggest that future research might consider the adoption of sexual arousal concordance as a relevant endpoint in treatment outcome research of women with sexual desire/arousal concerns.

Brotto (2013) says that the potential for mindfulness to help men have better sex goes far beyond this. According to Brotto "mindfulness can also be extended to the treatment of men with premature ejaculation, delayed ejaculation, and low sexual desire."

Brotto *et al.* (2018) team enrolled 10 men suffering erection difficulties in a four-week mindfulness-based treatment program that included information about ED, counseling, and mindfulness meditation practiced in therapy sessions and daily at home. Most of the men reported significant improvement.

Brotto also has a multi-year study underway exploring the impact of mindfulness on the sexual functioning of male prostate cancer survivors, a group she believes could benefit from this treatment approach tremendously. Prostate cancer is the most common cancer diagnosed in men, affecting nearly 200,000 new men each year in the United States alone. Although survival rates are high, treatments for prostate cancer often result in sexual side effects. Brotto suggests that mindfulness has the potential to help these men considerably, because the sexual difficulties they face are compounded by sexual anxiety, changes in body image following treatment, and distress from having been diagnosed with cancer. In other words, male cancer survivors are a group that may be especially in need of tools that can help them get out of their heads and into the moment when they are in the bedroom. Mindful meditation mitigates their problem as suggested by the investigation of Ott *et al.* (2006).

If you're interested in using mindfulness techniques to improve your own sex life, where do you begin? "Start by doing 10 minutes per day of formal mindful practice in your chair. Choose one time and do it every day," Brotto says. "During those 10 minutes guide your attention to different locations in your body and ask yourself 'what do I feel?' Always focus on the sensations themselves, not the story behind the sensations."

Brotto adds that, after a few weeks of practice, and gaining more proficiency for using that mindful muscle, you can begin incorporating that skill into sex itself and ask yourself the same question: "What do I feel? Where do I feel it? Can I pay close enough attention to detect subtle changes in those sensations?" she says. "And when the mind distracts, gently guide it back. Over and over."

Castleman (2019) reported that Investigators at Willamette University in Oregon analyzed 11 studies of mindfulness involving 449 women who complained of low libido and arousal and orgasm difficulties. "All aspects of sexual function and well-being—exhibited significant improvement."

A study by Bossio *et al.* (2018) found that mindfulness may be a useful approach for treating erectile dysfunction. This was a small study with just 10 men, participated in a month-long mindfulness training group. However, the results pointed to improvement in erectile functioning and sexual satisfaction over time.

A study by Sunnen (1977) at New York University on nine men with a mean age of 32 found that as little as two 15 minute sessions of meditation a day transformed the men so that all but two of them could achieve "erectile competence." The study worked by training the men how to deflect negative thought patterns from their mind through meditation.

Jaderek *et al.* (2019) studies indicate that mindful based intervention (MBT) led to improvement in subjectively evaluated arousal and desire, sexual satisfaction, and a reduction of fear linked with sexual activity, as well as improving the consistency between the subjectively perceived arousal and genital response in women. The research indicated that MBT did not make a significant change in a reduction of pain during sexual activities. Evidence-based data were found on the efficacy of MBT in the treatment of male erectile dysfunction in one study. The effects of MBT in female sexual dysfunctions are promising. In future studies, the mindfulness-based monotherapies should be implemented to verify their potential in reducing symptoms of sexual dysfunction. More research is needed to explore the potential of MBT in the treatment of male sexual dysfunction.

Vincent Giampapa, a famous anti-aging researcher, found that meditators' DHEA levels were higher by at least 40%! DHEA also boosts the level of endorphins. Some even had DHEA increases of up to 90%. DHEA is the only hormone that diminishes with age. It is described as a powerful anti-ageing hormone and is a key determinant of our physiological age. It guards against disease, increases sexual libido, and increases the feeling of wellbeing and youthful vitality. Meditation also increases melatonin and decrease cortisol. Melatonin, besides being a sleep hormone, is a very powerful antioxidant, anti-ageing agent, immuno-regulator and anti-depressant. It slows cell damage, improves energy and may even inhibit the growth of cancer cells. In addition to being present during sexual arousal and even orgasm, these euphoric neurotransmitters have been proven to reduce anxiety and depression which adversely affect the sex drive (Ross 2016).

Meditation and Sex Addiction:
Sex addiction is a disorder that can have serious adverse functional consequences. Treatment effectiveness research for sex addiction is currently underdeveloped, and interventions are generally

based on the guidelines for treating other behavioral (as well as chemical) addictions. Consequently, there is a need to clinically evaluate tailored treatments that target the specific symptoms of sex addiction. It has been proposed that second-generation mindfulness-based interventions (SG-MBIs) may be an appropriate treatment for sex addiction because in addition to helping individuals increase perceptual distance from craving for desired objects and experiences. An in-depth clinical case study was conducted by Gordon *et al* (2016) involving an adult male suffering from sex addiction that underwent treatment utilizing an SG-MBI known as Meditation Awareness Training (MAT). Following completion of MAT, the participant demonstrated clinically significant improvements in addictive sexual behavior, as well as reductions in depression and psychological distress. The MAT intervention also led to improvements in sleep quality, job satisfaction, and non-attachment to self and experiences. Salutary outcomes were maintained at 6-month follow-up. The current study extends the literature exploring the applications of mindfulness for treating behavioral addiction, and findings indicate that further clinical investigation into the role of mindfulness for treating sex addiction is warranted.

Meditation Helps in Porn Addiction:

Castleman reported (2019) that Creighton University investigators took 38 men who were convinced they were porn addicts to a rustic retreat center for eight days. They spent 32 hours in cognitive-behavioral therapy (CBT). During CBT sessions, the researchers endeavored to correct participants' sexual misconceptions, such as: Sexual thoughts and fantasies are wrong, harmful, and sinful. Only bad people masturbate. My porn watching proves I'm evil. The therapists endeavored to correct those mistaken beliefs: There's nothing wrong with sexual thoughts and fantasies. Everyone has them. They are perfectly normal and a key element of great sex. Almost everyone masturbates, particularly men who feel stressed. Unless it interferes with life responsibilities or partner lovemaking, there is nothing wrong with it, even frequently, even daily. Virtually every Internet-connected man on Earth has seen porn, many frequently, some daily. Viewing it does not make you evil. Porn is a cartoon version of men's fantasies of effortless sexual abundance. The researchers also taught participants mindfulness meditation, which they practiced several times a day. After the retreat, their sexual anxiety and porn viewing decreased significantly. Anxiety contributes to many sexual problems. That is why "Am I normal?" is one of the most common questions sex experts get. Many people feel nervous about their fantasies, bodies, libidos, sexual repertoire, and ability to negotiate functional sexual relationships. That nervousness causes stress, which, as mentioned, impairs sexual desire and function.

When sex experts correct people's misconceptions, sometimes that is all necessary to resolve their issues. But quite often, sexual issues cause chronic stress not relieved just by learning the truth. Sometimes, people need the truth plus tools to relieve their sexual stress. That's where mindfulness and other relaxing activities help: deep breathing, hot baths, massage, yoga, tai chi, dance, hiking, and other exercises. They break the vicious cycle of stress-dysfunction-more stress-worse dysfunction and replace it with refreshing calmness. Sex unfolds most pleasurably when people feel calm, centered, and focused on pleasure—their own and their partners'. Even those free of sex problems can benefit from deep relaxation through meditation.

Conclusion:
Meditation is an ancient behavioral intervention, however, its benefits for achieving holistic health have been highlighted in recent times with rigorous scientific studies revealing its benefits in many chronic diseases. Discussion in this chapter on the benefits of meditation has been verified with scientific data.

Meditation is a complex phenomenon involving change in cognition, memory, and social and emotional control, and causes improvement in various cardiovascular, neurological, autoimmune, and renal pathologies. Meditation is now widely used in medical and psychological treatment therapies for stress-related physical and mental disorders. Nevertheless, meditation has been accepted in the mainstream of alternative methods as complementary medicine. A literature search revealed that 14 medical schools teach mindfulness meditation to medical and dental students and residents in USA, Canada, and Australia.

Survey of literature revealed, most of the studies on meditation have shown wide range of benefits on human physiology starting from brain to erectile dysfunction. It has been specially found useful in neurodegenerative diseases and recent evidence points to the positive effects of meditation in preserving gray and white matter in the adult brain. It is also a potential therapy to downregulate processes implicated in brain aging and confer "neuroprotection"--something beneficial for glaucoma patients. It sounds to be an elixir for all kinds of ailments suggesting a prospective future. However, some of the studies are contradictory and a few of them are inconclusive owing to limitations such as small groups and lack of statistical evaluations. Significant gaps in the research are identified, including weak research design, poor methodology quality, and inconsistency in measurement of outcomes, small sample sizes, and lack of standardized meditation protocols including blind studies. Nevertheless, some of the studies conducted have no information on variations regarding the age, gender, race of the participants and their genetic history.

Arias *et al.* (2006) reviewed the efficacy of meditation techniques as treatments for medical illness. From a total of 82 identified studies, 20 randomized controlled trials their criteria. The studies included 958 subjects total (397 experimentally treated, 561 controls). Studies on normal healthy populations were not included. Their results support the safety and potential efficacy of meditative practices for treating certain illnesses, particularly in nonpsychotic mood and anxiety disorders. Benefit was also demonstrated for mood and anxiety disorders, autoimmune illness, and emotional disturbance in neoplastic disease. However, clear and reproducible evidence supporting efficacy from large, methodologically sound studies is lacking.

Despite all the progress made on meditation, biological mechanisms in terms of effect on brain and body are poorly understood. Research on meditation is still in embryonic stage, extensive research is required to completely comprehend the structure of meditation and mechanism of action on the body. Future research on meditation practices should be more meticulous and comprehensive in the design and execution of studies including analyzing and reporting of results.

Different religions practice meditation in different ways. Spiritual practice is not limited to any faith or religion – anyone can follow a guided spiritual meditation. The blessings of spiritual meditation have a ripple effect: as our awareness and spiritual confidence increase, so do our desire and ability to be of benefit to others. For as long as we humans have been embarking on spiritual journeys, we have relied on the guidance of spiritual teachers. The hallmarks of a genuine spiritual teacher are wisdom, kindness, spiritual power, and humility.

The journey to spiritual awareness through meditation takes time. Progress is not achieved overnight; promises of a quick fix are implausible at best. It takes plenty of discipline and practice to achieve spiritual realization, but the long-term benefits are incomparable. For those whose spiritual lives are important to them, there is no more worthy effort than meditation.

"To understand the absolute reality, the mind must be in absolute stillness, that comes through meditation." —Ravi K. Puri

Chapter Six:
The Dark Side of Meditation

"Every adversity, every failure, every heartache carries with it the seed of an equal or greater benefit." – Napoleon Hill

D uring the survey of the literature on meditation, some adverse effects came across like a bolt from the blue sky. So far, only the benefits were focused on and never realized about the dark side of meditation.

Truly, little is known about the negative effects of meditation. It was difficult to assimilate this concept that meditation can cause health problems also. However, it is equally important to recognize the potential hazards of meditation, which might arise during practice. This is especially relevant to beginners, who might experience one of the challenges discussed below and think that there is something wrong. It is also vital for meditation teachers to be aware of these potential dangers, as their students might encounter similar challenges and need support. If the possible perils of meditation are known, it would be easy to deal with the challenges in a healthy manner, instead of terminating meditation practice.

No doubt, extremely limited research has been done on potentially harmful effects of meditation. During recent years, some serious negative effects have come on the surface and caught the attention of scientists. West (1979) and Epstein and Lieff (1981), Kuijpers *et al.* (2007), Lustyk *et al.* (2009) and Shonin *et al.* (2014) reviews on the negative effects of meditation were eye-openers for the supporters of meditation. Most recently, Lomas *et al.* (2015) exploded the various adverse effects of meditation. In their publication, they reported the experiences of some participants with Mindfulness Meditation. Participants faced difficulties such as learning meditation on, troubling experiences of self, psychological problems being aggravated, reality being challenged, and compensatory positive experiences. In-depth interviews were conducted by the main author with 30 male meditators. Having originally set out simply to inquire about the impact of various meditation practices including but not limited to mindfulness on men's wellbeing, they uncovered psychological challenges associated with its practice. Their review focuses specifically on these issues to alert health professionals to potential challenges associated with meditation. Four main problems of increasing severity were uncovered: Meditation was a difficult skill to learn and practice; participants encountered troubling thoughts and feelings which were hard to manage; meditation reportedly aggravated mental health issues, such as depression and anxiety; and in a few cases, meditation was associated with psychotic episodes. Their publications raise important issues around safeguarding those who practice meditation, both within therapeutic settings and in the community.

Some of the expressions of the experienced meditators interviewed by Lomas *et al.* (2015) are as follow: Their first names are given in parentheses. These expressions have been taken from his review.

Difficulties Learning Meditation:
*An experienced meditator categorized himself as inattentive: *"Meditation is never easy. I almost feel, 'Why am I doing this? I'm rubbish at it, I just can't concentrate, there's too much going on in my head.'* — (William).

"I have had many struggles in meditating...The special moments happened in the contest of just plodding along, making mistakes, going down dead ends. That what happens most of the time really."— (Sam).

A Troubled Sense of Self:
* *"You're coming face to face with your own heart and mind, fear, anger, hatred, confusion, frustration and anxiety, all the difficult*

emotions. ...That's the whole point. ... It was certainly challenging. "— (Andrew).

*"I suddenly got the sense that all my life I had been buffeted around by experience, and that I had no control over what I was feeling, or what my conscious mind was doing." — (William).

*"[Mindfulness involves] listen[ing] to yourself, and sometimes you don't like to hear what is coming out. You think "Gosh, my mind is so horrible, I've got so much work to do and I don't know where to start." — (Walter).

*"With "painful feelings" relating to a childhood trauma one had suppressed for years. "I saw the depth of the pain that is buried. ... things that have happened to me that have not been dealt with properly. It can be very scary to know there's that very strong thing in there." — (Henry).

Exacerbating Psychological Issues

*"Doing mindfulness, you don't like yourself sometimes. You just become aware, "Actually. I'm a bit of a shit." If you've got a tendency towards negativity, that can make you feel not too good about yourself. ... You're developing awareness of things that set you off down the negative route. You're opening a can of worms." —(Dean).

*"I do not do much of it (Lave kind meditation). It has a strong effect. I find it painful. I experience very strong emotions, and don't always have the awareness and robustness to deal with those."— (Adam).

*As Kris said, "It's brought up a bit of fear, of violence, of [how] things you take for granted you could lose..... At work I'm more sensitive to [clients'] distress, I feel their pain."

*("Very intense, very painful ... scared [by] how dark this absence of light can be."). Mindfulness was not helpful during these times, as depression had divested them of the strength to manage their negative subjective experience. I'd feel pain, and [think], "What the hell's

happened to me? I'm a complete wreck." You can get stuck in that. [I lacked] the energy to turn my mind around. I would just experience suffering, and wasn't able to do anything with it."— (Walter)

"Getting into deep meditation just made you more sensitive, when actually your whole system would cry out, 'Stop doing this, it's mad.' I needed to do things that took me out of myself. Better to go and see a friend." —(Adam)

Reality Being Challenged

*Sam had a "vision" of a "golden and vibrating" sphere "hovering" in his chest: "I felt confident that if I'd manage throughout my life to make a path to reach that source, [then]my spiritual development would unfold naturally."

*"I crashed, lying on the floor sobbing. I had a really strong sense of impermanence without the context, without the positivity. The crushing experience of despair was very strong. ... You just feel like you don't exist, you're nothing, there's nothing really there. It's nihilistic, pretty terrifying." —(Adam)

*"coming back into the 'real world,' what happens [is] the tide goes out, and what you see is all the rotting prams, the dead dogs, the smells, the sewage....I asked for it, and I got it, and I have to deal with it. So, the last 10 years of my life has been about integrating that, being able to bear the suffering of the world. Harry felt such experiences were "crazy-making, he felt close to psychosis," —(Harry)

*"Dwelling on my own thoughts, thinking I was the Centre of the universe, and was going to be the next Buddha", which he believed had contributed his breakdown. I sat on the pavement and tried to meditate. I got picked up by the police. ... I went from bad to worse. I wanted to kill myself and tried to throw myself out the window. I got given drugs, a high dosage. I was violent." —(Alan)

*"*Meditation is great, [but] if you're not skilled, or don't get the right guidance, which I wasn't getting, it can go down a slippery path. You have to be cautious."* — (Alan)

Compensatory Positive Experience

"The natural corollary" of the "joyfulness" one had been feeling: The sun was streaming through; the light was clear. My hair was standing up on end. Then from inside, a wave of ecstasy, just a complete feeling of love and warmth and more than joy." —(Alan)

In view of the above, it was thought desirable, to investigate the adverse effects of meditation to comprehend the various pros and cons of meditation for aspirants of meditation.

Most of the data found on adverse effects was from the western culture. In the east, meditation is a part of life and its practice is being incorporated during childhood. Almost in every function of the family starting from birthday, wedding, wedding anniversary, birth and death including all the festivities throughout the year, meditation in the form of short *religion function* is very essential. This system sets a foundation for meditation. Thus, people from east are accustomed to meditation and have very rarely adverse effects. However, exceptions are there. There is a general assumption and belief that meditation is a secular technique and is good for everyone. *It is also true now that practice of meditation is not for everybody.*

The first report of negative side effects of meditation revealed from former Buddhist Monk Christopher Titmuss, a former senior Theravada Buddhist monk, offers Dharma teachings on mindfulness, insight meditation (Vipassana) and a Buddhist critique on social. According to him, some of his students experience trauma and require medical services. Some of them have been hospitalized when the other experienced, "Alienation from reality and short-lived terrors." Likewise, Zen meditation teacher Dowson (2011) reported that 20 people had mental disaster, panic attack, depressive and manic episodes. He further articulates, "Meditation centers need to look more closely at taking responsibility for who is accepted into retreats. If someone went to a solarium and developed a melanoma does that mean that the solarium bears no responsibility? In many cases there may be a genetic pre-disposition, but exposure to excessive radiation, which could have otherwise been avoided, arguably caused the melanoma." Booth (2014) reported in his article entitled "Mindful therapy comes at a high price for some, says experts." The concern comes not from critics of mindfulness but from supporters, Florian Ruths, consultant psychiatrist at the Maudsley Hospital in south London. He has launched an investigation into adverse reactions to MBCT (Mindfulness-Based Cognitive Therapy) which have included rare cases of "depersonalisation", where people feel like they are watching themselves in a film. "There is a lot of enthusiasm for mindfulness-based therapies and they are very powerful interventions," Ruths said. "But they can also have side-effects. Mindfulness is delivered to potentially vulnerable people with mental illness, including depression and anxiety, so it needs to be taught by people who know the basics about those illnesses, and when to refer people for specialist help."

Schlosser *et al.* (2019) reported unpleasant meditation related experiences in regular meditators. The aim of their study was to report the prevalence of particularly unpleasant meditation related experiences in a large international sample of regular meditators, and to explore the association of these experiences with demographic characteristics, meditation practice, repetitive negative thinking, mindfulness, and self-expression. Using a cross-selected online survey, 1232 regular meditators with at least two months of meditation experience (mean age 44.8 years, 56.6% female) responded to one question about particularly unpleasant meditation-related experiences. A total of 315 participants reported having had particularly unpleasant meditation-related experiences, which they thought may have been caused by their meditation practice. Logistic regression models indicated that unpleasant meditation-related experiences were less likely to occur in female participants, and religious participants. Participants with higher levels of repetitive negative thinking, those who only engaged in deconstructive types of meditation such as inside meditation and those who had attended a meditation retreat at any point in their life were more likely to report unpleasant meditation-related experiences.

Sharma *et al* (2019) reviewed the Meditation-Induced Psychosis. A total of 19 studies and 28 cases were included in the review. The patients described had an age range of 18–57 years; there was equal distribution of males and females. The diagnoses included acute psychosis in 14 cases, schizophrenia in 7 cases, mania with psychotic symptoms in 3 cases, and schizoaffective disorder in 1 case. The types of meditation described were Transcendent, Mindfulness, Buddhist Meditation like Qigong, Zen, and Theraveda, and others like Bikram yoga, Pranic Healing, and Hindustan Type meditation. Of the 28 cases reported, 14 patients had certain precipitating factors like insomnia, lack of food intake, history of mental illness, stress, and psychoactive substance use.

There are case reports of psychotic disorder arising in association with meditative practice; however, it is difficult to attribute a causal relationship between the two. At the same time, there is a body of research describing the beneficial effect of meditative practice in clinical settings for patients with psychotic disorders. Appropriately designed studies are needed to further investigate the relationship between meditative practice and psychosis.

Meditation centers need to be subject to the same scrutiny as other organizations on the question of whether they are putting profit before the welfare of people for whom they provide a service. Many meditation centers are organized based on values of altruism rather than profit, but this does not mean that they are free from making ill-informed decisions. Good judgement can also be clouded by blind faith and evangelism and the attitude 'that one size fits all'. There are 42 best mental health retreats of various categories in USA. Their charges vary from $197- 6500 (2- 30 days)

Brown University neuroscientist Willoughby Britton, who has published research demonstrating how meditation can be used in depression, is currently carrying out what she calls the "dark night" project, which will explore the rockier parts of the mindfulness path. Britton was inspired to do the research in part by two patients she treated during her psychiatry residency. Both were participating in a meditation retreat and had to be hospitalized for symptoms they developed during their contemplation. She later attended a retreat—and experienced for herself what it was like to follow meditation into an extreme and distressing mental state. As she described it in an online interview —

"I thought that I had gone crazy. I thought I was having a nervous breakdown. I mean I really had no idea why I was suddenly having all these...like terror was big symptom of mine."

A man committed suicide by jumping from the roof of a hotel after completing a thirty-day Tibetan Buddhist meditation course from Kathmandu, Nepal. There was another report about a twenty-five-year-old woman committing suicide after attending a ten-day Vipassana meditation course. She wasn't the first to commit suicide after intensive meditation, there are stories all across the web of students who have come out of an intensive course, seemed okay but commit suicide within a month after. There are also many cases of students coming out and experiencing mental health issues that were not present before their meditation course.

Roche, an eminent Joyous Meditation teacher, says a major problem arises from the way meditators interpret Buddhist and Hindu teachings. He pointed out that meditation techniques that encourage detachment from the world were intended only for monks and nuns. He has spent thirty years doing interviews with people who meditate regularly. He concluded, most of them were depressed and they have tried to detach themselves from their desires, their loves, and their passion. Roche further articulated "Depression is a natural result of loss, and if you internalize teachings that poison you against the world, then of course you will become depressed."

The Dalai Lama also said that Eastern forms of meditation must be handled carefully. According to him, "Westerners who proceed too quickly to deep meditation should learn more about Eastern traditions and get better training than they usually do. Otherwise, certain physical or mental difficulties appear."

Sarah Bowen, a researcher at the University of Washington, recommends that people who have a history of depression or anxiety should only meditate under expert guidance in case stressful, painful, or upsetting thoughts do arise.

Nancy Hayes, a neurobiologist at Robert Wood Johnson Medical School in New Jersey says, "Patients with emotional disorders may have adverse reactions to meditation."

A distinguished neuroscientist, Solomon Snyder, Director of the Department of Neuroscience at Johns Hopkins Medical School, expressed that meditation may increase serotonin neurotransmitter in the brain. He believes that certain techniques of meditation raise the level of serotonin in the brain which can cause anxiety. He has noted that some people with emotional disorders, experience distress and panic attacks while meditating, and patients who have schizophrenia can experience psychosis as a direct result of the practice.

Jaseja (2005) reported that meditation is potentially capable of increasing susceptibility to epilepsy. Neuro-imaging techniques were used to study the effect of meditation practice in epileptic people. Studies revealed that meditative states alter neurochemistry and neurophysiology of the brain and can lead to epileptogenesis. Epilepsy is caused by hyper synchrony of EEG activity and the rise in brain glutamate and serotonin. Some Psychiatrists believe that meditation involving concentration could cause seizures. On the other hand, David Orme-Johnson (2006) contradicted that Transcendental Meditation program prevented or decreased diseases of the nervous system and was specifically beneficial for epilepsy. There is no evidence that the Transcendental Meditation technique increases glutamate, which has been associated with epilepsy. Regarding serotonin, the relationship of serotonin to epilepsy must be viewed in the context of the abnormal brain tissue that causes epilepsy. The serotonin increase that may occur through meditation have been associated with only beneficial effects.

Neuroscientist Michael Persinger at the Laurentian University of Canada investigated the relationship between seizures and meditation. In 1993 he studied 1,018 meditators and the results showed that meditation could lead to symptoms of partial epilepsy, including hearing voices, feeling vibrations, and experiencing visual abnormalities. Epileptic patients suffer from auditory and visual hallucinations, with many believing that they have spiritual experiences, including speaking with God. Persinger also investigated the experience of so-called "spiritual events." In his tests, Persinger had patients wear helmets through which were passed electrical signals that led to magnetically induced seizures. Four out of every five of his test subjects stated that they had experienced a spiritual event.

Researchers at the Brown University and the University of California analyzed the experiences of 60 meditation practitioners. It revealed that meditation can cause surprising negative side effects, affecting participants' emotions, sensory perception, social interaction, sense of self, and more. Some of the study subjects reported hallucinations, panic, a total loss of motivation, and the re-living of traumatic memories.

Many meditators scuffle to focus the mind during practice. The effort to change mental state is met with psychological confrontation and the aspiration to keep things unchanged. This struggle causes psychological and physical tension that can cause headaches.

One detail (Szalavitz 2013) among the many reports emerging about Aaron Alexis, the 34-year-old man suspected of killing 12 people in a shooting at the Washington Navy Yard, stood out: he was a regular meditator. How does someone who engages in meditation, which is supposed to focus the mind, and is often associated with efforts to diffuse violence, rather than instigate it, perform the acts that Alexis is accused of executing? Alexis had a record of violent crime and his father informed the Wall Street Journal that his son had anger issues related to post-traumatic stress from participating in rescue efforts during the 9/11 attacks. A former boss, who met Alexis at a Buddhist temple in the Fort Worth, Texas area, said Alexis was also a heavy drinker who came to chanting and meditation sessions regularly.

At worst, most people see meditation as flaky, boring, self-involved, or harmless. But as research starts to document how it can help to fight stress, high blood pressure, addictions, and many other mental and physical disorders, it is also becoming clear that meditating isn't always so benign — particularly if it's used against a background of existing mental illness. That is why University of Washington researcher Sarah Bowen suggests that people with depression or trauma issues who want to benefit from meditation should try it with expert guidance. "If you get stuck in ruts like rumination, there are ways to work with that," she says, "It's important to have teachers who are very familiar with meditation to guide you as you are learning." Experts can let people know what to expect and offer emotional support to help them through rough patches.

Harrison, a qualified known teacher of meditation noted that certain techniques—Third Eye Chakra Dhyana, for instance—involve quite compellingly focusing the mind. So, headaches are a common negative side effect of meditation. For beginner meditators focusing the mind can be a challenge. If they are not used to focusing the mind, it can lead to headaches (thedailymeditation.com).

Perhaps the most critical factor in understanding the link between meditation and headaches is the serious transformation that takes place in the brain. For some people, it can be quite jolting to go from a natural state to a meditative state and then back again. The sudden change in state is another cause of strain.

Sometimes meditation brings painful memories of the past. During meditation, mind relaxes more than usual. Many people who are new to the practice have never experienced such a deep level of inner stillness. They become more aware of their mind and thoughts. Some of those thoughts are unpleasant and they may notice painful memories, which might upset them emotionally.

Britton, the Director of the Clinical and Affective Neuroscience Laboratory at Brown University, runs a support group for people for whom meditation has caused a psychological and physical crisis. Each week, she gets more emails from people who are struggling, asking for her help. "I'm seeing a lot of casualties," she says. To understand the range of experiences encountered among Western Buddhists practicing meditation, Britton, Lindahl and their co-authors interviewed nearly 100 meditators and meditation teachers from each of three main traditions: Theravāda, Zen and Tibetan. Each interview told a story, which the researchers meticulously coded and analyzed using qualitative research methodology. A significant portion of the interviewees stated that they had been experiencing hypersensitivity to light and sound, as well as insomnia, occasional involuntary movements, and feelings of fear, anxiety, and panic. The degree of the hypersensitivity to light and sound, and the extremity of insomnia, ranged between different people. Some people were much less sensitive to sounds and light than others. Jared Lindahl, visiting assistant professor at Brown's Cogut Center for Humanities said, "We're not trying to scare people away from trying meditation. There is data that many people find tremendous benefits of these practices." He states that it is essential to have a good idea of the pros and cons of meditating before beginning.

Newberg (2010) at the University of Pennsylvania studied the brains of long-term meditators and observed that blood flow to the posterior superior parietal lobe decreased during meditation is the part of the brain involved with navigating our environment. He stated, "Patients with damaged posterior superior parietal lobes often cannot move without falling." According to him, "oneness (the state in which we feel we are one with our surroundings) could have hidden negative side effects. By blocking blood flow to the posterior superior parietal lobe, you "lose the boundary between yourself and the rest of the world." This can lead to disorientation and falls.

Arthur Chappell, a former devotee of Maharaj Prem Rawat, an Indian American also known as Guru Maharajji, and Bal-Yogeshwar, believes that the practice of meditation "Deprives the mind of stimulus", leading to sensory deprivation. Many methods stimulate the mind and create awareness. When we are more aware of our surroundings, we find more stimulation, not less.

This is undoubtedly true for a great many techniques, but it depends on the specific procedure. Sitting for hours on end focusing on your breathing (as retreats do) is depriving your brain of stimuli. When this is carried out for long periods, it can lead to sensory deprivation and even atrophy of the brain. Therefore, many people who practice for long periods have complained of an inability to perform cognitive functions, like arithmetic and remembering names.

Some people believe that meditative exercises hinder imagination and creativity. However, there is little evidence to support this. This can result only in mindfulness meditation where the focus is on the present only. It prevents the meditator from seeing reality *otherwise*, results in lack of imagination and creativity. In *open meditations* (where your mind is open to the entirety of your surroundings), one will boost both creativity and imagination. It can Up Painful Memories. New meditators have never experienced such a level of inner stillness and become more aware of their mind and thoughts.

After spending almost a decade in India and living in many Ashrams in India such as Guru Maharaj (Prem Rawat) Ashram, Rishikesh, Haridwar, S. N. Goenka. (Vipassana meditation), Patna, Iskcon, Brindaban, Osho commune in Pune and learning the various kinds of meditations with extensive retreats, Garden (2007) a freelance journalist and author of the book *Rising of the Serpent* articulates, "I meditated a lot in the 1970s and thought I was superior to those who didn't. Thankfully, I did not have a breakdown (though sometimes I was surely "out of my mind"). I had all sorts of bizarre and strange experiences and in the early days often felt bliss and ecstasy. There were a few occasions where I felt as though I was "one with the universe", and I once began hallucinating that the trees outside were vibrating with white light, convinced I could hear the sacred *Om* sound booming through the Himalayan night."

She further concludes, "Exercise may be better for physical and mental well-being than meditation. I just love my morning swims in the local pool. After my Indian odyssey and my return to worldly life in 1979, I have found being back in the world not such a bad thing after all. I no longer regard the world as a place from which to escape or detach myself. My mind is no longer something to conquer or to cleanse of impurities. In fact, my life is immeasurably richer without meditation."

There are contradictory statements on meditation even from an individual like Mary Garden (2007). It is exceedingly difficult to conclude whether it is a cure or curse. Most of them are in favor of meditation and some are against as per their experiences. Mostly, the negative effects were noticed in meditators who have been in a long duration of meditation treats. These treats are extremely strict, tiring, boring and focus on meditation almost 24 hours a day. A kind of imprisonment for the meditators. Under that environment some weak-minded people can flip.

Most of the adverse studies did not disentangle the effects of meditation from pre-existing psychological issues. Thus, the few studies that do acknowledge risks around meditation do so usually in terms of it being contraindicated for clinical groups, such as those with a history of schizophrenia. There is less understanding of the potential for meditation to trigger problems in people without pre-existing conditions. More than 5000 years old practice of meditation cannot be a curse without cure.

How to Avoid Adverse Effects of Meditation:

In view of the above discussion, there are health risks of meditation. Now how to avoid them. Meditators need to find the suitable method of meditation among many available in the literature. Find the one which suits to an individual.

Many people start meditating without proper instructions. Practice of meditation should be carried out under the guidance of a trained teacher.

There should be a proper questionnaire to be filled out before starting any practice comprising any mental and physical illness. Lois Vanderkooi, a clinical psychologist who has published on meditation-related psychosis, points out that screening is important when intensive meditation is involved and suggests that it can be done easily with a questionnaire that asks about psychiatric history. Lustyk *et al.* (2009) published a comprehensive detail of adverse reactions of mindfulness meditation along safety concerns of MM practice including issues of participants screening and safety procedures.

Do not force the technique. Start slowly with five minutes per day and increase to 10, 15 and 20 as the time goes. Proper instruction reduces the potential side effects of meditation. Avoid going to long hours retreat. The Dalai Lama has also warned against too casual an approach to practice. The opposite of the casual approach is the intense approach, which has dire consequences. This is when people meditate too much or go too deep. Many people begin practicing and sign themselves up for a retreat. Retreats involve practicing for entire days, for up to fourteen hours. The aim is to create equanimity and enlightenment. Such retreats are suitable for advanced practitioners only. For the uninitiated, they are potential death traps. The sheer number of hours these retreats practice for is simply too much meditation for the average person. The result can range from seizures to psychosis and even death.

Meditative practices and techniques are powerful and have the potential to do tremendous good for us. Still, there are some potential dangers, and they should be acknowledged. The biggest problem is the way people learn to practice. Jumping in headfirst without guidance could lead to significant health problems. Majority of these people follow this approach.

The false advertisements from different communes are responsible for feeding a meditation craze, and millions of people are trapped to practice and join these groups. These are awfully expensive too. Retired and old people with some mental and physical problems become the prey to these traps. Long duration meditation through periodical retreats should be avoided.

The science behind meditation is still in early stages. Previous research has found that mindful meditation, which focuses on breathing, can reduce pain. Certain types of meditation, combined with exercise, can ease symptoms of depression, according to a recent study. Sharon Salzberg, a famous meditation teacher and co-founder of the Insight Meditation Society in Barre, Massachusetts, acknowledged that unexpected or uncomfortable experiences can sometimes arise during meditation and applauded the study for examining an under-researched area. "Certainly, people at different times may go through some degree of difficulty. But it is not everybody," said Saltzberg. "I wouldn't go into meditation thinking it's going to be dreadful. The quality of instructor, the nature of the community and the ongoing support system makes a difference in how we handle the feelings that arise."

The results of negative effects also challenge other common causal attributions, such as the assumption that meditation-related difficulties *only* happen to individuals with a pre-existing condition (psychiatric or trauma history), who are on long or intensive retreats, who are poorly supervised, who are practicing incorrectly, or who have inadequate preparation. Everybody has his own story to tell. However, a growing number of reports indicate that psychologically unpleasant experiences can occur in the context of meditation practice. Extraordinarily little is known about the prevalence and potential causes of these experiences. More investigations are required on the unpleasant effects of meditation to confirm that it is a curse not a cure. Over 11000 years old meditation cannot be a curse but a cure.

"Laughter is the only medicine without side effects."
— *Shannon L. Alde*

Chapter Seven:
Meditation: Myth or Reality

"There is no reality without a Myth." — Ravi K. Puri

Before going into the discussion of the subject of meditation. Let us find out the meaning of 'Myth'. What is a 'Myth'? During primordial time, the term 'myth' was considered as a 'true story' which revealed some precious, sacred, and significant possession. However, with the passage of time and scientific developments the term was used as 'fable' or 'illusion' on account of lack of scientific validations. It is exceedingly difficult to illustrate the definition of myth that would satisfy majority of the scholars. Moreover, there is no way to find one meaningful definition that would cover all types and functions of myths in all traditions and cultures. Myth is an extremely complex cultural reality that can be comprehend and interpreted differently. Myth narrates a sacred cultural history which took place in primordial time and illustrates the phenomenon of 'reality' through supernatural powers. Sometimes, it is extremely challenging to assimilate this 'reality' for lack of validations. According to the myth, earth was flat and stationary. The Sun rises in the east and sets in the west. The Moon has its own light. These myths were false, though some have meaningful approach. Science unveiled many myths into facts. However, all the miracles of myth have some latent messages waiting to be discovered by the latest technology.

Meditation has been practiced by people of various religions throughout the world since the conception of civilization. There are many questions which arise in the mind such as the origin, source, validated benefits and above all the idea of meditation. It is not easy to answer these questions for lack of correct data. It traces back to about 5000 years in India. The earliest records of meditation practice date from approximately 1500 years BCE (Before Common Era). It appears to have been an essential part of the earliest forms of the Vedic Schools in India. In the 6th to 4th centuries BCE, the Chinese Taoist and Indian Buddhist traditions began to develop and organize meditation practice. In the west, meditation was introduced by Philo of Alexandria, the Desert Fathers of the Middle East, and Saint Augustine. The History of meditation until today has been discussed earlier in chapter two of this text.

During recent years there is a sudden spur in the practice of meditation. According to a survey by the National Institutes of Health, 10 percent of respondents—representing more than 20 million adult Americans—tried meditating between 2006 and 2007, a 1.8 percent increase from a similar survey in 2002. At that rate, by 2017, there may be more than 27 million American adults with a recent meditation experience.

Pickert (2014), *Time* magazine featured a cover story on "The Mindful Revolution," an account of the extent to which mindfulness meditation has diffused into the largest sectors of modern society. Used by "Silicon Valley entrepreneurs, Fortune 500 titans, Pentagon chiefs, and more," mindfulness meditation is promoted to help Americans, work mindfully, eat mindfully, parent mindfully, teach mindfully, take standardized tests mindfully, spend money mindfully, and go to war mindfully.

Thus, tremendous research is being carried out on meditation and science claims some incredibly significant results beneficial to mankind. The findings accelerated the practice of meditation. However, on the other hand, some people are very skeptical and consider meditation as 'myth'. There are many myths surrounding meditation. Some people think, it is a mystery. Some people emphatically emphasized, "If we can't hallucinate, see amazing colors, images, could not aspire to levitate, then it is not worth doing meditation or one has not accomplished anything". Others think they should achieve some magic powers, superhuman powers or get connected with God. If they are not getting or visualizing those superpowers there is no need of carrying out meditation. For them it is a fiction. Some people have cravings to see God through meditation or seek self- realization. If it is not possible, they are not interested. They think it is a waste of time and effort. Mary Gardner, author, and journalist spent 10 years in India in search of self-realization and enlightenment, visited various communes, attended various meditation treats like Vipassana, dynamic meditation of Osho and Hare Rama and Hare Krishna Ashram at Vrindavan, Mathura, and finally came back and settled in Australia. Now she realizes, meditation is a waste of time. She can better utilize that time in physical exercise. Strange, it took her ten years to reach this conclusion after going through all the odds during her stay in India.

Regarding the misconception of the people, they need to understand the term meditation, its phenomenon and practice. First, there is a need to understand--what is meditation? Secondly, why does an individual want to do it? Finally, the process and techniques of meditations.

Meditation means to "know thyself." After knowing the true nature of self, the solution for sufferings can be found. It means our happiness depends only on the internal world not the external world. All our lives from childhood to old age, we are running around and manipulating to please others to find happiness. Even if we find it, it is going to be short lived. Meditation is a means for purifying the mind, eliminating attachments, delusion and desires that causes pain, sufferings, and unhappiness. Meditation technique does not depend upon the external world or external power but only on our own efforts, internal world which gives permanent bliss. Meditation is a wonderful journey into the inner world. It is a silent conversation within and a way to explore and re-discover oneself.

The Hallmark of meditation is based on the present moment— while staying in the now, enjoying the present. It consists of observing body and mind with bare attention. The biggest problem is mind which is full of thoughts. A constant flow of the memories of the past or the fear of the future going through the mind. Your worst enemy cannot harm you as much as your own thoughts unguarded. Controlling mind is not a one day's job but it needs a regular and systematic practice. It comes under control when there is a feeling of oneness with God.

All these senses, external and internal, must be under the disciple's control. By hard practice, meditator must arrive at the stage where he can assert his mind against the senses, against the commands of nature. He should be able to say to his mind, "You are mine; I order you, do not see or hear anything", and the mind will not see or hear anything — no form or sound will react on the mind. The flow of this continuous control of the mind becomes steady when practiced day after day, and the mind obtains the faculty of constant concentration.

Now the question arises, how to control or deviate the mind, The solution is amazingly simple, sit quietly and let the mind wander where it wants to go. Keep a strong faith and watch the mind drifting in all random directions. The mind is not you or me. It comprises thoughts only. Now try connecting with self but not with any worldly thing or relationship. After some time, the mind will calm down like a serene lake. This will slow down the wandering of mind. Each day practice this and identify yourself. With time, the mind will be under your control. The body is an extraordinarily strong weapon. Consider your mind to be equally strong as only with strong mind and body you will be able to cross the ocean of life. Have a sturdy faith in yourself, your body and mind.

Secondly, be spiritual. This will make the person happy and his or her mind will be under control. The mind is like a lake, and every stone that drops into it raises ripples. These ripples do not let us see the bottom. After these calm, one can see the bottom. Similarly, we must seize this unstable mind and drag it from its wanderings and fix it on one idea. Repeatedly this must be done. By power of will get hold of the mind and make it stop and reflect upon the glory of

God. Let the mind be cheerful but calm. Never let it run into excesses because every excess will be followed by a reaction. We must realize that thoughts appear and disappear in our consciousness. Our consciousness is like a screen. Do not accept delivery of all the wrong ideas that keep coming to you. Rest quietly in the feeling of "I am", which is consciousness, and cultivate the attitude that all thoughts, all perceptions, are "not me". When you know that everything that is happening is only appearing on the screen of consciousness, and that you yourself are the screen on which it all appears, nothing can touch you, harm you or make you afraid. Mental problems feed on the attention that you give them. The more you worry about them, the stronger they become. If you ignore them, they lose their power and finally vanish.

Thoughts are the root cause of all the problems in life including diseases. Thoughts give rise to actions and repeated actions become a habit. Repeated habit becomes the second nature of the person which leads to the character of a person. For example, if a person starts eating ice cream, it will lead to craving of ice cream every day and he is addicted to ice cream or any other desert. Ultimately it causes insulin resistance regardless the person is diabetic or prediabetes, and the extra sugar in the body would accumulate in the form of visceral fat stored within the abdominal cavity and several vital organs including liver, stomach, and intestines. It can also build up in the arteries. Excess visceral fat can raise blood pressure, cause heart attack, stroke, breast cancer and Alzheimer's disease. In females, in addition to visceral fat, steatopygia fat accumulates around buttock region that even extends to the thighs.

Similarly, the addiction of alcohol results to liver damage or cirrhosis. Likewise, smoking habit leads to lung cancer. Use of narcotic and psychedelic substances, are habit forming and destroy the nervous system. Negative thoughts give rise to mental stress and repeated negative thoughts day and night produce fear and panic attacks. Stress is another root cause of many diseases. It stimulates cortisol level in the body. A high concentration of cortisol in the body can suppress immunity, raise blood pressure, reduce libido, increase obesity and blood sugar levels. Sugar binds to proteins and lipids through "glycation," it makes the skin wrinkled to enhance aging.

That means nothing is good or bad thinking makes it so. Good thoughts will make your life whereas bad ones can mar your life. Meditation is the excellent technique to deviate the negative thoughts that controls the mind and finally affect the body. Thoughts appear and disappear in our consciousness. Do not attach to wrong ideas coming to the mind. Mind is a modified consciousness; one should stay in the consciousness. Thoughts are only perceptions on the screen of consciousness, just like a movie on the screen. So, ignore them and focus on meditation.

Do not worry about whether you are making progress or not in meditation. Just keep your attention on the Self twenty-four hours a day. Meditation is not something that should be done in a particular position at a particular time. It is an awareness and an attitude that must persist through the day. Meditation must be continuous. The current of meditation must be present in all your activities. If you pay attention to thoughts and feelings while you meditate and try to use them to evaluate how well or how badly you are meditating, you will never reach the ultimate silence. Instead you will just get bogged down in mental concepts. If you can be continuously aware of each thought as it rises, and if you can be so indifferent to it that it does not sprout or flourish, you are well on the way to escaping from the entanglements of mind.

Benefits of meditation on the various organs of the body with scientific validations have been discussed in the chapter five. The significant studies on meditation were carried out on stress, depression, anxiety, cardiovascular diseases, Alzheimer, ulcerative colitis, cancer, and chronic pain etc. Most cases show that meditation helps through controlling the mind. It controls the various hormones such as cortisol, adrenaline, dopamine, endorphin, responsible for various diseases. Meditation has been in practice more than 5000 years in the various parts of the word. Several studies have been done by private and government agencies to use meditation as an alternative method of treatment or complementary medicine. Ample money in the form of Grants has been given to various institutions and hospitals to study the effects of various meditations on the human diseases. Some of the data is favorable where other is contradictory. The results are inconclusive. Some of the studies were done on small scale. Large scale studies lack statistical evaluations. Science is still in infancy stage and must catch up to speed to know about meditation. Since the studies are done on human beings, there are many variabilities such as age, race, genes. heredity, and pre-existing illness. When conventional medicine cannot help much in improving the health of a person, then people turn to alternative complementary holistic healing practices. One of them is meditation. It is quite interesting that people resort to meditation as a last option when meditation has already been practiced for thousands of years, with its limitless benefits being understood by all who have done any research.

On the other hand, we cannot depend upon meditation only for the treatment of chronic or infectious diseases. They need to be treated with proper medication. As far as meditation is concerned, it is good for mental relaxation to treat anxiety, depression, and stress. For the treatment of CVD, diabetes, arthritis, cancer, pneumonia, sexually transmitted diseases (STD) and other chronic diseases, proper allopathic treatment is required. Meditation can be used as a complementary treatment. Meditation alone cannot do the job. For example, in case of high blood pressure, regular medicine is required along meditation. If meditation is working, then slowly one can leave the medicine.

So, what does it all mean? Obviously, a few studies on several dozen meditators are not the final answer as to how meditation produces changes in mood and biological functions. Though it is a wonderful tool, no one should expect meditation to work miracles, cautioned psychologist and medical sociologist Barrie Cassileth, chief of the integrative medicine service at Memorial Sloan-Kettering

Cancer Center in New York, articulated, "It cannot bring about levitation. It cannot control cellular activity in the sense of getting rid of disease. It's not going to let you fly to Europe on your own without a plane." (Freeman 2003).

In view of the above, and going through the enormous, published data available in the literature on meditation, it is concluded that meditation is an excellent practice to protect our thoughts from controlling our mind. Meditation is not the way to find heaven or God. One cannot achieve any superpower with it. Searching God is just like peeling an anion. You do not get anything in the end. So, stop searching and deviate the negative thoughts who are controlling your mind and your destiny.

Meditation is the ineffable longing of the Inner Self for the divine. Every individual is inquisitive to know the unknown divinity. It is impossible to achieve that. How one can see God when all the religion conclude that God is shapeless. birthless and self-illuminating. Some enlightened mystics have expressed the unknown divinity seen as white flooded light or sound, that is understandable. First came the sound followed by light. Meditation is not a myth. It is a technique to know thyself. Through meditation, the Higher Self is experienced, that higher self is absolute consciousness.

Some people do not believe in meditation and feel it is a sheer waste of time. That is fine too. They should leave meditation completely but do not let the mind hold on to anything negative.

Studies on meditation suggest that the subjective experience of meditation may prove capable of being understood objectively as well. Spending your entire life on your cellphone or laptop, is not enough. Spending time with friends and family is exceedingly critical, too. Meditation by itself is not enough. Although there are numerous life-changing benefits of meditation. Meditation is a wonderful practice and a fantastic exercise for the mind. The body benefits by movements whereas the mind benefits by stillness. That stillness comes through meditation. With the passage of time, myth of meditation is becoming reality. But it is not a cure-all, and it should be complemented with additional healthy habits. A regular exercise, restricting your calories, eating healthy, sleeping on time, avoiding alcohol, intoxicating substances and smoking are essential habits along meditation. Above all, be compassionate, kind to others and help the needy. Then we can say meditation is over medication and it is not a myth but reality.

> *It is difficult to separate, at times, the Myth from the Reality.*
> *—Bob Kane.*

Chapter Eight:
Search for the Unknown

"Unknown is shapeless, colorless, birth less, deathless, neither created nor destroyed, omnipresent, omniscient and omnipotent. What people are searching for I don't have any idea." — Ravi K. Puri

Most of the people have some misconceptions, confusions or doubts about meditation and ask questions. Some of the questions are being answered below.

Q: Does meditation live up to the hype?
A: Over 5000 year's old tradition of practicing meditation must live up to the hype. If it has no significance, it could have vanished by now. The science is very much in an embryonic state for meditation. It has to catch up to understand the structure of meditation. Meditation plays an important role for the maintenance of well-being.

Q: Meditation is a religious practice. It is meant for monks, saints, yogis, and priest only.
A: This is a wrong concept. No doubt, meditation is linked with certain religions and cultures. However, everybody can practice meditation regardless of his or her religion and can gain benefits physically, intellectually, and spiritually.

Q: It is exceedingly difficult to practice meditation due to its uncomfortable lotus position with straight spine.
A: It is a misconception. Though, sitting in lotus position with straight spine during meditation helps easy natural breathing, but it is not mandatory. One can do meditation in any easy position, seated in a chair, sofa or in bed, even while moving or exercising. One can follow any position suitable to him. Meditation should be considered as fun not punishment.

Q: I can't do meditation due to lack of concentration. It is not easy to quiet the mind. Thoughts move in the past and future. One cannot get rid of thoughts.

A: Yes, it is exceedingly difficult to get rid of the thoughts. Mind is clinging to the past and living in the future. It causes frustration when one cannot calm his or her mind. There is no way we can stop thinking. Thoughts are like heart beats. They continue like heart beating. Descartes said, "Cogito Ergo Sum --I think, therefore I live." The same goes with the heart, it is functioning with the heartbeat. Let the thoughts flow in your mind while sitting in meditation, just watch them and do not attach with them or judge them. Focus on an object, such as the breath or mantra or physical sensations, while remaining aware of the present feelings, thoughts and sensations that arise in the mind. Notice when your mind wanders and avoid stressing about it – just gently bring your attention back to the breath or the object. With daily and regular practice thoughts will not bother and mind will start relaxing. Act of noticing and coming back to the object is the key to meditation.

Q: Is Chanting necessary in meditation?

A: Some forms of meditation include chanting, though it is not essential. One can select some other form of meditation where one can focus on an object or breathing only. If you are not comfortable chanting. You can also chant silently in your mind.

Q Is there any scientific proof of mantras effects?

A. Yes, studies have been done on certain popular mantras. Dissimilar mantras have different effects and benefits. Each mantra possesses characteristic vibrations.

Q: Is it essential to follow certain rituals, wear saffron color clothes, burn incense, keep some flowers, turmeric, rice, coconuts etc. for performing meditation?

A: It is not required. If you like, you can do it. These things are to purify the environment.

Q: **Should Meditation be performed in a temple, or a special secluded place only?**
A: Not required, one can do anywhere he or she likes.

Q: **Does Meditation require to abandon my life and become a Sanyasi or monk?**
A: It is not required; it is not like that. One can meditate in any profession. No need of leaving anything. One can performs all his duties along with 10-15 minutes meditation per day.

Q: Does one need a master or Guru to learn and meditate?
A: Not really. You can learn from books or video, and U-Tube. Guru is not required; it is an option.

Q: Is Meditation escapism / running away from the problems of the world?
A: No. It is rather the opposite of it. It will help you to solve your problems.

Q: Is the use of Psychedelics an easy way to reach an altered state of consciousness?
A: The use of Psychedelics is not new. It has been mentioned even in Yoga Sutra of Patanjali, too. For thousands of years the ancient mystics, priests, monks, and yogis used to consume them to reach altered state of consciousness. Their use is not required in meditation. Some people take Ayahuasca or LSD to acquire the altered state of consciousness. I think it is an excuse or inquisitiveness to know the altered state of consciousness. Its use has some toxic effects.

Q: People think if they leave the hustle and bustle of life and go in the mountains or forest, they can do contemplating practice seriously.
A: One can do meditation anywhere. Going into the mountains or forest is an escapism. Peace is within not without.

Q: If everyone meditates the world would be a much better place. Is it true?

A: Most of the mystics say this including Dalai Lama. There are some scientific data in sport of this statement. However, there is no clear scientific evidence that meditation is more effective than other spiritual or psychological practices. Data on this topic has serious methodological and theoretical limitations and biases. Anyway, regular practice of meditation changes the nature of a practitioner and makes him or her a better human being.

Q: Does Meditation produce an altered state of consciousness?

A: Meditation does not produce an altered state of consciousness. There is no concrete scientific proof of it. Some people tried hallucinogenic or psychedelic plants to experience altered state of consciousness. These psychedelics only cause euphoria which they call it as altered state of consciousness.

Q: Do we achieve ecstasy through meditation?

A: Meditation is not a matter of trying to achieve ecstasy, spiritual bliss, or tranquility. It is simply the creation of a space in which we can expose and undo our neurotic games, our self-deception, our hidden fears, and hopes. So, meditation is a way of churning out the neuroses of mind and using them as part of our practice.

Q: Do we control our mind in Meditation?

In meditation practice, we neither hold the mind very tightly nor let it go completely. If we try to control the mind, then its energy will rebound back to us. If we let the mind go completely, then it will become very wild and chaotic. So, we let the mind go but there is some discipline involved. Precisely being in the moment, neither suppressing nor wildly letting go, but being exactly aware of what you are. The mind is so complicated, so exotic craving all sorts of entertainment constantly, the only way to deal with it is to channel it into a disciplined path without sidetracks.

Q. Can I get spiritual power through meditation?

A. No sir, you cannot. Some people have misconception of practicing spiritual meditation. They think, meditation is to acquire *superpowers* such as, the ability to heal people, knowledge of past lives, visions of the future, levitation etc. and so on. It is nothing like that. However, there are cons Gurus who will promise almost anything to people as long as they follow them or donate money to their communes. Meditation is to achieve spiritual awareness which starts with being honest and kind, and with our commitment to becoming the best human being we can be. Gentle appreciation of the present moment and an outlook of compassion towards all human beings are the real signs of spiritual awakening.

Q. What is spiritual awakening?

A. It is the dissolving of the illusion that you are separate from oneness. Expansion of consciousness in a new realm. When you have the feeling of oneness with God, you are spiritually awakened. Spiritual awakening is a kind of flowering of consciousness. When consciousness expands and opens into a new expression, it is called a spiritual awakening. Very nicely explained by an Indian mystic Nissargadatta, "There are some steps to self-realization. There is nothing gradual about it. It happens suddenly and is irrevocably. You rotate in a new dimension, seen from which the previous ones are mere abstractions. Just like on sunrise you see things as they are, so on self-realization you see everything as it is. The world of illusion is left behind."

Q. What is spiritual meditation?

A. Spiritual meditation is the mindful practice of connection to something that is greater, vaster, and deeper than the individual self. The path to that connection passes through honest self-reflection. Mindful practice is not limited to any particular faith or religion – anyone can follow a guided spiritual meditation. The blessings of spiritual meditation have a ripple effect: as our awareness and spiritual confidence increase, so do our desire and ability to be of benefit to others.

Q. What is spiritual Transformation?

A. Spiritual transformation refers primarily to a fundamental change in the place of the sacred or the character of the sacred as an object of significance in life, and secondarily to a fundamental change in the pathways the individual takes to the sacred.

Q. What happens during Spiritual Transformation?

A. When going through a spiritual transformation, one begins to question the traditional rules and beliefs that one grew up with. For example, one may begin to question their own religious or spiritual beliefs and seek for confirmation or a deeper understanding.

Q. What are the signs of Spiritual Transformation (ST)?

A. A person in the ST starts realizing his negative thoughts and emotional reactions to certain events and circumstances and tries to find the solution whereas a common person accepts these as a way of life or his karmas theory.

Q. What are the signs of a spiritual person?

An ST person does not have interest in gossip or drama and materialistic comforts such as going to resorts, parties, fun and frolics. He is more inclined to learn about self-realization. He likes to be in a more quiet and peaceful environments and can spend lots of time alone without feeling lonely. He has no attraction for external world and is more focused on to diving deeper into himself. The noise of the world becomes more of a distraction. Solitude becomes more attractive, and he feels spending a lot of time alone "lonely" at all. He is attached more towards nature and its silent beauty. His desire for freedom becomes stronger. He wants to be independent in his views instead of a being a follower. People going through a spiritual transformation often have an intuitive sense that something wonderful is waiting for them just outside of their comfort zone. He starts questioning everything about certain myths and religions. He tries to seek confirmation or a deeper understanding of religion or spiritual beliefs. He asks more and more questions, there is no end to these. Negativity and violence become less enticing and more repulsive to him. An especially important sign is sometimes he can enter deep depressions which have no apparent reason that are followed by periods of unexpected happiness and inner peace.

He has no fears. Fearlessness is the first sign of a **spiritual person** which is not easy to attain.

The person sees things as they are. ...
*Does not speak ill of others or gossip. ...
* Is loving and kind. ... does not hate anyone.
*Believes that the soul is eternal. ...
*Meditates regularly....
*Feels his life has a purpose. ...
*Takes care of his mental and physical health.
*Speaks the truth. Compassionate and kind to others.
*Does not hurt people by his words and is rather kind, helpful to the needy.

Q. Some people talk about seeing the "White Light" during? meditation. Is it enlightenment?
A. You might have heard stories about people who say they see a white light or feel like they are flying as a free spirit when they meditate. Although this might be an experiential side effect of meditation, seeking such experiences is unhelpful. You would be frustrated when you did not get the experience you were hoping for. Meditate and let everything else take its natural course.

Q. Is Meditation a therapy?
Mediation is for healing and nourishing. However, if someone is facing health problems and seeking help, meditation might not offer the support. They need to see a therapist.

Q. What is nonattachment in meditation?

Non-attachment is very essential in meditation. It is the skill of taking a step back from whatever happens, or whatever we feel, acknowledging that it is transient, and accepting that it will soon change and transform. This quality of non-attachment is important, as it helps us to get rid of the "drama" of life and to remain calm and peaceful. Since we have no control on inevitability, we must cooperate with the circumstances. However, such non-attachment does not mean avoiding, repressing, or disregarding anything. We should not detach ourselves from the people, relatives, friends and activities we love and enjoy, nor should we become passive or inactive. Non-attachment simply changes the quality of the relationship with life.

Q Can meditation cause seizures?

It is rare, but some reports are in the literature causing seizures. It can be due to preexisting conditions. It can be due to certain mental problems or related illness. Meditation for twenty minutes will not cause epilepsy. Long retreats can create problems that are possibly due to preexisting illness.

Q. What is Karma?

A. It is a Sanskrit word, meaning, *action,* originated from Hinduism and Buddhism. It can be summarized as the sum of a person's actions in this and previous states of existence, viewed as deciding their fate in future existences.

Q. What is the difference between Mukti and Moksha?

Mukti: In Mukti, there is no desires or expectations in life. It is a state where a person is no more attached to emotions like anger, happiness, sadness, love, greed. Also, where one is not attached with any of the relationship may be father, mother, son, daughter, wife, friends etc. A State where there is no attachment with materialistic things.

Moksha: Moksha is getting released or liberated from 'samsara'. Samsara is a cycle of birth and death, rebirth, and death. This birth and death cycle will continue until one's karmas are not dissolved. Karmas done in past life is the main reason for the rebirth. So, the "purpose of life" is to complete karmic cycle of past life.

Q. When will I complete this life Karma?
A. In your next life. This continues for a long time. The day when you dissolve all your karmas there is no need of your rebirth forever. This state is called moksha.

Q How are Mukti and Mokksh related?
A. Mukthi and Moksha relation· Now if you are in a state of mukthi there are very less chances that you do a lot of actions or karma so automatically your previous karmas get drained and new karmas will not come back. It is obvious that at one point of time you will reach moksha.

Q. Do Meditators require to practice Celibacy?
A. Not really. It all depends upon an individual.

Q. Can we obtain Salvation through Sex?
A. Osho has written a book "From Sex to Super Consciousness." He had elaborated in a better way.

Q Is Meditation Safe?
When practiced daily for a limited period, meditation is safe for healthy people. Herbert Benson, a cardiologist who founded the *Relaxation Response*, studied meditation for many years and stated that he had seen no unfavorable side effects when people practiced 20-30 minutes two times a day.

"There are things known and there are things unknown, and in between are the doors of perception."
— *Aldous Huxley*

References

Alidina S (2010) "Mindfulness for Dummies." Tantor Media Inc. CT.

Arias AJ, Steinberg K, Banga A, Trestman RL (2006) Systematic review of the efficacy of meditation techniques as treatments for medical illness. *Altern Complement Med* **12**(8):817-32.

Arruda JM, Bogetz AL, Vellanki S, Wren A, Yeh AM (2018) Yoga as adjunct therapy for adolescents with inflammatory bowel disease: A pilot clinical trial. *Complement Thera Med* **41**:99-104.

Asda Good living (2016) Mindfulness meditation could be the answer to losing weight. - Asda *Good Living*, 29 March.

Ashley-Farrand T (1999) Healing Mantras: Using Sound Affirmations for Personal Power. *Creativity and Healing*. Ballantine Wellspring. The Ballantine publishing Group, NY.

Aubrey A (2008) To Lower Blood Pressure, Open Up and Say *'Om':* NPR, August 21, 12:43 AM ET, Heard on Morning Edition.

Baijal S, Narayanan S (2010) Theta activity and meditative states: spectral changes during concentrative meditation. *Cognitive Processing* **11**(1):31-38.

Bakalar N (2006) Regimens: High Blood Pressure? Meditation May Help, *New York Times*, June 13.

Ball EF, Sharizan ENSM, Franklin G, Rogozińska E (2017) Does mindfulness meditation improve chronic pain? A systematic review. *Curr Opin Obstet* Gynecol **29**(6):359-366.

Ball J, Carry J, Mitchel P (2007) Mindfulness Meditation and Bipolar Disorder Chapter 3, in "Innovation and advances in Cognitive Behavior Therapy", ed Einstein DA, Australia Academic Press, Australia.

Bansal A, Mittal A, and Seth V (2016) Osho Dynamic Meditation's Effect on Serum Cortisol Level. *J Clin Diagn Res* **10**(11):05-08.

Benson H, and Proctor W (2010) "Relaxation Revolution," Simon and Schuster, Inc., NY.

Bernardi L·Sleight P, Bandinelli G, Cencetti S, Fattorini L, Wdowczyc-Szulc J, Lagi A (2001) Effect of rosary prayer and yoga mantras on autonomic cardiovascular rhythms: comparative study. *BMJ* **323**(7327):1446-9.

Berrill JW, Sadlier M· Hood K· Green JT (2014) Mindfulness-based therapy for inflammatory bowel disease patients with functional abdominal symptoms or high perceived stress levels. *Crohns Colitis* **8**(9):945-55.

Biegler KA, Chaoul MA, Cohen L (2009) Cancer, cognitive impairment, and meditation, *Acta Oncol* **48**(1):18-26.

Blom K, Baker B, How H, Dai M, Irvine J, Abbey S, Abramson BL, Myers MG, Kiss A, Perkins NJ, Tobe SW (2014) Hypertension analysis of stress reduction using mindfulness meditation and yoga: results from the harmony randomized controlled trial. *Am J Hypertens* **27**(1):122-9.

Booth R (2014) Mindfulness therapy comes at a high price for some, say experts. *Mental Health*, August 25.

Bossio JA, Basson R, Driscoli M, Correia S, Brotto L (2018) Mindfulness-Based Group Therapy for Men with Situational Erectile

Dysfunction: A Mixed-Methods Feasibility Analysis and Pilot Study. *J Sex Med* **15:**1478.

Bounous G, and Molson JH (2003) The Antioxidant System. *Anticancer Res* **23**(2B):1411-5.

Bowen S, Witkiewitz K, Dillworth TM, Chawla N, Simpson TL, Ostafin BD, Larimer ME, Blume AW, Parks GA, Marlatt GA (2006) Mindfulness meditation and substance use in an incarcerated population. *Psychol Addict Behav* **20**(3):343-7.

Brady B, and Stevens L (2000) Binaural-beat induced theta EEG activity and hypnotic susceptibility. *American Journal of Clinical Hypnosis* **43**(1):53-69.

Brand S, Holsboer-Trachsler E, Naranjo JR, Schmidt S (2012) Influence of mindfulness practice on cortisol and sleep in long-term and short-term meditators. *Neuropsychobiology* **65** (3):109-18.

Bränström R, Kvillemo P, Akersted T (2013) Effects of mindfulness training on levels of cortisol in cancer patients. *Psychosomatics* **54**(2):158-64.

Brash D (2014) A recent study finds that meditation can be neuro therapeutic. *Psychology today* Posted Jan 11.

Brenner J, LeBlang S, Lizotte-Waniewski M, Schmidt B, Espinosa PS, DeMets DL, Newberg A, Hennekens CH (2020) Mindfulness with paced breathing reduces blood pressure. *Medical Hypotheses* **142**:109780.

Brotto LA (2013) Mindful Sex, *Canadian J Human Sexuality* **22**(2): 63-68.

Brotto LA (2018) "Better Sex Through Mindfulness," Greystone Books, Vancouver. Canada.

Brotto LA, Basson R (2014) Group Mindfulness-Based Therapy Significantly Improves Sexual Desire in Women. *Behavior Research and Therapy* **57**:43.

Brotto LA, Basson R, Luria M (2008) A Mindfulness-Based Group Psychoeducational Intervention Targeting Sexual Arousal Disorder in Women. *J Sex Med* **5**(7):1646-59.

Brotto LA, Chivers ML, Millman RD, Albert A (2016) Mindfulness-Based Sex Therapy Improves Genital-Subjective Arousal Concordance in Women with Sexual Desire/Arousal Difficulties. *Archiv Sex Behav* **45**(8):1907-1921.

Brotto LA, Seal BN, Rellini A (2012) Pilot Study of a Brief Cognitive Behavioral Versus Mindfulness-Based Intervention for Women with Sexual Distress and a History of Childhood Sexual Abuse. *J Sex Marital Ther* **38**(1): 1-27.

Cahn BR, Goodman MS, Peterson CT, Maturi R, Mills PJ (2017) Yoga, Meditation and Mind-Body Health: Increased BDNF, Cortisol Awakening Response, and Altered Inflammatory Marker Expression after a 3-Month Yoga and Meditation Retreat. *Front. Hum. Neurosci* **11**:315.

Cameron D (2014) Medical School geneticist David Sinclair has been named by Time magazine as one of the 100 most influential people in the world. *Time magazine* July 2014.

Camilleri GM, Méjean C, Bellisle F, Andreeva VA, Kesse-Guyot E, Hercberg S, Péneau S (2016) Intuitive eating is inversely associated with body weight status in the general population-based NutriNet-Santé study. *Obesity* (Silver Spring) **24** (5):1154-61

Camilleri GM, Méjean C, Bellisle F, Hercberg S, and Péneau S (2015) Association between Mindfulness and Weight Status in a

General Population from the NutriNet-Santé Study. *PLoS One.* **10**(6): e0127447

Carim-Todd L, Mitchell SH, Oken BS (2013) Mind-body practices: an alternative, drug-free treatment for smoking cessation? A systematic review of the literature *Drug Alcohol Depend* **132**(3):399-410.

Carlson LE, Beattie TL, Giese-Davis J, Faris P, Tamagawa R, Fick LJ, Degelman ES, Speca M. (2014) Mindfulness-based cancer recovery and supportive-expressive therapy maintain telomerase length relative controls to distressed breast cancer survivors. *Cancer* **121**(3): 476-484.

Castleman M (2019) Mindfulness Meditation Helps Resolve Many Sex Problems. *Psychology Today,* posted May 01.

Chadwick P, Kaur H, Swelam M, Ross S, Ellett L (2011) Experience of mindfulness in people with bipolar disorder: A qualitative study. *Psychotherapy Research* **21** (3):277-285.

Chaieb L, Wilpert EC, Reber TP, Fell J (2015) Auditory beat stimulation and its effects on cognition and mood states. *Front Psychiatry* **6**:70.

Conger K (2009) Scientists discover new mechanism behind aging in mice. *Stanford Report* January 14.

Cooper R, Joffe BI, Lamprey JM, Botha A, Shires R, Baker SG, H C Seftel (1985) Hormonal and biochemical responses to transcendental meditation. *Postgrad Med J* **61**(714):301-4.

Cramer H, Rabsilber S, Lauche R, Kümmel S, Dobos G, Cramer H, *et al.* (2015) Yoga and meditation for menopausal symptoms in breast cancer 6: survivors-A randomized controlled trial. *Cancer* **121**(13):2175-84.

Crescentini C, Matiz A, Cimenti M, Pascoli E, Eleopra R, Fabbro F (2018) Effect of Mindfulness Meditation on Personality and Psychological Well-being in Patients with Multiple Sclerosis. *Int J MS Care* **20**(3):101-108,

Dada T, Ramesh P, Shakrawal J (2020) Meditation: A Polypill for Comprehensive Management of Glaucoma Patients. *J. Glaucoma* **29**:133-140.

Dascalu L, Brotto LA (2018) Sexual Functioning in Experienced Meditators. *J Sex Marital Ther* **44**(5):459-467.

Davidson R, Lutz A (2008) Buddha's Brain: Neuroplasticity and Meditation. *Signal Processing Magazine* **25**(1):176-174.

Davidson RJ, Kabat-Zinn J, Schumacher J, Rosenkranz M, Daniel M, Santorelli, SF, Urbanowski F, Harrington A, Bonus K, Sheridan, JF (2003) Alterations in Brain and ImmuneFunction Produced by Mindfulness Meditation. *Psychosomatic Medicine* **65** (4) 564-570.

Demarin V, Bedeković MR, Puretić MB, Pašić MB (2016) Arts, Brain and Cognition. *Psychiatr Danub* **28**(4):343-348.

Desai R, Tailor A, Tanvi Bhatt T (2015) Effects of yoga on brain waves and structural activation: A review. *Complement Ther Clin Prac* **21:**112-8.

Desbordes GL, T Negi, Thaddeus W, *et al.* (2012) Effects of Mindful-attention and Compassion Meditation Training on Amygdala Response to Emotional Stimuli in an Ordinary, Non-meditative State. *Frontiers Human Neuroscience* **6**:292.

Dowson G (2011) Mental Health and Intensive Retreats, Psych, the bulletin of the Australian Psychological Society Ltd, April 24. https://zensydney.com/Mental-Health-and-Intensive-Meditation-Retreats.

Dunlop J (2015) Meditation, stress relief, and well-being. *Radiol Technol* **86**(5):535-55.

Dusek JA, Hibberd PL, Buczynski B, Chang B, Dusek KC, Johnston JM, Wohlhueter AL, Benson H, Zusman RM (2008) Stress management versus lifestyle modification on systolic hypertension and medication elimination: a randomized trial. *J Altern Complement Med* **14**(2):129-38.

Elias AN, Wilson AF (1995) Serum hormonal concentrations following transcendental meditation--potential role of gamma aminobutyric acid. *Med Hypotheses* **44**(4):287-91.

Ellingsen (2010) Brain waves and Meditation, *ScienceDaily,* March 31.

Epel E, Daubenmier J, Moskowitz JT, Folkman S, Blackburn E (2009) Can Meditation Slow Rate of Cellular Aging? Cognitive Stress, Mindfulness, and Telomeres. *Annals New York Academy Sciences.* **1172**:3453.

Epstein MD, and Lieff JD (1981) Psychiatric complications of meditation practice. *J Transper psychol* **13**:137-147.

Ford AC, Moayyedi P, Lacy BE, *et al.* (2014) American College of Gastroenterology monograph on the management of irritable bowel syndrome and chronic idiopathic constipation. *Am J Gastroenterol* **109** (1): S2-S26.

Foreman J (2003) A look at Science Behind Meditation. *The Boston Globe*, April 22.

Galantino ML(2019) Tiger R, Brooks J, Jang S, Wilson K, Impact of Somatic Yoga and Meditation on Fall Risk, Function, and Quality of Life for Chemotherapy-Induced Peripheral Neuropathy Syndrome in Cancer Survivors. *Integr Cancer Ther* **18**:1534735419850627.

Garden M (2007) Can meditation be bad. *The September, The Humanist.com*

Garden M (2003) "The Serpent Rising, A journey of Spiritual Seduction," Sid Harta Publishers, Victoria, Australia.

Gaylord SA, Palsson OS, Garland EL, *et al.* (2011) Mindfulness training reduces the severity of irritable bowel syndrome in women: results of a randomized controlled trial. *Am J Gastroenterol* **106**(9):1678-1688.

Gerbarg PL, Jacob VE, Stevens L, Bosworth BP, Chabouni F, DeFilippis EM, Warren R, Trivellas M, Patel PV, Webb CD, Harbus MD, Christos PJ, Brown RP, Scherl EJ (2015) The Effect of Breathing, Movement, and Meditation on Psychological and Physical Symptoms and Inflammatory Biomarkers in Inflammatory Bowel Disease: A Randomized Controlled Trial. *Inflamm Bowel Dis* **21**(12):2886-96.

Glaser JL, Brind JL, Vogelman JH, Eisner MJ, Dillbeck MC, Wallace RK, Chopra D, Orentreich N (1992) Elevated serum dehydroepiandrosterone sulfate levels in practitioners of the Transcendental Meditation (TM) and TM-Sidhi programs. *J Behav Med* **15**(4):327-41.

Goldstein KM, Shepherd-Banigan M, Coeytaux RR, McDuffie JR, Adam S, Befus D, Goode AP, Kosinski AS, Masilamani V, Williams JW Jr. (2017) Use of mindfulness, Goldstein meditation and relaxation to treat vasomotor symptoms. *Climacteric* **20**(2):178-182.

Goldstein RZ, Volkow ND (2002) Drug addiction and its underlying neurobiological basis: neuroimaging evidence for the involvement of the frontal cortex. *Am J Psychiatry* **159**(10):1642-52.

Golechha GR, Sethi IG, Deshpande M, Rani U (1991) Agnihotra in the treatment of alcoholism *Indian J Psychiatry* **33**(1):20-6.

Goodman MJ, Schorling JB (2012) A mindfulness course decreases burnout and improves well-being among healthcare providers. *Int J Psychiatry Med* **43**(2):119-28.

Gordon WV, Shonin E, Griffiths MD (2016) Meditation Awareness Training for the Treatment of Sex Addiction: A Case Study. *J Behav Addict* **5**(2):363-72.

Grossman P, Kappos L, Gensicke H, D'Souza M, Mohr DC, Penner IK, Steiner C (2010) MS quality of life, depression, and fatigue improve after mindfulness training: a randomized trial. *Neurology* **75**(13):141-9.

Gryffin PA, Chen WC (2013) Implications of t'ai chi for smoking cessation. *J Altern Complement Med* **9**(2):141-5.

Gutman J (2019) "The Comprehensive Guide to Glutathione." GSH Books Inc., 5th ed. Canada.

Hairston KG, Vitolins MZ, Norris JM, Anderson AM, Hanley AJ, Wagenknecht LE (2012) Lifestyle factors and 5-year abdominal fat accumulation in a minority cohort: the IRAS Family Study. *Obesity* (Silver Spring) **20**(2):421-7.

Harrison P. 9Meditation Side Effects: Excerpts on What You Need to Know (*thedailymeditation.com*)

Harte JL, Eifert GH, Smith R (1995) The effects of running and meditation on beta-endorphin, corticotropin-releasing hormone and cortisol in plasma, and on mood. *Biological Psychology* **40** (3):251-265.

Harvard Health (2013) Meditation offers significant heart benefits. August .

Harvard Health (2018) Mindfulness can improve heart health. Feb 18.

Hilton L, Hempel S, Ewing BA, Apaydin E, Xenakis L, Newberry S, Colaiaco B, Maher AR, Shanman RM, Sorbero ME, Maglione MA (2017) Mindfulness Meditation for Chronic Pain: Systematic Review and Meta-analysis. *Ann Behav Med* **51**(2):199–213.

Hoffman L, Hutt R, Tsui Y, Zorokong K, Marfeo E (2020) Meditation-Based Interventions for Adults with Dementia: A Scoping Review, *Am J Occup Ther* **74**(3): 7403205010p.

Hoge EA, Chen MM, Orr E, Metcalf CA, Fischer LE, Pollack MH, Vivo ID, Simon NM (2013) Loving-Kindness Meditation practice associated with longer telomeres in women. *Brain Behav Immun* **32**:159-63.

HuffPost (2012) Chronic Pain Affects 47 Percent of U.S. Adults,

Hughes J, Fresco DA, Myerscough R, Dulmen MHM, Carlson LE, Josephson R (2013) Randomized controlled trial of mindfulness-based stress reduction for prehypertension *Psychosom Med* **75**(8):721-8.

Hyman M (2011) Glutathione: The Mother of All Antioxidants, *Huffington Post* 06/10/2010.

Jacobs TL, Epel ES, Lin J, Blackburn EH, Wolkowitz OM, Bridwell DA, Zanesco AP, Aichele SR, Sahdra BK, MacLean KA, King BG, Shaver PR, Rosenberg EL, Ferrer E, Wallace BA, Saron CD (2011) Intensive meditation training, immune cell telomerase activity, and psychological meditators, *Psychoneuroloendocrinology* **36**(5): 664-681.

Jacobs TL, Shaver PR, Epel ES, Zanesco AP, Aichele SR, Bridwell, DA, Rosenberg EL, King BG, Maclean KA, Sahdra BK, Kemeny, ME, Wallace, BA, Saron, CD (2013) Self-reported mindfulness and cortisol during a Shamatha meditation retreat, *Health Psychol* **32**(10):1104-9.

Jaderek I, Lew-Starowicz M (2019) A Systematic Review on Mindfulness Meditation-Based Interventions for Sexual Dysfunctions. *J Sex Med* **16**:1581-1596.

Janeyoga (2010) Benefits of Chanting: Yoga of Sound leads to positive effects. Janeyoga.com

Jaseja H (2005) Meditation may predispose to epilepsy: an insight into the alteration in brain environment induced by meditation. *Med Hypotheses* **64**(3):464-7.

Jayadevappa R, Johnson JC, Bloom BS, Nidich S, Desai S, Chhatre S, Raziano DB, Schneider R, (2007) Effectiveness of transcendental meditation on functional capacity and quality of life of African Americans with congestive heart failure: a randomized control study. *Ethn Dis* **17**(1):72-7.

Johnston BC, Kanters S, Bandayrel K *et al.* (2014) Comparison of Weight Loss Among Named Diet Programs in Overweight and Obese Adults: A Meta-analysis. *JAMA* **312**(9):923-933.

Kaliman P, Alvarez-Lopez MJ, Cosin-Tomas M, Rosenkranz MA, Lutz A, Davidson R (2014) Rapid changes in histone deacetylases and inflammatory gene expression in expert meditators. *Psychoneuroendocrinology* **40**:96-107.

Katie A. Posted on Support Network Blog, Jeff Breece – As FDR Said, "There is Nothing to Fear Except Fear Itself." June 13, 2016, 8:24am EST.

Keefer L, Blanchard EB (2002) A one year follow-up of relaxation response meditation as a treatment for irritable bowel syndrome *Behav Res Ther* **40**(5):541-6.

Kemper KJ, Powell D, Helms CC (2015) Loving-Kindness Meditation's Effects on Nitric Oxide and Perceived Well-being: A

Pilot Study in Experienced and Inexperienced Meditators. *Explore* (NY) **11**(1):32-9.

Khalsa DK (2015) Meditation, and Alzheimer's Disease Prevention: Where the Evidence Stands, *J Alzheimer's Dis* **48**(1):1-12.

Khalsa DS, Daniel AD, Hanks C, Money N, Newberg A (2009) Cerebral blood flow changes during chanting meditation. *Nucl Med Commun* **30**(12):956-61.

Khanna S, Greeson JM (2013) A narrative review of yoga and mindfulness as complementary therapies for addiction. *Complement Ther Med* **21**(3):244-52.

Kim DH, Moon YS, Kim HS, Jung JS, Park HM, Suh HW, Kim YH, Song DK (2005*)*

Effect of Zen Meditation on serum nitric oxide activity and lipid peroxidation. *Prog Neuropsychopharmacol Biol Psychiatry.* **29**(2):327-31

Kjaer TW, Bertelsen C, Piccini P, Brooks D, Alving J, Lou HC (2002) Increased dopamine tone during meditation-induced change of consciousness. *Brain Res Cogn Brain Res* **13**(2):255-9.

Kristeller JL, Hallett CB (1999) An Exploratory Study of a Meditation-Based Intervention for Binge Eating Disorder. *J Health Psychol* **4** (3):357-363.

Krittanawong C, Kumar A, Wang Z, Narasimhan B, Jneid H, Virani SS, Levine GN. (2020) Meditation and Cardiovascular Health in US. *Am J. Cardiol* **131**:23-2.

Kuijpers HJH, Heijden FMMA, Tuiner S, Verhoeven WMM (2007) Meditation- Induced Psychosis. *Psychopathology* **40**:461-464.

Kumar K, Kumar D, Singh V, Pandey M, Divya PT (2018) Role of yoga and meditation on serum DHEAS level in first year medical students. *Inter J Research Med Sciences* **6**(3).

Kumar R, Kumar A, Sardhara J (2018) Pineal Gland—A Spiritual Third Eye: An Odyssey of Antiquity to Modern Chronomedicine. *Indian J Neurosurg* **7**(1):1-4.

Kuo B, Bhasin M, Jacquart J, Scult MA, Slipp L, Riklin EIK, *et al.* (2015) Genomic and Clinical Effects Associated with a Relaxation Response Mind-Body Intervention in Patients with Irritable Bowel Syndrome and Inflammatory Bowel Disease. *PLoS One* **10**(4): e0123861.

Kurth F, Cherbuin N and Luders E (2017) Promising Links between Meditation and Reduced (Brain) Aging: An Attempt to Bridge Some Gaps between the Alleged Fountain of Youth and the Youth of the Field. *Front Psychol* 30 May.

Lagopoulos J, Xu J, Rasmussen I, Vik A, Malhi GS, Eliassen CF, Arntsen IE, Saether JG, Hollup S, Holen A, Davanger S, Ellingsen Ø. (2009) Increased theta and alpha EEG activity during nondirective meditation. *J Altern Complement Med* **15**(11): 1187-1192.

Lai HM, Liu MSY, Lin TJ, Tsai YL, Chien EJ (2017) Higher DHEAS Levels Associated with Long-Term Practicing of Tai Chi. *Chin J Physio* **60**(2):124-130.

Last N, Tufts E, Auger LE (2017) The Effects of Meditation on Grey Matter Atrophy and Neurodegeneration: A Systematic Review. *J. Alzheimer's Dis* **56***(1):*275-86.

Laures-Gore J, Marshall RS (2016) Mindfulness meditation in aphasia: A case report. *NeuroRehabilitation* **38**(4):321-9.

Lawrence M, Celestino Junior FT, Matozinho HH, Govan L, Booth J, Beecher J, (2017) Yoga for Stroke, Rehabilitation. *Cochrane Database Syst Rev* **12**(12):CD011483.

Lazar S, Kerr C, Wasserman R, Gray J, *et al.* (2005) Meditation experience is associated with increased cortical thickness. *Neuroreport* **16**(17):1893-1897.

Levine GN, Lange RA, Bairey-Merz CN, Davidson RJ, Jamerson K, Mehta PK, Michos ED, Norris K, Ray IB, Saban KL, Shah T, Stein R, Smith SC Jr. (2017) Meditation and Cardiovascular Risk Reduction: A Scientific Statement from the American Heart Association. *J Am Heart Assoc* **6** (10), 117.

Linderburg S (2019) Stress and Weight Gain: Understanding the Connection. *Healthline*, November.

Lindsay EK, Young S, Warren Brown K, Joshua M Smyth JM, Creswell J (2019) Mindfulness training reduces loneliness and increases social contact in a randomized controlled trial. *Proc Natl Acad Sci USA* **116**(9):3488-3493.

Ljótsson B, Andréewitch S, Hedman E, Rück C, Andersson G, Lindefors N (2010) Exposure and mindfulness based therapy for irritable bowel syndrome--an open pilot study. *J Behav Ther Exp Psychiatry* **41**(3):185-90

Ljótsson B, Hedman E, Lindfors P, Hursti T, Lindefors N, Andersson G, Rück C (2011) Long-term follow-up of internet-delivered exposure and mindfulness based treatment for irritable bowel syndrome. *Behav Res Ther* **49**(1):58-61.

Lomas T, Cartwright T, Edginton T, Ridge D (2015) A Qualitative Analysis of Experiential Challenges Associated with Meditation Practice. *Mindfulness* **6**:848–860.

Longo VD, Antebi A, Bartke A, Barzilai N, Brown-Borg HM, Caruso C, Curiel TJ, de Cabo R, Franceschi C, Gems D, Ingram DK, Johnson TE, Kennedy BK, Kenyon C, Klein S, Kopchick JJ, Loucks EB, Britton WB, Howe CJ, Gutman R, Gilman SE, Brewer J, Eaton CB, Buka SL (2016) Associations of Dispositional Mindfulness with Obesity and Central Adiposity: the New England Family Study. *International J Behavioral Medicine* **23**:224–233.

Luders E· Phillips OR, Clark K, Kurth F, Toga AW, Narr KL (2012) Bridging the hemispheres in meditation: thicker callosal regions and enhanced fractional anisotropy (FA) in long-term practitioners. *Neuroimage* **61**(1):181-7.

Lustyk MK, Chawla N, Roger S. Nolan RS, Marlatt Ga (2009) Mindful Meditation Research: Issues of Participant Screening Safety Procedures, and Research Training. *Advan mind-body Med* **24**(1): 20-30.

Maglione MA· Maher AR· Ewing B, Colaiaco B, Newberry S, Kandrack R· Shanman RM· Sorbero ME, Hempel S (2017) Efficacy of mindfulness meditation for smoking cessation: A systematic review and meta-analysis. *Addict Behav* **69**:27-34.

Mahagita C (2010) Roles of meditation on alleviation of oxidative stress and improvement of antioxidant system. *J Med Assoc Thai* **93** (6): S242-54.

Malaktaris A, Lang AJ, Casmar P, Baca S, Hurst S, Jeste DV, Palmer BW (2020) Pilot Study of Compassion Meditation Training to Improve Well-being Among Older Adults. *Clin Gerontol* **12**:1-14.

Mann CC (2011), "The Birth of Religion," *National Geography.* **216** (6):34.

Mantzios M, and Egan HM (2020), New Research Examines Whether Mindfulness Can Help Tackle Obesity,

Psychreg :07 October 2020, https://medicalxpress.com/news/2020-10-mindfulness-tackle-obesity.

Márquez PHP, Feliu-Soler A, José Solé-Villa M, Matas-Pericas L, Filella-Agullo D, Ruiz-Herrerias M, Soler-Ribaudi J, Coll AR, Antonio Arroyo-Díaz J (2019) Benefits of mindfulness meditation in reducing blood pressure and stress in patients with arterial hypertension. *J Hum Hypertens Mar* **33**(3):237-247.

Marshall RS, Laures-Gore J, Love K (2018) Brief mindfulness meditation group training in aphasia: exploring attention, language and psychophysiological outcomes. *Int J Lang Commun Disord* **53**(1):40-54.

Massion AO, Teas J, Hebert JR, Wertheimer MD, Kabat-Zinn J (1995) Meditation, melatonin and breast/prostate cancer: Hypothesis and preliminary data. *Med Hypotheses* **44**(1):39-46.

Morris EL (2001) The relationship of Spirituality to Coronary Heart Disease. *Altern Therp Health Med* **7**(5): 96-8.

Muthukrishnan S, Jain R, Kohli S, Batra S (2016) Effect of mindfulness meditation on perceived stress scores and autonomic function tests of pregnant Indian women. *J Clin Diagn Res* **10**(4).

Nagendra RP, Maruthai N, Kutty BM (2012) Meditation and its regulatory role on sleep. *Front Neurol* **3**:54.

Narendran S, Nagarathna R, Narendran V, Gunasheela S, *et al.*(2005) Efficacy of Yoga on Pregnancy Outcome. *J Altern Complement Med* **11**(2).

Newburg A (2010) "Principles of Neurotheology." Ashgate Publishing, UK.

Nidich SI, Rainforth MV, Haaga DA, Hagelin J, Salerno JW, Travis F, Tanner M, Gaylord-King C, Grosswald S, Schneider RH (2009) A randomized controlled trial on effects of the Transcendental Meditation program on blood pressure, psychological distress, and coping in young adults. *Am J Hypertens* **22**(12):1326-31.

Orenstein E, Basilakos A, Marshall RS (2012) Effects of mindfulness meditation on three individuals with aphasia. *Int J Lang Commun Disord* **47**(6):673-84.

Orme-Johnson D (2006) Evidence that the Transcendental Meditation program prevents or decreases diseases of the nervous system and is specifically beneficial for epilepsy. *Med Hypotheses* **67**(2):240-6.

Oscar AG (2010) Loneliness Among Older Adults: A National Survey of Adults 45+.Washington, DC: AARP Research.September2010. https://doi.org/10.26419/res.00064.001

Ott MJ, Norris RL, Bauer-Wu SM (2006) Mindfulness meditation for oncology patients: a discussion and critical review. *Integr Cancer Ther* **5**(2):98-108.

Pace WW, Negi LT, Adame DD, Cole SP, Brown TD, Sivilli TI, Issae MJ, Raisona CL (2009) Effect of compassion meditation on neuroendocrine, innate immune and behavioral responses to psychosocial stress. *Psychoneuroendocrinology* **34**(1):87-98.

Pagnoni G, Cekic M (2007) Age effects on gray matter volume and attentional performance in Zen meditation. *Neurobiology of aging* **28** (10):1623-1627.

Pandya SP *(2019)* Meditation for treating adults with bipolar disorder II: A multi-city study. *Clin Psychol Psychother* **26**(2):252-261.

Paul-Labrador M Polk D, Dwyer HJ, Velasquez I, Nidich S, Rainforth M, Schneider R, Noel C, Merz B (2006) Effects of a randomized controlled trial of transcendental meditation on components of the metabolic syndrome in subjects with coronary heart disease. *Arch Intern Med* **166**(11):1218-24.

Perich T, Manicavasagar V, Mitchell PB, Ball IR (2013) The association between meditation practice and treatment outcome in Mindfulness-based Cognitive Therapy for bipolar disorder. *Behavior Research and Therapy* **51**:338: e343

Perreau-Linck E, Beauregard M, Gravel P, *et al* (2007) In vivo measurements of brain trapping of α-[^{11}C]methyl-L-tryptophan during acute changes in mood states. *J Psychiatry Neurosci* **32**:430-4.

Perreau-Linck, E *et al.* (2004) "Serotonin Metabolism During Self-Induced Sadness and Happiness in Professional Actors," program 669.3 presented at the 34th annual meeting of the *Society for Neuroscience*, San Diego, Calif., October 23-27.

Pickert K (2014) The Mindful Revolution. *Time*, February 3.

Platt LM, Whitburn AI, Platt-Koch AG, Koch RL (2016) Nonpharmacological Alternatives to Benzodiazepine Drugs for the Treatment of Anxiety in Outpatient Populations: A Literature Review. *J Psychosoc Nurs Ment Health Serv* **54**(8):35-42.

PoChan K (2014) Prenatal Meditation Influences Infant behaviors *Infant Behavior and Development* **37**(4):556-561.

Pradhan B, Derle SM (2012) Comparison of effect of Gayatri Mantra and Poem Chanting on Digit Letter Substitution Task. *Anc Sci Life* **32**(2):89-92.

Pramanik T, Pudasaini, B and Prajapati, R (2010) Immediate effect of a slow pace breathing exercise *Bhramari pranayama* on blood pressure and heart rate. *Nepal Med Coll J* **12**(3): 154-157.

Rathore M, Abraham J (2018) Implication of Asana, Pranayama and Meditation on Telomere Stability. *Int J Yoga.* **11**(3):186-193.

Rogers KA, MacDonald MJ (2015) Therapeutic Yoga: Symptom Management for Multiple Sclerosis. *Altern Complement Med.* **21**(11):655-9.

Root S (2021) Can Meditation Heal Ulcerative Colitis & Crohn's Disease? *Stevenroot.com.*

Ross A (2016) Fight off Aging with Meditation, *Bodyandsoul.com. au* June 2016.

Roth B (2018) "Strength in Stillness: The Power of Transcendental Meditation" Simon and Schuster, NY.

Satyanarayana M, Rajeswari KR, Rani NJ, Krishna CS, Rao PV (1992) Effect of Santhi Kriya on certain psychophysiological parameters: a preliminary study. *Indian J Physiol Pharmacol*, **36**(2):88-92.

Schlosser M, Sparby T, Voros S, Jones R, Marchant NL (2019) Unpleasant meditation -related experiences in regular meditators: Prevalence, Predictors, and concepted considerations. *PLoS One* **14** (5) e0216643.

Schnaubelt S, Hammer A, Koller L, Niederdoeckl J, Kazem N, Spiel A, Niessner A, Sulzgruber P (2019) Meditation and cardiovascular Health: what is the link, *European Cardiology Review* **14**(3):161–4.

Schulte EM, Avena NM, Gearhard AN (2015) Which Foods May Be Addictive? The Roles of Processing, Fat Content, and Glycemic Load. *PLoS One* **10**(2) e0117959.

Schwartz JM, Gladding R (2012) You are not Your Brain. Avery, a member of Penguin Group (USA) inc.

Scott WC, Kaiser D, Othmer S, Sideroff SI (2005) Effects of an EEG biofeedback protocol on a mixed substance abusing population. *Am J Drug Alcohol Abuse* **31**(3):455-69.

Sharma P, Mahapatra A. Gupta R (2019) Meditation-induced psychosis: a narrative review and individual patient data analysis. *Ir J Psychol Med* Oct 31, pp. 1 – 7.

Shonin E, and Van Gordon W (2014) Mindfulness of Death. *Mindfulness,* doi: 10.1007/s12671-014-0290-6

Sinha S, Singh SN, Monga YP, and Ray US, Improvement of Glutathione and Total Antioxidant Status with Yoga. *J Altern Complement Medicine* **13**(10) 1085-90

Somersell AC, and Bounous G (1999) "Breakthrough in Cell-Defense." GOLDENeight Publishing.

Streeter CC, Jensen JE, Perlmutter RM, Cabral HJ, Tian H, Terhune DB, Ciraulo DA, Renshaw PF (2007)Yoga Asana sessions increase brain GABA levels: a pilot study. *J Altern Complement Med* **13**(4):419-26.

Streeter CC, Whitfield TH, Owen L, Rein T, Karri SK, Yakhkind A, Perlmutter R, Prescot A, Renshaw PF, Ciraulo DA, Jensen JE (2010) Effects of Yoga Versus Walking on Mood, Anxiety, and Brain GABA Levels: A Randomized Controlled MRS Study. *J Altern Complement Med* **16**(11):1145–1152.

Sudsuang R, Chentanez V, and Veluvan K (1991) Effect of Buddhist meditation on serum cortisol and total protein levels, blood pressure, pulse rate, lung volume and reaction time. *Physiology & Behavior* **50** (3):543-548.

Sui CK (2005) "SuperYoga," Institute for Inner Studies Publishing Foundation, Inc.; Quezon City, Philippines 1st edition..

Sung MK, Lee US, Ha NH, Koh E, Yang HJ (2020) A potential association of meditation with menopausal symptoms and blood chemistry in healthy women: A pilot cross-sectional study. *Medicine* (Baltimore) **99**(36): e22048.

Sunnen GV (1977) Meditative Treatment for Erectile Dysfunction, Love and Attraction, edited, Mark Cook & Glenn Wilson, Pergamon Press.

Szalavitz M (2013) Aaron Alexis and the Dark Side of Meditation. *Mental Health*, Sept 17,

Tang YY, Tang R, Posner MI (2013) Brief meditation training induces smoking reduction. *Proc Proc Natl Acad Sci USA* **110** (34):13971-5.

Tang YY, Hölzel BK, Posner M (2015) The neuroscience of mindfulness meditation *Nat Rev Neurosci* **16**(4):213-25.

Tang YY, Tang R, Rothbart MK, Posner MI (2019) Frontal theta activity and white matter plasticity following mindfulness meditation. *Curr Opin Pshycol 28:294-297.*

Tapper K (2018) Mindfulness and craving: effects and mechanisms. *Clin Psychol Rev* **59**:101-117.

Taren AA, Gianaros PJ, Greco CM, Lindsay EK, Fairgrieve A, Brown KW, Rosen RK, Ferris JL, Julson E, Marsland AL, BursleyAK, Ramsburg J, Creswell, JD (2015) Mindfulness meditation training alters stress-related amygdala resting state functional connectivity: a randomized controlled trial. *Soc Cogn Affect Neurosci* **10**(12):1758–1768.

Telles S, Nagarathna R, Nagendra HR (1995) Autonomic changes during "OM" meditation. *Indian J Physiol Pharmacol* **39**(4):418-20.

Thakur P, Mohammad A, Rastogi YR, Saini RV, Saini AK (2020) Yoga as an intervention to manage multiple sclerosis symptoms. *J Ayurveda Integr Med* (2):114-117.

Thimmapuram J, Pargament R, Bell T, Schurk H, Madhusudhan DK (2021) Heartfulness meditation improves loneliness and sleep in physicians and advance practice providers during COVID-19 pandemic. *Hosp Pract Mar* **17**:1-9.

Tolahunase M, Sagar R, and Dada R (2017) Impact of Yoga and Meditation on Cellular Aging in Apparently Healthy Individuals: A Prospective, Open-Label Single-Arm Exploratory Study, *Oxidative Medicine and Cellular Longevity*, Article ID 7928981, 9 pages

Tomasino B, Fregona S, Skrap M, Fabbro F (2013) Meditation-related activations are modulated by the practices needed to obtain it and by the expertise: an ALE meta-analysis study. *Front Hum Neurosci* **6**:346.

Tonob D, and Melby MK (2017) Broadening our perspectives on complementary and alternative medicine for menopause: A narrative review. *Maturitas.* **99**:79-85.

Tooley GA, Armstrong SM, Norman TR, Sali A (2000) Acute increases in night-time plasma melatonin levels following a period of meditation. *Biol Psychol* **53**(1):69-78.

Torkos S, and Waseff F (2003) "Breaking the Age Barrier" Penguin, Global.

Turakitwanakan W, Mekseepralard C, Busarakumtragul P (2013) Effects of Mindfulness Meditation on Serum Cortisol of Medical Students, *J Med Assoc Thai* **96** (1): S90-S95,

US Army Research (2018) Army study quantifies changes in stress after meditation, shows positive effects of mindfulness, Research Laboratory Public Affairs. June 27.

Vaze N, and Joshi S.J (2010) Yoga and Menopause Transition. *Midlife Health* (2):56-8.

Vella E (2019) Reducing stress and burnout in the public-sector work environment: A mindfulness meditation pilot study. *Health Promot J Austr* **30**(2):219-227.

Veronese N, Galvano D, D'Antiga F, Vecchiato C, Furegon E, Allocco R, Smith L, Gelmini G, Gareri P, Solmi M, Yang L, Trabucchi M, DeLeo D, Demurtas J. (2020) Interventions for reducing loneliness: An umbrella review of intervention studies. *Health Soc Care Community* Dec 5.

Vestergaard-Poulsen P, Van Beek M, Skewes J, Bjarkam CR, Stubberup M, Bertelsen J, and Roepstorff A (2009) Long-Term Meditation is Associated with Increased Gray Matter Density in the Brain Stem, *Neuroreport* **20**(2):170-174.

Wansink B, and Johnson KA (2015) The clean plate club: about 92% of self-served food is eaten. *International Journal of Obesity* **39**,371–374.

Watkins J, and Wulaningsih W (2016) Obesity: A by-product of Trade or Attitude? *Obesity* (Silver Spring) **24**(12):2445-2446.

Wein S (2012) Between solitude and loneliness: a meditation. *Palliat Support Care* **10**(2):71-3.

Werner OR, Wallace RK, Charles B, Janssen G, T Stryker T, Chalmers RA (1986) Long-term endocrinologic changes in subjects practicing the Transcendental Meditation and TM-Sidhi program. *Psychosom Med* **48**: 42-58.

West MA (1979) Meditation: a review. *Br J Psychiatry* **135**: 457-467.

Xiao C, Mou C, Zhou X (2019) Effect of mindfulness meditation training on anxiety, depression, and sleep quality in perimenopausal women. *Nan Fang Yi Ke Da Xue Xue Ba* **39**(8):998-1002.

Yang CC, Barrós-Loscertales A, Pinazo D, Ventura-Campos N, Borchardt V, Bustamante JC, Rodríguez-Pujadas A, Fuentes-Claramonte P, Balaguer R, Ávila C, Walter M (2016) State and Training Effects of Mindfulness Meditation on Brain Networks Reflect Neuronal Mechanisms of Its Antidepressant Effect, *Neural Plasticity* Research Article 9504642.

Zeidan F, Martucci KT, Kraft RA, Gordon RS, McHaffie JG, Coghill RC (2011) Brain mechanisms supporting the modulation of pain by mindfulness meditation. *J Neuroscience* **31**(14):5540-5548

Afterword

It is a challenging undertaking to write this book. To prove Meditation over Medication is not an easy task without scientific validations. Survey of literature consumed ample time to collect the meaningful data. Moreover, in the presence of adverse effects of meditation it is rather more difficult to bring meditation into limelight. On the other hand, numerous published data on the benefits of meditation was sufficient to prove that with the passage of time meditation would take over medication particularly in mental disorders.

Meditation-related cognitive and physiological mechanisms involving refining the attention, enhancing attention skills, and developing very sophisticated means for investigating the nature of the mind have been consistently addressed by neuroscience regarding its potential benefit for mental and physical health.

Practicing meditation is considered a way of training the mind. Thoughts can make and mar your life. Meditation is a way to prevent the thoughts to control your body. Your life reflects your thoughts, if you change your thoughts, you can change your life.

You are today where your thoughts have brought you, you will be tomorrow where your thoughts take you.
—James Allen

Printed in the United States
by Baker & Taylor Publisher Services